SOCIAL WORK, CRITICAL REF
LEARNING ORGAN.

Social Work, Critical Reflection and the Learning Organization

Edited by

NICK GOULD and MARK BALDWIN
University of Bath

ASHGATE

Published by
Ashgate Publishing Limited
Gower House
Croft Road
Aldershot
Hants GU11 3HR
England

Ashgate Publishing Company
Suite 420
101 Cherry Street
Burlington, VT 05401-4405
USA

Ashgate website: http://www.ashgate.com

British Library Cataloguing in Publication Data
Social work, critical reflection and the learning
    organization
    1.Social work education 2.Social workers - Supervision of
    3.Self knowledge, Theory of 4.Organizational learning
    I.Gould, Nick II.Baldwin, Mark, Dr
    361.3'071

Library of Congress Cataloging-in-Publication Data
Social work, critical reflection, and the learning organization / edited by Nick
    Gould and Mark Baldwin.
        p. cm
    Includes bibliographical references and index.
    ISBN 0-7546-3165-6 – ISBN 0-7546-3167-2
        1.Social work education. 2.Organizational learning. 3.Experimental learning.
    4.Social workers–Supervision of. 5.Social service–Evaluation. I. Gould, Nick.
    II. Baldwin, Mark, Dr.

HV11S5873 2004
361.3'068'4–dc22

2003062844

ISBN 0 7546 3165 6 (Hbk)
ISBN 0 7546 3167 2 (Pbk)

Typeset by Bournemouth Colour Press, Parkstone, Poole
Printed and bound in Great Britain by MPG Books Ltd, Bodmin.

Contents

Contributors   vii

Introduction: The Learning Organization and Reflective Practice
– the Emergence of a Concept   1
Nick Gould

1   Supervision, Learning and Transformative Practices   11
    Martyn Jones
2   Social Work Supervision: Contributing to Innovative Knowledge
    Production and Open Expertise   23
    Synnöve Karvinen-Niinikoski
3   Critical Reflection: Opportunities and Threats to Professional
    Learning and Service Development in Social Work Organizations   41
    Mark Baldwin
4   Critical Reflection and Organizational Learning and Change: A Case
    Study   57
    Jan Fook
5   Multi-professional Teams and the Learning Organization   75
    Imogen Taylor
6   Sustaining Reflective Practice in the Workplace   87
    Hilary Sage and Mary Allan
7   Using 'Critical Incident Analysis' to Promote Critical Reflection
    and Holistic Assessment   101
    Judith Thomas
8   Evaluation for a Learning Organization?   117
    Ian Shaw
9   Reflecting on Practice: Exploring Individual and Organizational
    Learning through a Reflective Teaching Model   129
    Bairbre Redmond
10 Living out Histories and Identities in Organizations: A Case Study
    from Three Perspectives   143
    Harjeet Badwall, Patricia O'Connor and Amy Rossiter
11 Conclusions: Optimism and the Art of the Possible   161
    Mark Baldwin

Bibliography   177
Index   199

Contributors

Mary Allan worked for Stonham Housing Association for 15 years. For much of that time she managed an offender project before taking up the newly created role of Practice Development Adviser for the West Region in 1999. Mary completed the Diploma in Social Work on a part time basis in 1998, having previously gained the Central Council for Education and Training in Social Work (CCETSW) Practice Teacher Award and subsequently went on to gain her degree at the University of the West of England while continuing to work full time. She is involved in union activities and holds the National Learning Representative role. Much of her current work involves training other professionals in social care. She also continues to practice teach social work students in placement.

Harjeet Badwall has been practising social work for several years. She has worked in the areas of youth, women's issues, anti-violence, HIV/AIDS, with ethno-specific communities and larger community activism. Harjeet has worked as an anti-racism and anti-oppression facilitator in organizations and academic settings. She has lectured in university settings on critical reflective practice from an anti-oppressive framework. Currently, Harjeet is working as a Sexual Assault Counsellor in a local hospital in Toronto.

Mark Baldwin is senior lecturer in social work at the University of Bath. He is interested in the part that professional practitioners play in the development of policy through the use of discretion. He is currently investigating how this is affecting the introduction of integrated services in the health and social care field. He has worked with co-operative inquiry groups within statutory and voluntary organizations to investigate the possibilities for developing good practice. He is committed to the importance of service user involvement and has worked with the Wiltshire Service User Network for a number of years to bring their perspective into social work education.

Jan Fook has taught social work students for most of her career. Her most abiding interest is in practice, particularly how it is best researched and developed from the perspective of the practitioner. In her current position as Professor/Director of the Centre for Professional Development at La Trobe University, a major role is providing continuing education for human service professionals in the area of critical reflective practice. She is known nationally and internationally for her work in this area, and is regularly invited to speak in the UK and other parts of Europe. She has published eight books and over 40 journal articles and book chapters. Her first book, *Radical Casework* (Allen & Unwin, 1993), is one of the most widely used social work texts in Australia, and *The Reflective Researcher* (Allen & Unwin, 1996) is used by many different professional groups. Her most recent book is *Social Work: Critical Theory and Practice* (Sage, 2002).

Nick Gould is professor of social work at the University of Bath, and fellow in social care with the National Institute for Mental Health (England) and Social Care Institute for Excellence. A qualified social worker, he has worked in generic and mental health settings. He has published widely in the fields of professional learning, social informatics and research methodology. His most recent book, edited with Ian Shaw, is *Qualitative Research in Social Work* (Sage, 2001).

Martyn Jones is associate professor in field education at RMIT University Melbourne and was previously acting Director of Social Work at Deakin University, Australia. He has previously been employed in social work education and practice in the UK. He has engaged in a number of collaborative research projects concerned with the professional identity, knowledge and organizational change. His teaching interests include the place of critical reflection and reflexivity in professional development. Currently, he is working on a book (with Heather D'Cruz) entitled *Social Work Research: A Political and Ethical Practice?*, to be published in 2004.

Synnöve Karvinen-Niinikoski is professor of social work at the University of Helsinki, Finland. Earlier she has worked in the universities of Kuopio and Turku. She is a qualified and practising social work supervisor and has also done developmental work on the training of social work supervisors and practice teachers. She has written on reflective practice in social work and on the theory of supervision, and she is engaged in research on social work research and epistemological issues and issues of expertise and knowledge production.

Patricia O'Connor has a career as a social worker which spans 30 years and a wide variety of positions – child welfare, neighbourhood centre work, community education and local service planning. She has been involved in undergraduate social work education for many years as a teacher and as a field instructor. She currently is a front-line worker in a community health centre in downtown Toronto, where she continues to be challenged and stimulated by the complexity of the work and the diversity of the people and tasks. Writing this chapter with Harjeet and Amy was a much welcomed opportunity for reflection and growth.

Bairbre Redmond is Director of Social Work Training in the Department of Social Policy and Social Work at University College, Dublin; she has also worked as a senior social worker in the intellectual disability services. Her research interests include the development of better relationships between health service professionals and service users. She has a particular interest in developing new, innovative teaching approaches to professional training and development at university level. She is the author of *Reflection in Action* (Ashgate, 2004).

Amy Rossiter is a professor in the School of Social Work at York University in

Toronto. She is interested in critical approaches to social work theory and practice, with particular emphasis on postmodern perspectives. She explores the possibilities and contradictions of critical approaches in the context of social work education. She is also working on the effects of corporate globalization on the social work profession. Amy has two terrific adult children, a dysfunctional cat, and a garden that is the result of her enthusiastic but sadly untalented ministrations.

Hilary Sage is practice learning co-ordinator and tutor for the social work course at the University of Bristol. She has written about, and evaluated the use of, portfolios for the assessment of practice and professional development. From her previous experience as a social worker and care manager in Gloucestershire she has developed an interest in, and carried out research into, the housing context for the delivery of health and social care services and inter-agency work. She is currently developing enquiry-based learning units to link with a greater variety of practice settings for the new postgraduate social work award.

Ian Shaw is professor of social work at the University of York, England. He has spent most of his career working in Wales at Cardiff University. His interests include developing social work research methodology, in relation to evaluation, action research, qualitative methods and practitioner research. He writes on issues at the borders of health and social care, and publishes in social work, housing, education, sociology and health journals. He is author or editor of 10 or so books. He has led on the development of eLearning packages in social work practice and community care, and co-edits the journal *Qualitative Social Work*.

Imogen Taylor joined the University of Sussex as professor of social work and social care in 2001. Prior to this she was a Senior Lecturer at the University of Bristol where she completed her doctorate. She is also Co-Director of the UK Learning and Teaching Support Network Subject Centre in Social Policy and Social Work. Imogen qualified as a social worker in Toronto where she practised before joining the Faculty of the School of Social Work there. Her research interests include: learning for professional and interprofessional practice; gender in learning and practice; non-traditional learners; and, critically reflective learning. Her book, *Developing Learning in Professional Education: Partnerships for Practice* (SRHE and Open University Press, 1997), was an outcome of these interests. More recently she has become interested in the learning organization. She is a member of the Editorial Board of *Social Work Education*. In recognition of her work, Imogen was awarded a National Teaching Fellowship in 2003.

Judith Thomas worked in residential work with children, also as a specialist mental health social worker, then as a training officer and practice learning organizer in various local authorities. Over the past 10 years Judith has worked closely with social services agencies to develop practice teacher training and is now programme leader for the BSc(Hons) Social Work at the University of the West of England, Bristol. Judith is particularly interested in exploring creative ways of looking at the connections between research and practice, and how we can all make the most of our learning from the rich and challenging experiences of life. Research and writing include self and peer assessment, action learning and problem-solving. Currently, Judith is researching inter-professional education and working and is co-editing a book on this subject.

Introduction: The Learning Organization and Reflective Practice – the Emergence of a Concept

Nick Gould

The late Peter Cook, the British comedian, was asked in a sketch about his failed restaurant, The Frog and Peach, the menu of which contained only two dishes, 'peche à la frog' and 'frog à la peche', whether as a restaurateur he had learned from his mistakes? He replied forthrightly that, 'I have definitely learned from my mistakes ... and I could repeat all of them exactly again.' At the risk of being flippant, this could be said to encapsulate the problem which has been addressed in recent years by a significant body of writing about the need in social work to develop forms of professional learning that helped practice to move beyond mere routine towards creative and critical problem-solving. Much of this writing and research has fallen within the rubric of 'reflective learning', broadly drawing on the seminal work of Donald Schön (1983; 1987) but often also informed by wider areas of critical theory. In 1996 Imogen Taylor and I edited *Reflective Learning for Social Work* (Gould and Taylor, 1996), the first volume in the social work literature to draw together contributions on the application of Schön's ideas in social work, and it has become widely cited. In the introductory chapter to that volume I commented that, 'There is always a danger that a concept such as reflective learning will become little more than a slogan' (Gould and Taylor, 1996: 2). Some may argue that it has, but there can be no denial that within social work, as in many other professional domains, reflection has become an established element in the professional discourse, and is found everywhere from the competence requirements for professional qualification to mainstream textbooks for students and practitioners.

For several reasons it seems timely to revisit, but particularly to develop, the debates about reflective learning and practice. Sadly, at the time of writing this chapter, the British social care community is yet again absorbing the report from the latest major public inquiry into the abusive death of a child, Victoria Climbié, and the perceived failures of the child protection system. This report comes 30 years after the death of Maria Colwell, a tragedy which in many ways established the terms of reference for the subsequent debates around social work and the protection of children. Numerous commentaries have made observations about the repetitive nature of the mistakes that have characterized many of the child abuse inquiries during the intervening years (Chief Secretary to the Treasury, 2003: 5). Many of the

Colwell inquiry preoccupations are reiterated in Lord Laming's report on the death of Victoria Climbié, and yet there are also additional dimensions in Laming's analysis (Laming, 2003). Specifically, Laming places the circumstances of direct practice within a wide organizational context, and raises difficult questions about the responsibilities of senior managers for the effectiveness of front-line practice, the role of professional supervision in the development of practice, continuing systemic failures of communication and accountability, and the need to develop a whole-system approach to work with children and adults who are vulnerable.

Although this volume is not a direct response to these events, it does engage in a timely way with many of these issues; by reconnecting with the reflective learning debates it seeks to address the need to locate the learning and expertise of individual practitioners within the wider organizational context. A convenient label to refer to the development of that organizational framework is 'the learning organization', initially associated in the early 1990s with the writings of Peter Senge, and later adopted by other management theorists. In some ways, which we will elaborate shortly, the concept of the learning organization is problematic for social work and social care; it originated in response to the needs of commercial enterprises under conditions of market turbulence to achieve continuous improvement in productivity and profit. Nevertheless, the learning organization's engagement with systemic thinking, teamwork and work-based learning are also relevant to social services and social work, and are themes which, as some chapters in this book point out, are hardly new in the literature of social work. In addition to this, social work is in a position to make significant contributions to the wider understanding of the learning organization through its concerns with the effects of power and the structural disadvantage of marginalized individuals and groups, issues which are signally missing from the generic management literature.

This chapter briefly summarizes the provenance of the concept of the learning organization, and tries to identify some of the links between individual reflection and organizational learning. Some immanent critiques of these positions are reviewed and, finally, the structure of the book and thrust of individual chapters are explained.

The Theory of the Learning Organization

Although the literature on the learning organization is relatively recent, it builds on a longer sociological tradition of theorization of the relationship between organizational structure and behaviour. In Weber's classic theory of bureaucracy, learning is strongly associated with traditional notions of professionalization, where stratification separates the educated and qualified 'thinkers' from the 'doers'. The implications of this are that, primarily, learning for the job has taken place through qualifying education and any 'topping up' is focused on managerial levels of the organization. In later scientific views of organizations, associated with Fordism and Taylorism, the emphasis was on the acquisition of technical skills for task efficiency. Individuals were trained to perform a segment of the production process within a highly standardized system. Over time a tension was to emerge between the dehumanizing effects of Taylorism (see Beynon's 1973 account of life on the Ford production track) and the human relations movement of the 1960s and 1970s within which writers such as Maslow (1968) and McGregor focused attention on meeting human needs through personal development, job enrichment and the quality of working life.

Contemporaneous with the development of human relations thinking was an identification of learning as a specific issue within management development, particularly associated with the action-learning theories of Revans (1980), that is, the view that learning for management can be experiential, achieved through shared problem-solving (Margerison, 1994). Revans had been responsible for training in the British mining industry during the Second World War. Scarcity of human resources made him realize that conventional training programmes were impractical because of the cost and interruptions to production resulting from taking managers away from the workplace to attend training events. Revans began to develop structured problem-based approaches to learning on the job, or 'action learning' (Revans, 1980). Revans's 'law' anticipates much of the theory of the learning organization: 'For an organisation to survive its rate of learning must be equal to or greater than the rate of change in its external environment.'

Continuous change has also been a theme of sociologists and futurologists such as Alvin Toffler (1971) and Daniel Bell (1973), and it has emerged in the work of theorists of strategic management such as Charles Handy (1989), who challenged managers to accept that change had become a continuous reality and not something which temporarily interrupted periods of stability. Associated with this shift is an implicit change of metaphor for conceptualizing organizational life, from the dominant Taylorist image of the organization as a machine towards the metaphor of the organization as a system, one that has to adapt through learning to the changing demands created by its environment.

At the heart of this progression of organizational theory is the problematic concept of learning; what it means, how it relates to organizational structure and behaviour, and whether there are real differences behind the managerialist slogans of 'organizational learning' (the processes through which learning takes place) and the 'learning organization' (the characteristics of an organization that learns). The overlap between these concepts seems to be large, and to make a rigid analytical distinction between them probably just reifies academic turf wars rather than making a useful analytical distinction. What seems to be shared between these fields are two fundamental premises. First, individual learning is a necessary but not sufficient condition for organizational learning – the latter is a collective process which means that the organization has not automatically learned as a result of an individual's learning. Second, the learning experience is more pervasive and distributed than that delivered through a specific, designated training or educational event; learning incorporates the broad dynamics of adaptation, change and environmental alignment of organizations, takes place across multiple levels within the organization, and involves the construction and reconstruction of meanings and world views within the organization (Gould, 2000).

Reflection in the Learning Organization

This recognition that learning is experiential and organizationally embedded potentially connects the concept of the learning organization with the process of reflective practice. The fundamental premises of reflective learning can be summarized as emerging from three critiques of technical rational models of problem-solving (Gould, 1999). First, expert practitioners might draw upon the findings of formal research to guide their interventions, but their strategies for problem-solving are acquired through experience. It is the practice of novices that tends to be characterized by more slavish and explicit use of formal or propositional knowledge but, with the development of expertise, practitioner knowledge typically becomes more tacit, demonstrated and communicated through the practice itself (Benner, 1984; Dreyfus and Dreyfus, 1986; Fook, Ryan and Hawkins, 2000). Second, the conventional understanding of practice as applied formal knowledge, underestimates the context of practice as a formative influence in knowledge-use and creation by practitioners. Despite the widespread reference to skill transfer as a core competence in social work and other practitioner fields, the empirical evidence shows that practice knowledge is very context specific and most learning is not directly transferable without interpretation and adaptation. Third, what constitutes a problem is itself a matter of interpretation and construction within a specific context. Rule-based or cookery-book approaches to practice tend to assume that it is self-evident that we can recognize particular types of problem to which a predetermined solution can be applied. Schön (1983), in a metaphor which has often been cited, argued that this rationalistic view of problem-setting is typically from the high ground occupied by managers and academics, while practitioners are situated in the swampy lowlands having to negotiate from a complex and confusing plethora of circumstances an understanding of what constitutes 'the problem'.

These core premises of the reflective approach to expert practice chime strongly with the generic premise of learning organization approaches that much (though not all) learning needs to be ongoing and embedded in the organizational context. What is implied is a shift from seeing learning in the workplace as something only derived from going on a course or taking a distance learning module, to recognizing that most workplace learning is non-formal and unplanned (Eraut et al., 1998; 1999) where learning happens all the time, but is often not identified as learning because what people learn is their practice. 'Learning is the engine of practice and practice is the history of that learning' (Wenger, 1998: 96). The prioritization of practice as the crucible of learning has to address at least two issues which emerge from this – the relationship of formal knowledge (the evidence-base derived from empirical research and scholarly outputs) to practice, and the connections between individual learning or practice and the organization. To ignore the former disregards evidence that practitioners, including social workers, are influenced by formal knowledge (Gould, 2000), while the second issue reminds us that we cannot view organizations as anthropomorphic entities which have a mystical life of their own. Simons and Ruijters (2001) suggest a model of work-related learning which links individuals, groups and organizations. Their model constructs a three-stage process of learning:

- elaboration – where competences are elaborated on by learning from and in practice;
- expansion – where formal knowledge and insight are expanded by learning from research; and
- externalizing – where building on practical and theoretical insights contributes to the development of the organization and the profession.

This model allows for learning between different professions (increasingly the scenario in social care) and for the linkage between individual and collective learning. It theorizes organizational collective learning as people sharing a common interest in the organization, and professional collective learning as people sharing a common interest in learning, but not necessarily in the same organization; individual learning becomes collective when groups reflect on common implicit outcomes, reflect on or plan common learning outcomes and define common plans for externalization.

The Learning Organization as Contested Theory

Of course, there are many criticisms of the learning organization. Some of these are related to the highly normative orientation of writers such as Senge, arguing that theirs is a theory that is strongly driven by ideological values of the market, competition and a functionalist perspective on social life. Gherardi (1999), for instance, has argued that the 'learning organization' is produced out of the real social relations that exist in organizations; these will include relationships of class, gender, race, disability and any of the other social fault lines that characterize inequality. By ignoring these dimensions but claiming that organizational life is based on participation and self-development, it is claimed that the learning organization becomes a form of rhetorical discourse that obscures the mobilization of top-down change: 'The literature on LO has been suspected of colluding with the "ruling courts" which govern organizations, and of employing, in an ideological manner, a discourse of democracy and liberation' (Gherardi, 1999: 105).

Coopey characterizes these more negative readings of the learning organisation as the 'Foucauldian gloom' perspective, according to which the liberal, humanist possibilities of voice and participation offered by learning organization theory (the 'Utopian sunshine' perspective) can be subverted into unilateral control, disempowerment and abuse (cited in Driver, 2002: 37). Obviously, social work writers, and particularly those represented in this volume, would fundamentally reject any standpoint which did not endorse a social work perspective which was incompatible with values of promoting equality and empowerment; but neither would we be comfortable with an approach that was naive and wholly ideological, the 'Utopian sunshine' option. To some degree this polarization has been reinforced by two distinct camps within empirical organizational research (Tsang, 1997). One such camp is characterized by descriptive studies, often produced by academics with limited possibilities of generating practice guidance, the other, typically produced by consultants, is prescriptive with insufficient empirical detail to allow readers to judge how transferable or generalizable the findings may be.

As Driver argues, the need is to find a middle-ground perspective that is informed by the scepticism of the more pessimistic theoretical Foucauldian analyses, but sufficiently respectful of 'real world' needs of agencies and their service users to offer practical suggestions for promoting learning in organizations. This is about holding the creative tension between the idea of a learning organization as an aspirational goal, while realizing that if an organization is seeking continuously to learn from and influence an always changing environment, then by definition the learning organization itself will always be changing. This is recognized by Nyhan et al. (2003) who have argued:

> The prescriptive and simplistic formula-based view of the learning organisation does nothing more than discredit the concept. A learning organisation cannot be created by applying a formula. It can only be brought to life by the people who work and learn in the organisation. This is not about applying an external theory but rather a construction process based on a lived collective practice. Each organisation has to devise its own unique theory based on its own distinctive practice. (Nyhan et al., 2003: 14)

The Contribution of this Volume

The aspiration in editing this book has been to assemble an overview that brings reflective and learning organization perspectives to bear on social work, but does so from critical standpoints. All the chapters 'touch base' with the contributions of seminal writers such as Schön and Senge, but they are also informed by a range of insights that are grounded in academic theory but also in the realpolitik of practice in various parts of the world as, arguably, the drive for continuous change is in part a response to processes of globalization and connected pressures upon welfare states (Pugh and Gould, 2001).

The first two chapters, from Australia and Finland, both take supervision as core processes in the transformation of practice and organizational learning. Thus, Martyn Jones argues that supervision in social services is fundamental to both professional and organizational fortunes. Starting from the observation that discussions of supervision in the social work professional literature have focused largely upon principles of good practice and have been detached from the social context of their performance, he seeks to situate supervision within the wider organizational and professional field. Locating the historical development of mainstream models of supervision within the social relations of liberal welfare regimes, he then draws on the lessons from his own research and consultancy to challenge those assumptions. Referring to contemporary analyses of governance he calls into question the conventional model of supervision as a vehicle for regulating social workers. Instead, he cites the pivotal concepts of 'accountability' and 'indeterminacy' as levers for opening up future directions for supervision that are responsive to both professional and organizational concerns. In this recasting of supervision, critical reflectivity and generative learning cultures are highlighted as important indicators of transformative social work practices.

Synnöve Karvinen-Niinikoski's chapter also locates supervision in its organizational and professional context, and for many readers, it will probably introduce them to important theories of experiential learning which remain largely unknown to social work readers. Karvinen-Niinikoski sees supervision as a method of reflection with long traditions in social work which can be an integrating factor between the individual practitioner and his or her organizational setting. Setting out the theory of 'expansive learning', she argues that this provides a conceptual tool for critical reflection and the construction of reflexive practices and expertise in human services. Against a backdrop of postmodernity and rapid change, social workers increasingly will have to look for innovative solutions rather than drawing on a repertoire of prototype professional methods, in effect inventing new models and methods of working. The seeds of these innovative practices often emerge from everyday experiences of practitioners and their clients. The challenge for supervision is to support these creative processes in the daily construction of professional practice. Supervision, it is argued, provides an essential forum for reflection on practice, research, experimentation and evaluation in the development of innovation.

Supervision is one of the professional arenas within which social workers reflect on the use of their discretion and judgement. The work of Lipsky on 'street-level bureaucrats' has tended to cast discretion in a negative light as indicative of the insertion of unprofessional subjectivity into practice. In Chapter 3, Mark Baldwin argues for the reframing of discretion as something that is fundamental to the development of effective practice. The pejorative view of discretion is ascribed to three factors: managerialist practices which seek to deny the role of judgement in decision-making; the emphasis on technical-rationalist understandings of what constitutes 'evidence' in the quest for evidence-based practice; and the impacts of an audit culture which prioritizes outcome measurements while devaluing the significance for practitioners and service users of process evaluation. Drawing on his own co-operative inquiry research in social work agencies, Baldwin identifies opportunities for reflective learning which facilitate the creative use of discretion for more effective practice.

Jan Fook's chapter (Chapter 4), has significant parallels with Chapter 3, similarly drawing upon her own inquiries which were established with groups of practitioners in agencies, to suggest ways in which critical reflection can support organizational change. The first section of her chapter describes a 'critical reflection programme' involving small groups of workers who met over a four-month period, during which a supportive group climate was built to facilitate maximum reflectiveness and receptivity to scrutiny. Fook then discusses the issues that arise both from the programme and its formal evaluation, particularly identifying the implications for improvement of practice, identification of best practice, staff development, supervision and management.

All of these earlier chapters are generic in their scope, they are not directed at any particular area of social work specialism. Arguably, at least in the UK, mental health has in recent years been an interesting crucible for 'modernization' of health and social care services. Government-driven organizational change, notably merging of services, is forcing a re-examination of the distinct contribution that social work can make to multi-professional teams. At the same time, an increasingly organized service user movement is also expecting that it will be involved in service planning, delivery and review. In Chapter 5, Taylor explores the dual implications of learning in multi-professional settings and the involvement of service users in that process. Drawing on Wenger's work on communities of practice, she identifies some of the strategies to develop the 'learning architecture' of these new kinds of service organizations, as well as the gaps in our knowledge about how they are effected by the interactions of power, trust and confidentiality.

The two chapters that follow these can be read as case studies that help ground our understanding of implementing reflective approaches within specific organizations. They make important contributions to appreciating some of the challenges that have to be surmounted in, first, embedding reflection in the mainstream practices of the organization and, secondly, sustaining commitment to them. In Chapter 6, Mary Allan and Hilary Sage report on a partnership between a university department and housing association which had as an initial aim the development of student placements within the association. This happened to coincide with the association's adoption of a new staff training strategy which emphasized reflective practice; the synergy between the university and agency was used as an opportunity for developing lifelong learning for the workforce and new skill and role development.

Chapter 7, authored by Judith Thomas, also starts from an interest in the development of practice teaching, and is based on five years' experience of using 'critical incident analysis' in the development of effective practice. Critical incident analysis uses problematic or challenging scenarios from practitioners' own caseloads as the focus for reflexive analysis. Thomas argues that social workers' anxiety about relating practice to theory partly derives from their limited perception of different types of theory, viewing it in terms of 'grand theory' or 'theories of practice'. Innovative practice in areas such as community development and anti-discriminatory practice has, however, often developed from analysing and evaluating everyday working practices; without opportunities for critical reflection, practitioners lose the skill of being able to articulate and identify the theories and methods of intervention they are using.

Evaluation has already been mentioned several times as an inalienable element of practitioner and organizational learning, and there are contributions to the learning organization literature that suggest that embedding evaluation in the organization, and creating feedback loops from evaluation into practice development, are defining features of the learning organization (Preskill and Torres, 1999b). Ian Shaw, in Chapter 8, questions the extent to which evaluation in social work has taken into account organizational learning dimensions. He distinguishes between formal evaluation (whether external or internal to the organization) and informal practitioner experiences and understandings of the evaluative dimension of daily practice, and includes not only methodology-led approaches, but also advocacy and justice-driven models. Despite the initial pessimism of Shaw's overview, he draws on his own research experience to argue that identifiable practice and service improvements do flow from bringing to bear on organizations a diverse range of evaluation standpoints that might include reflective and participatory inquiry, organizational research and so on.

Bringing experience from another national context, Ireland, Bairbre Redmond analyses in Chapter 9 a model of reflective teaching and learning she has developed in working with learning disability practitioners. Using an action research methodology, the author and her co-inquirers elaborated a model which included an exploration of the organizational contexts in which the practitioners operated and techniques for helping them investigate the influence on their practice of the structures in which they work. The chapter describes the organizational barriers to change as perceived by this multi-professional group and some of the ways in which they challenged those obstacles. Redmond considers the theoretical and practical implications of exploring organizational issues within a reflective practicum, the implications of reflective practice models that are focused not only on the individual but also the agency level, and the knock-on effects on organizational learning when practitioners return to practice settings empowered by their experience of reflective learning.

In a powerful chapter that is co-authored by a counsellor and anti-racist educator (Harjeet Badwall), social work practitioner (Patricia O'Connor) and academic (Amy Rossiter), the issues of organizational change in a Canadian community health centre are examined. This was a project that grew out of organizational tensions in a centre that demonstrated difficult issues of race, class and status played out among the workers and users of the centre. The chapter combines the voices of the three authors and describes how their respective positions engendered different vantage points. They are able to utilize their multiple points of view to illuminate the structural, organizational and personal complexities of reflective change in organizations.

Finally, in Chapter 11 Mark Baldwin takes an overview of the messages that emerge from these contributions in an attempt to identify core aspects of the learning organization, as understood from social work perspectives. These include the embedding of value-based critical reflection within the organization, the inculcation of critical reflexivity through new understandings of professional supervision, the participation of all stakeholders but especially service users in the development of services, and the critical analysis of approaches to performance management that ignore the reflective process.

Chapter 1

Supervision, Learning and Transformative Practices

Martyn Jones

Introduction

Professional and management discourses often share a similar feature, the tendency to take a prescriptive approach towards practice. Of course, in many respects this would be expected in applied domains that involve purposive action. Furthermore, it might be argued that educating for professional and management practice involves socializing members into methodologies and technologies of practice as an integral part of the acculturation process. At the same time, a corresponding theme in professional and management discourse concerns 'the gap' – the gap between theory and practice, rhetoric and reality, the espoused and the enacted. Among other things, the gap speaks of a disjuncture between the imperatives for practice that are to be read off of encoded models and theories, and the circumstances of their supposed application. In the face of this disjuncture, practitioners might speak of finding compromises between the ideals and the realities, or they might abandon the encoded models and theories as ones that belong to a different order – an order sometimes perceived as the comfortable and somewhat protected world of those who generate them.

In this chapter, the models and theories of professional supervision and learning organizations are considered in relation to one another, but also in regard to the critiques that have surrounded them. It is suggested that these critiques largely reflect the limitations of prescriptive models and theories, detached from the contexts of their application. In particular, the chapter suggests that professional and management discourses are more properly understood by situating them within the historical and political contexts in which they have arisen.

Contextualizing Professional Supervision in Human Services

Supervision in human services holds a pivotal place in professional and organizational fortunes (Jones, 1999). On the one hand, supervision has been considered crucial to professional development and effective practice. While the forms it might assume have varied according to the dominant practice models of the day (Tsui, 1997a), the presence of good supervisory structures and processes has been taken as an indicator of the relative health of the professional body (Tsui,

1997b). At the same time, supervision has also been considered an important component in the administration of professional activity, and a means of aligning the work of semi-autonomous members with organizational goals and procedures (Jones and May, 1992). The question as to how these objectives might best be achieved has given rise to a discourse on supervision which exhorts principles of good practice in this field.

Every so often, the generation of such discourse has received added momentum through public inquiries into high profile tragedies. Hughes and Pengelly (1997) have spoken of the reports into child deaths, for example, which have 'highlighted with depressing repetitiveness the failures of supervision in social work ... and re-emphasised the central importance of effective supervision in promoting safe practice' (ibid.: 26). Effectiveness has been associated with 'the marrying of managerial and professional aspects of supervision' and 'a proactive supervisory stance in thorough decision-making, relating to workers' feelings, and so on' (Hughes and Pengelly, 1997: 26–7). The intrinsically stressful nature of much of social work has been emphasized consistently in such considerations, and importance attached to supervision as a way of assisting staff to deal with the emotional impact of the job (Stanley and Goddard, 1993).

Something of an orthodoxy has evolved on supervision, inspired largely by the work of Kadushin, who has systematically and in considerable depth promoted and researched the nature of supervision. Kadushin (1992) defined its three primary functions as administrative, educational and supportive, and these have become widely accepted as the hallmarks of good supervisory practice. Others have augmented and refined this framework, adding the function of mediation for example (Austin, 1988; Morrison, 1993), yet the appeal has remained relatively constant through to recent times.

The appeal lies in part with the persuasive way in which this prescriptive framework for supervision has been congruent with the prevailing policy and organizational context. The social settlement of many western welfare agencies provided for a trade-off between pervasive management practices and the professional cohort (Jones, 1999). The regulation of professional behaviour was to be conducted through the supervision of front-line practitioners, a role largely performed by staff with professional experience promoted into management positions. Embodying both professional and organizational concerns, supervision existed at the interface, sufficient to satisfy organizational requirements while retaining licence for the exercise and moderation of professional judgement and support.

This configuration was not without its points of tension. The heavy reliance on the capabilities of the supervisor to 'pull it off' created considerable sources of strain (Clare, 1988). The 'piggy in the middle' dynamic, common to most supervisory positions, was compounded by the conflict of moral commitments, fuelled through connection with a sense of professional mission and longstanding antagonisms between the professionals and the managers (Laragy, 1997). Furthermore, the arrangement provided no ready place for the inclusion of user/client perspectives and arguably carried the contradiction of colonizing-liberating praxis (Ife, 1997).

Following a period of relative stability for this social settlement, there has been significant and continuing disruption. The nexus has been broken, dislocating supervision and making it available for appropriation by competing interests. The waves of new public management ideologies that swept through the human services industry, when challenged to break alleged cycles of welfare dependency and self-serving professionalism, inevitably caught supervision in their wake (Hough, 2003; Lewis, 1998). A series of studies have described how these new systems of governance have reconstructed the role and relations of professionals within changing organizational contexts (Scarborough, 1996).

Commentaries on the implications for supervision have been offered at various transitional phases. Early studies, for example, that were critical of the perceived commodification of social welfare saw a parallel process occurring within the welfare workforce. The emphasis upon efficient and effective achievement of outcomes, it was held, resulted in a convergence of neo-Taylorist management principles with neo-liberal market ideologies (Dominelli, 1997). Workforce planning went 'back to basics' by delineating position descriptions according to pre-specified competences required for those tasks necessary to achieve the objectives defined in the organization's strategic plans. The training for and supervision of competent practice became a focus for controversy and one of the contested sites in redrawing a place for the human services professional (Shapiro, 2000).

The advent of the quality movement provided a further site for contest. Potentially an oppositional discourse to the quantification of outcomes, there were perceived possibilities here to claim a legitimate place for professional knowledge, skills and judgement-making. With quality defined into strategic planning, the professional contribution might be reincorporated not only into practice, but also into policy development. Professional supervision might be retained as the incubator for distinctive perspectives and social practices on which the organization could draw for its achievements of quality. In the event, as we shall see, the possibilities here have proved somewhat slippery, with quality often proving to be rather more politicized than initially it may have appeared (Reed, 1995).

A third area to note concerns the impact upon professional identities. Some observers characterized the professional response to welfare transformations rather in terms of a passive-aggressive reaction to threats – that is to say, loss of territory, loss of income, loss of security. While this interpretation is consistent with an analysis of the professional body as essentially self rather than other serving, it runs a little crudely over the moral sensibilities that appeared to be at stake (Jones, 2000). Practitioners' accounts of despair, disillusionment and even fear spoke of a different kind of threat, threat to the values which signify a more altruistic dimension of professional identity – the values, for instance, of compassion, humanity, justice. The moderation of value conflicts through supervisory process was felt to be compromised by the erosion of these considerations in the pursuit of predetermined, instrumental outcomes by increasingly generic managers.

Responses to Changing Times

The approach to reinventing supervision for the changing contexts of practice has been varied. The variations themselves reflect alternative political strategies in the transforming relations between the professional workforce and their employing agencies.

One strategy has been to align supervision with the organizational mission (Beddoe, 1997; Kearney, 1996; Scott and Farrow, 1993). Where aspirations to quality are written into organizational goals, for example, there are possibilities for supervision itself to appear in the list of Key Performance Indicators (KPIs), at least in those instances where supervision has retained sufficient profile as a contributor to desired organizational performance. Once on the KPI list, a place is secured for the production of a Supervision Policy for the organization, which may well include requirements for the form and frequency of supervisory practice. Enshrined in policy, staff throughout the organization that are subject to it can be monitored for their compliance with it.

Working within the parameters of organizational governance processes, this strategy may well be successful in keeping supervision on the map. However, it is primarily pursued within the formal structures of the organization. As such, it provides no guarantee as to what transpires within supervision itself. That is to say, it does not necessarily touch the cultural life of the organization and so may have little influence on the interactions between supervisors and supervisees. Consequently, despite being formally anchored in quality, supervisory practices may still be perfunctory, attending more to correct technical performance and little to learning and development (Clare, 2001; Gibbs, 2001; Morrison, 2001).

In some respects, this raises the question as to what counts as supervision. A study by Syrett, Jones and Sercombe (1996) is indicative of a related strategy. The approach here was to split administrative from educational/supportive functions of supervision, locating each within complementary organizational positions of 'team managers' and 'practice supervisors' to ensure due attention was paid to both sets of functions. The study suggested that practitioners did indeed express satisfaction over the opportunity this afforded to focus with their practice supervisor on practice-related issues and developmental needs.

Perhaps predictably, the overall satisfaction with this arrangement was dependent upon the degree of 'partnership' established between the team manager and their practice supervisor. Partnerships were seen to vary in the extent to which the partners were appreciative of the perspectives and priorities of one another. In the worst case scenario, practitioners described themselves as caught between warring parties. Interestingly, the organizational structure clearly situated the practice supervisor as hierarchically subordinate to the team manager, leaving the former feeling somewhat vulnerable to being undermined by the latter. The gendered aspects of such a partnership would have been a relevant topic for further study (Hearn, 1992).

Contemporaneously, a rather different approach was being advocated elsewhere (Bunker and Wijnberg, 1988). This involved a more wholesale redesign of supervision for human services. The starting point was an assumption that high-performing (and by implication, best fit to survive) organizations were ones which could be responsive to an ever-changing environment. Moreover, there was an assumption that in so doing staff were the organization's greatest resource, and that therefore the engagement of staff in both day-to-day service delivery and ongoing organizational development was vital. The position of supervisor now became highly significant in linking staff with a whole range of organizational processes. In this scenario, supervision took on multiple functions and provided a conduit for information upon which organizational performance depended.

Within this approach, one feature particularly pertinent for the present discussion concerned the reconceptualizing of administrative, professional and inter-personal dimensions as streams of information that were to feed into organizational knowledge management. This represented a break with prior thinking. The functions of supervision became extended (with up to 10 being identified) and were derived from the goals of organizational performance, involving information of differing kinds being duly processed. The significance of this is twofold. First, it locates professional members as contributors to organizational performance. Simplistically, professionals are there to serve the organization rather than vice versa. Secondly, it suggests that the organization's repositories of professional knowledge are not contained solely within the occupants of professional positions. The information streams that contain professional knowledge may have numerous sources. For example, the dissemination of research through the organization would potentially become a source of professional knowledge; or, the encoding of 'best practice' within legal or procedural protocols would provide another form of embodiment of professional knowledge (Jones and Jordan, 1996).

Interestingly, when considering high performance in human service organizations, the authors underwrote this approach with the understanding that such organizations would be pursuing a social mission (Bunker and Wijnberg, 1988: 44). Given this, professional and practitioner knowledge, as well as information that flows from clients and users of the services, were assumed to be invaluable to effective organizational development and performance. This assumption, however, is somewhat problematic. The approach does situate human service organizations systemically within a competitive environment that requires continual adaptation, and it redefines supervision accordingly. Here, the professional contribution finds its safeguard in the convergence of professional and organizational missions rather than in the organizational presence of professionals. Yet, this overlooks the ways in which organizational missions themselves are responsive to their contexts, as well as presuming that such missions have a pervasive influence upon organizational activity.

Observations from a Study of Supervision

Led on by the idea that perhaps something important was happening to supervision, indicative of broader changes to the professional role and relation within human service organizations, a small-scale exploratory study was undertaken recently in the state of Victoria, Australia. The aim was to ascertain the perspectives of supervisors and supervisees across a range of human service organizations, government and non-government, on the ways in which supervisory functions and practices may or may not be changing. The study was limited to front-line practitioners and managers. A questionnaire was distributed (25 respondents), which included an invitation to participate in a subsequent group discussion. Two such discussions were convened (16 participants in total).

The questionnaires were analysed through simple counting procedures, and the discussions subjected to thematic analysis. As an exploratory study, the purpose was to understand what was happening to supervision from the perspectives of the parties directly involved. The findings echoed messages from elsewhere that supervision (broadly conceived) in human services was finding itself somewhat on the defensive. The administrative aspects of supervision (associated with accountability, compliance with organizational procedures and oversight of task performance) were viewed by participants as having increasingly squeezed out educational and supportive aspects. Interestingly, this was what most had now come to expect from supervision, though such an expectation diverged greatly from what most staff thought supervision still ought to be providing. Commitment of time to supervision, allowing for more in-depth examination of practice, was seen to be fragile within an ever busy working environment. Access to supervisors who were felt to understand the nature of practice was not to be taken for granted. For some, the growing presence of computer technologies in the workplace was superseding certain of the more instrumental aspects of the supervisory role.

The study also pointed to a proliferation in the forms of supervision that practitioners were now embracing. The more traditional one-to-one model, while still the most predominant formal arrangement, was for many no longer the mainstay of their supervisory experience. Informal and formal peer group supervision was cited as a way of gaining assistance with current practice dilemmas and exploring longer-term issues. The use of external consultants, via a variety of agreements, was a new departure for a handful of others. Activities undertaken jointly provided another platform for mutual support and feedback, previously outside the realm of the lone practitioner. Generally, the concept of 'network learning' would not be an inappropriate term to describe what many felt to be initiatives taken in response to the perceived erosion of supervision. For some, this extended to networks of like-minded but diversely qualified practitioners. For some too, the term did also signify the imaginative use of information and communication technologies to further their professional development.

The study is suggestive, then, of a transitional phase in the meaning and forms of supervision. A tentative conclusion points to supervision being constituted within a more tightly regulated administration of practice accompanied by a growing array of sites and sources for learning. The tensions here are evident, and speak to the changing contexts of not only accountability but also of learning within human services.

Contextualizing Learning within Human Services

While the concept of learning might generally carry benign connotations – with a tendency to be seen as intrinsically 'a good thing' – the recent upheavals in human services have perhaps exposed some of its more contentious aspects. In this section, the discussion turns to learning as a political and ethical practice, intimately concerned with the exercise of power and with social values.

In the conventional, triad model propounded by Kadushin (1992), the educational function of supervision stood alongside the administrative and supportive function. Given this combination approach, the positions of learner and educator were hierarchically inscribed by the organizational location of each. Clearly this presented certain dilemmas of its own regarding the learning processes that could pertain between the two. The potential existed, particularly where supervisors transferred hierarchical models of practice into the conduct of their supervisory role, for the relationship to be one of subtle or not so subtle control. Kadushin himself was not unaware of this, contributing to folklore his observations on 'games people play in supervision', albeit using a psychological rather than social focus for his analysis (Kadushin, 1968).

As previously described, however, this configuration occurred within welfare regimes in which supervision provided a necessary social glue between the professional workforce and their employing organizations. Subsequently, each factor in this equation has experienced, and continues to experience, substantive changes. The challenges for human service professionals in the 'new politics of welfare' (Jordan, 1998) have been extensively documented (Parton, 1994; Uttley, 1994). The emergence of different forms of governance has been transforming the management of the professional workforce (Harris, 1998; Newman, 2000). Yet, a significant and further dimension to these considerations is the place of learning within changing organizational and professional contexts.

While broader socio-economic changes were under way, the concept of workplace learning began to gain considerable ground (Marsick, 1987). It involved assembling ideas particularly from action learning (Revans, 1980) and experiential learning (Boud, Keogh and Walker, 1985; Kolb, 1984) and developing them further in regard to the work setting. It challenged the notion that training occurs at work and education occurs at school or university. Rather in the way of a new social movement, this would undermine any position of dominance held by educational institutions over knowledge-making in the professional and applied disciplines. There was now a promotion of the previously hidden learning that occurs within the workplace and, in some senses, a celebration of its worth and value. As a consequence, workplace learning implied recasting relations of knowledge and power between the workplace and external institutions with a claim over its practices, for example, between 'industry' and 'academia'. Affording legitimacy to workplace learning means that academia relinquishes any pretensions to be the socially dominant producer and transmitter of theory and knowledge relevant to the work setting.

Receptiveness to this position has been fostered by the parallel discourse of reflective learning, by the rapidity and extent of social changes, as well as by the pursuit of productivity. In a fashion somewhat complementary to workplace learning, the reflective approach was similarly reconceptualizing epistemologies of practice. The partnership between Schön, with his interest in professional practice, and Argyris, with his attention to organizational learning, captured much of this ground. Schön's depiction of the creativity inherent in practice responsive to unpredictable contingencies became influential in redesigning education across many professions, including nursing, teaching and social work (Schön, 1987). With Argyris, the two formulated analyses of learning within organizations informed by systemic theorizing that challenged individualistic models and began to link learning with wider cultural change in the organizational domain (Argyris and Schön, 1978).

Together, workplace and reflective learning are indicative of the shifts that were occurring. The workplace organization was presented as a legitimate producer of learning and also an agent in the learning process. The adoption of a reflective learning process, moreover, was seen to aid responsiveness to novel situations, and consequently viewed as highly appropriate in times of rapid social change. In a competitive environment, innovation was held as vital for organizational survival and advantageous performance. It is not surprising, therefore, to find that keen interest was emerging in the management of knowledge and the learning capacity of organizations.

The Fifth Discipline: The Art and Practice of the Learning Organization (Senge, 1990a) met with great enthusiasm. This landmark text was accessible, passionate and authoritative on the disciplines required by successful organizations of the future. The disciplines addressed the person, the team and the organization, and touched on all aspects of experience. Learning was to be total, and it was to be authentic and courageous. The analysis and rhetoric caught the spirit of the times. In the midst of downsizing, asset stripping and the single bottom line, there was a strident note of optimism. Organizations could be fulfilling, vibrant places with worthwhile and successful futures – and the key was learning.

With visions of the learning organization having emerged from the corporate sector, their relevance for human service organizations remained in question. The most self-evident areas of common ground concerned the imperatives to be responsive and innovative (Isaac-Henry, Painter and Barnes, 1997). The technologies of 'people-processing' organizations, especially the significance of teams and dialogue, has also been suggested as rendering them amenable for sculpting into learning organizations (Lewis et al., 2001). These external and internal considerations, however, again point to the importance of examining context in order to appreciate the shape that learning may or may not assume in the realities of the organizational world (Easterby-Smith, Araujo and Burgoyne, 1999).

Painting in these contextual considerations, Muetzelfeldt (2001) identified some trends. As he explains, critics of bureaucracy, including welfare bureaucracies, had long argued that 'a bureaucratic organization is an organization that cannot correct its behaviour by learning from errors' (Crozier, 1964: 187). Then, with the advent of new public management, similar criticisms emerged: 'managerialism inhibits or reduces the capacity for innovation' (Muetzelfeldt, 2001: 4). Yet, as Muetzelfeldt notes, 'the question of whether, and if so how, new public management can efficiently and effectively address knowledge management remains unasked and unanswered' (2001: 4). The backdrop here, provided by Gregory (1997: 202) is that human service organizations 'probably require greater capacity for learning and adaptation ... otherwise they may continue to categorise and act upon people in the light of inadequately examined, self validating, organisational (and professional) beliefs'. Yet, the working environment 'leave[s] little time and energy for critical reflection on the assumptions that underpin their work' and 'there may tend to be an inverse correlation between the certainty of task technology and the political sensitivity of that task' (ibid.). The tentative conclusion is that 'these types of organisations are likely to have little opportunity for systematic learning work, and what learning they can do is likely to be supplanted by the needs of their external political masters' (Muetzelfeldt, 2001: 5).

A further aspect of the internal context raised by Muetzelfeldt (2001) is that behind the aspirations towards learning in and by organizations there are:

> two brute facts: organisational change is always an exercise of power, and if it is to succeed there must be at least compliance and preferably commitment to it by people throughout the organisation ... . The learning organisation has – like many other organisational metaphors – been mobilised into the service of concealed organisational power plays .... (Ibid.: 3)

Prospects for Supervision and Learning

The contention is that the prospects for supervision and learning in human services are contingent upon the internal and external contexts in which they occur, and that analyses of power, knowledge and values are crucial to this task of contextualizing supervisory and learning practices. While prescriptive models may orient us towards preferred scenarios, the everyday construction of supervision and learning requires acting as part of the organizational, professional and policy contexts of practice. In assessing the current prospects, what are some of the key ideas? For the purposes of this discussion, it may be useful to group them under three headings: learning and indeterminacy, accountabilities and reflexivity.

Indeterminacy reaches into many parts of human services practice, from the micro engagement with the lives of individuals to the macro engagement with broader socio-political change. In contexts of uncertainty and change, predetermined responses do not address the uniqueness of the situations that confront professionals day by day. Yet, the drivers towards rule-governed practice are considerable, from the tenets of empiricist evidence-based practice, to the instructional software. Nevertheless, learning for professional expertise requires learning how to be 'rule-makers' as well as rule followers (Fook, Ryan and Hawkins, 2000). To some extent, this revisits the place for professional discretion.

There is some evidence that discretion may not have been so squeezed out of the picture by the restructuring of human service delivery and incorporation of new managerialism as had once been supposed (Baldwin, 2000a). People working with people, it appears, may feature an interactional dynamic that it would be misleading to construe as amenable to even the most sophisticated pre-programming and regulation. In the policy domain, moreover, both past and present configurations of service provision tell a complex story about the presence of discretionary activity. The fragmentation of services that has accompanied contractually based provision and now the partnership approaches of centre left politics have generated different channels of connectedness and communication which, it has been argued, result in new sets of conflicts and contradictions, posing alternative possibilities for discretion and interorganizational learning processes (Muetzelfeldt and Briskman, 2000).

However, discretion implies exercising judgement between criteria that are already fixed. Indeterminacy suggests that the criteria themselves have to be continually revised and re-created according to the emerging contexts of practice. The creation of new forms of professional practice and professionalism require not just being responsive to an incoming welfare regime but responsiveness to continually changing welfare settings and socio-political contexts (Rosenman, 2000). In the midst of this, the supervisor's role becomes one of facilitating learning networks within which practitioners can both receive and generate new knowledge. As intimated in the Victorian study referred to above, there is some evidence that such networks are embryonic within many human service organizations, energized in most instances by front-line staff themselves. The future existence and proliferation of such learning networks is tied to the possibilities for creating cultures of learning and research within and between human service organizations. This in itself would be convergent with agendas for establishing new relations between practitioners, educators, researchers and service users across the 'industry', professional bodies, educational institutions and local communities.

Learning in human services work is inseparably tied to questions of accountability. What is it that practitioners are learning to do, how well are they doing it and to whose benefit? Movements towards expansive and inclusive learning processes occur in the context of 'checks and balances' historically written into professional traditions and structurally produced through public policy. Transitions are evident in the forms of accountability prevalent in human services, and supervisors have been variously active and passive agents within this changing scene. Different forms of accountability have been aligned to the different traditions of 'confidence' or 'trust' (Smith, 2001) in commentaries on the rise of the 'audit culture' (Parton, 1998). In many instances, supervision has become a conduit for numerous and often standardized accountability procedures and policies (whether, for instance, performance management tools, quality assurance protocols, anti-harassment policies or community consultation forums) that have emanated from the upper echelons of the organization.

Maintaining multiple perspectives on accountabilities becomes a crucial task for the supervisor. The complexity of new forms of practice creates a range of 'stakeholders' who stand in varying power relations to the definitions and formats of accountable practice. Within this, accountabilities to service users and recipients might quickly become marginalized, and those to the wider professional and lay communities overlooked. Rather than remain a conduit alone, the supervisor can seek opportunities to become a mediator and arbiter of different forms of accountability, as well as engaging in processes which question and redefine the lines and content of accountability mechanisms. The exercise of leadership here is likely to be influential upon the organizational commitment of the work group, and will itself tend to reflect the quality of supervision that occurs throughout all levels of the organization (Hawkins and Shohet, 2000; Hughes and Pengelly, 1997).

In creating new practices through reinvented forms of supervision and learning, front-line practitioners and managers will be working with and within changing and uncertain contexts. As such, they are inevitably part of that context, informed by its traditions and with identities that have emerged from their own personal and professional histories (Jones, 2000). Seeing new possibilities and maintaining a critical eye on the strategies they pursue, and the values they espouse, requires an ability also to gaze upon themselves and the assumptions through which they make sense of their social worlds. Reflexivity speaks of this process, and the capacity it affords to position oneself within a fluid and changing environment, taking a critical look at the possibilities of the present and opportunities for action that are appropriate for the given time and place (Taylor and White, 2000).

The prospects for supervisory practice may well reside, then, in embracing expansive learning that reaches into a diverse range of networks, and inclusive learning that admits knowledge-building from many sites and sources. In this scenario, the role of supervisor becomes aligned to that of 'knowledge broker' (Muetzelfeldt, Briskman and Jones, 2002), and supervision represents a focal place in the circuits of knowledge/power in the networked organization. The processes by which this brokerage occurs will at the same time be sustaining and constructing the operations of accountability. By retaining openness to multiple perspectives on accountability, the supervisor can be an agent in the proactive pursuit of transformative professional practices that maintain possibilities for critical engagement within the organization and with service communities. Such openness is supported through the exercise of reflexivity. Potentially squeezed from top and bottom, and now stretched from side to side, reflexive analysis can assist the supervisor in developing purposive actions attuned to the immediate contexts of practice.

Conclusion

What should be the case with supervision and learning in human services is the subject of considerable debate. This chapter has reviewed prescribed models for advancing both areas of practice but has shown the importance of contextualizing the issues. Transformations in professions, human service organizations, public policies and the broader socio-political environment all contribute to the shape that supervision and learning can and will assume. An examination of their history and present location moves the debate from a normative one to a more analytic consideration of the possibilities. By siting themselves within these contexts, supervisors can take better hold of the opportunities that may be available to pursue forms of learning and supervision that are both viable and contribute to advancing the social values to which they aspire.

A particular reading of the present situation suggests that future prospects for supervision may well rest with the knowledge brokerage required when learning becomes an expansive and inclusive activity. Responsibilities turn to those concerning the legitimation of knowledge that is generated across networks and from diverse sources, and the use of multiple forms of accountability in the evaluation of knowledge and practice. There is an exercise of judgement implied here but one that requires positioning oneself within uncertain and changing contexts, a movement that can be assisted by the appropriation of reflexive modes of analysis and action. The challenges for effective supervision of transformative professional practice, therefore, are yet more complex and demanding. But, they remain ones of crucial importance for those working in human service organizations and the communities they seek to serve.

Acknowledgements

The ideas expressed here would not have been possible without the formative discussions held with Professor Michael Muetzelfeldt, Victoria University (Australia), and Associate Professor Linda Briskman, RMIT University; the participation of agency staff in the supervision research project conducted in south-west Victoria and the research assistance of Penny Jones; and, collaboration with Philip Gillingham, Department of Human Services, Barwon South Western Region, Victoria.

Chapter 2

Social Work Supervision: Contributing to Innovative Knowledge Production and Open Expertise

Synnöve Karvinen-Niinikoski

Introduction

The construction and development of knowledge and expertise has become the central focus of organizational development and organizational learning in the rapidly changing societies of our postmodern era. This is also opening a new role for professional supervision, especially in the field of social work. Our understanding of knowledge and knowledge creation is changing. Knowledge and expertise are understood to be in a new way reflexive by their nature very much due to contingency and ambiguity in our postmodern world. There is a shift from acquisition and transmission of knowledge to construction and invention of knowledge, towards innovative knowledge production. Expertise shows itself more and more as a mechanism of reframing problems, which incorporates not only scientific judgements or technical decisions but also more basic and deeper social and cultural predispositions and commitments (Eräsaari, 2003). In social work this shift towards constructive expertise matches the urge to cope with the ever-changing complexity that has to be dealt with in the everyday practices of the profession.

One could actually speak of a paradox of scientific and professional expertise (Nowotny, 2000). In our traditions of modernity we used to think about professional expertise as institutionalized and individually mastered specialist knowledge based on scientific evidence and reason. Today the trend is towards de-institutionalization, hybrid forms of organization and co-operative mastering of knowing and knowledge production, towards open expertise produced in multi-actor networks. The paradox concerns the need not only to support organizational and individual learning, but also to transfer knowledge and expertise into and from productive practice. The case is similar with organizations, which are being forced to adapt to continuous and rapid change in their environment. Structures and mechanisms for supporting reflexion, learning and innovative knowledge generation are of increasing interest, one of these being the learning organization. Supervision is also part of these processes, attaining a new role and scope.

In social work, supervision carries traditions of reflexive knowledge creation and learning. Coping with uncertainty and ambiguity is 'baked' into the very essence of social work as a professional practice dealing with social problems and people's everyday life. The new feature of 'expert knowledge being involved in social life and appropriated within everyday life itself' (Eräsaari, 2003) is a basic element in social work. Today, supervision and other reflective methods of supporting individual and organizational reflection and learning are becoming important to organizational development. This is after having been mainly used as methods for administration, individual support, learning and management of the psycho-socially loaded working tasks in social work (Abbott, 1988; 1995; Bruce and Austin, 2000; Engeström, 1987; 1992; Eräsaari, 1998; 2003; Fook, Ryan and Hawkins, 1997; Hakkarainen et al., 2003; Hawkins and Shohet, 2000; Juuti, 1999; Kadushin and Harkness, 2002; Karvinen, 1996; 1999; Parton and O'Byrne, 2000; Payne, 1991; 1999; Tynjälä et al., 1997).

Social work can be defined as a profession initiating change in social life in order to improve opportunities for a human life with dignity or for social sustainability, a concept used in discussion about eco-social social work (Karvinen, 1999; Närhi, Matthies and Ward, 2001; see also Besthorn, 2003; Smale, Tuson and Statham, 2000). Professional social work practice in postmodern society can be described as more reflexive in nature, which means that social workers increasingly have to look for flexible solutions in different situations and working contexts instead of leaning on given and existing professional methods in institutionalized settings (Satka and Karvinen, 1999). The great challenge and difficulty in social work is to cope with uncertainty and continuous change, the urge to interpret and create understanding according to the different and particular living situations of people, and to find optional ways and methods in solving and combating social problems. Treating cultural differences and gender identities in a respectful and sensitive way is also a big challenge for reflexivity in professional work (Karvinen, 1999). At the same time there is in the search for expertise in social work an internationally strengthening neo-positivistic trend towards controlled good practice based on scientific evidence (Webb, 2001). In any case the shared coefficient between these two is the need for organizational learning and (innovative) knowledge production in and through the practice context.

The aim of this chapter is to look at how supervision in social work with its long traditions and almost a pioneer role of supervision in human services (for example, Brown and Bourne, 1996; Karvinen, 1993; Middleman and Rhodes, 1985) could contribute to organizational learning and what would be the theoretical grounds for supervision promoting, critical and ethically sustainable professional developments and innovative knowledge production (for example, Banks, 1999; Ife, 1997; 2001).

I first look at the ideas of expertise and organizational learning. Secondly, I discuss the idea of the learning organization. Thirdly, I look at the traditions and theoretical understanding of social work supervision. The following section discusses the idea of reflexive supervision and expansive learning. In the final section supervision as a contributor to innovative knowledge production is discussed.

The Role of Supervision in Promoting Open Expertise

Traditional expertise, based on the three pillars of its constitution – scientific knowledge, professional agency and institutional traditions – can be considered to be in crisis because of rapid change, uncertainty and ambiguity in our societies. Institutions especially are in turbulence in postmodern societies, but also the nature of knowledge and scientific truth and knowledge generation are questioned. The crisis of expertise could be described as the crisis of expert institutions. Instead of traditional knowledge development, gradual accumulation of knowledge or constant epistemological revolutions, we now have to look for spatial arrangements and transformations in the relationships between these arrangements (Eräsaari, 2003). In the case of expertise as a particularly legitimate form of knowledge, the emphasis has moved on to contextualization or 'context-dependency' (Nowotny, 2000). That means also a new kind of interaction between 'practical knowledge' and 'explicit knowledge' taking place on individual and institutional levels in knowledge spirals or cycles of learning. The context has become an important source for generation and validation of knowledge. This development also raises different kinds of expertise such as open and closed expertise and lay and contra expertise (Eräsaari, 2003; Saaristo, 2000). In social work contextual practice there is an emerging concept in response to these changes in understanding expertise (Fook, 2002: 142–7). Supervision as a forum for reflecting and relating contextual knowledge seems to be gaining a new interest in managing social work.

Open expertise recognizes uncertainty and, instead of claiming to be the only one to possess proper knowledge and professional skills, it will be ready to question communication and even polemics as well as a willingness to negotiate and reconstruct expertise according to the different contexts of action. The context (the space for communication) is left open (to allow communication) (Eräsaari, 2003). In many cases expertise will be created together in multi-professional co-operation and communities, as traditional profession-centred solutions do not work. Expertise is created in the processes of learning and practising something that does not even exist yet, something that is in the process of evolution and potential in unrecognized or unrealized options. This makes tacit and experiential knowledge important constituents of expertise as well as scientific knowledge (Engeström, 1987; Eräsaari, 2003; Hakkarainen et al., 2003; Karvinen, 1993; Tynjälä et al., 1997). Closed, as opposed to open, expertise is 'a severe and unconditional strategy, ethos or mentality, which creates a strong link between core knowledge and specific advice or recommendations' (Eräsaari, 2003). This form of expertise prevails in the administrative traditions and may even be strengthening in social work through managerialist ideas of knowledge and evidence-based practices. In its very essence social work, however, inclines towards open expertise, for example, through being client centred or, to put it in more politically correct discourse, citizen centred (Lister, 1998). This is at least an issue for reflection, to ponder which kind of expertise supervision is promoting.

There is an urge and a wish for continuous, lifelong learning and professional development to be found in ideas of open and reflexive expertise. The importance of supervision in organizational learning can be seen in the emphases on experiential and tacit knowledge and the opportunity to learn from this knowledge through reflection, but also in the functions of supervision in looking after the well-being of practitioners in stressful work contexts (Baldwin, 2000b; Hakkarainen et al., 2003; Hawkins and Shohet, 2000; Kadushin and Harkness, 2002, Karvinen, 1993; Yliruka, 2000). The experience of partnership, the opportunity for dialogue and reflection provided in supervision can be considered as important contributors to 'organizational trust' (Kramer, 1999) and the reconstruction of professional identity in accordance with the demands of trust and co-operation in the networking organizations' knotworks (see Engeström, Engeström and Vähätalo, 1999).

There are several approaches for organizational learning and knowledge creation or innovative developmental work. There is lifelong adult learning and staff development (Tynjälä et al., 1997; Usher, Bryant and Johnson, 1997), knowledge management and knowledge creation (Nonaka, Toyama and Konno, 2000; Virkkunen, 2001), learning communities of practice (Wenger, 1998), the ideas of learning organizations (Gould, 2000; Frydman, Wilson and Wyer, 2000; Senge, 1990b, Senge et al., 1999), of expansive learning (Engeström, 1987; 1992) and of innovative knowledge communities (Bereiter, 2002; Hakkarainen et al., 2003). A central theme within these discourses is the search for models of collaborative and innovative learning allowing the search for alternative methods of action and innovation. Many of these models will include moments for research, critical reflection, studying, experimentation and evaluation following the same cyclical ideas that can be found in the Kolbian (Kolb, 1984) model of experiential learning or the ideas of reflective practices and the double-loop learning developed by Schön (1983; 1987) and Argyris and Schön (1974; 1996).

In social work much professional practice includes inventing new models and methods of working. The embryos for these innovative practices quite often can be found in the experiences of social workers and their clients in everyday practices. One of the dilemmas for developing social work thus lies in supporting these innovative processes, and much of that is dependant on organizational learning and developmental work for innovation (Gould, 2000). In social work the idea of open and innovative expertise (Eräsaari, 2003) or interpretative expertise (Bauman, 1992) is justified by the very nature of the professional ideal which recognizes and respects particularity and cultural difference in individual living situations as the starting point of professional practice (Karvinen, 1999; Raitakari, 2002). This kind of knowledge could be called 'orientation knowledge' (Eräsaari, 2003). There are, however, in the nature of social work and the institutions constituting professional jurisdiction, opposing factors which force much social work expertise to be closed (Eräsaari, 2003) or legislative (Bauman, 1992) in its nature. The Finnish researcher in expertise, Professor Risto Eräsaari (2003) warns professionals not to lose and close off differentiating and possibly unrecognized opportunities in the orientation processes of our postmodern life. He sees that opening and negotiating different perspectives is important. He encourages a certain lightness and imagination and awareness of the structures and processes of governance and power in society. In social work, as an institution of social welfare, there are elements of that kind of communication, 'first order seriousness' (Eräsaari, 2003: 29–35), which make social work in many senses 'closed' and preconditioned. Closed expertise as the opposite of open expertise, is according to Eräsaari (2003) 'a severe and unconditional strategy, ethos or mentality, which creates a strong link between core knowledge and specific advice or recommendations'. In social work with efforts to confirm expertise and credibility through evidence-based practices this is causing ethical conflicts and raising debate about the essence of the social work profession as a sensitive, critical and empowering democratic force in society. The ethical mission that, for example, Jim Ife (1997; 2000) or Walter Lorenz (2003) are posing for social work is looking for open and reflexive expertise. Reflexive expertise is a kind of orientation process relating experience to powerful meanings and calling for an epistemological standpoint in contextual and experiential factors of knowledge generation without excluding forms of counter-expertise or lay experience (Eräsaari, 2003). The social work profession is close to the critical point in society at the intersection of system and life world, indicating an ethical connection to the reflexive epistemological standpoint and knowledge generation in social work (Lorenz, 2003: 16).

Traditionally, supervision has been one of the main methods for supporting practitioners in the emotionally demanding work and the solutions and choices to be made in the manifold realities of clients. Also protection of 'closed practices', 'parochial and hierarchical mechanism' (Harris, 1998: 121; see also Kadushin and Harkness, 2002) for political and administrative control prevails in supervision. On the other side there also is the strong tradition of looking for autonomy and open development of expertise (Bruce and Austin, 2000). For example, Swedish social workers regard supervision as the most important source for reflection and support, learning and knowledge creation in social work (Nordlander and Björn, 2002). Supervision may in its essence become a method and forum for critical reflection on experiences gained from professional practice. But for it to face the contradictions of professional expertise, supervision needs to become more analytic and critical. There is also the need to sharpen understanding of the theoretical grounds for supervision and its capacity to develop expertise.

Organizational Learning and Supervision

There has been an extensive change in the constellation of organizations in postmodern society partly due to developments in expertise and knowledge production and, especially, due to globalization processes in the information society. The search has been towards flexible, light and innovative organizations like teams and networks or, to use the latest term, 'hybrid knotworks' (Engeström, Engeström and Vähätalo, 1999). This has led to the development of leadership and aroused the need to create more space and forums for dialogue and reflection. One could even speak about a new kind of empowering and collaborative leadership, with a strong emphasis on supervisory methods and mentoring (Frydman, Wilson and Wyer, 2000; Juuti, 1999). On the other hand, there has been an increasing need for new methods of governance and control, a development that managerialism is concerned with. In social work the idea of knowledge-based practices seems to have become the strategy of social services management even on the national level, for example,

Sweden (Socialstyrelsen, (2002), the UK (Walker, 2001; Webb, 2001) and Finland (Heikkilä, Kaakinen and Korpelainen, 2003). The idea is to promote expertise and quality of services through evidence-based knowledge for good practices. This development includes contradictory elements in regard to open and closed expertise. New managerialism is also using supervision (Harris, 1998), but more in the sense of governance and closed expertise. This trend may be strengthening in social work where the space for social worker autonomy is reduced and questioned by strengthening managerialism (Raunio, 2002).

Organizational development as the evolution of organizational culture and psychology (Schein, 1994) and of organizational learning (Argyris and Schön, 1974; 1996) has been discussed for decades. It has been a long process of paradigmatic development to the present situation where knowledge and expertise are understood to be constructed and negotiated through professional practice within their different contexts. Both individual experience and knowledge learned and transferred into a shared organizational knowledge and knowing have led to a search for methods of managing and promoting that learning – organizational learning. Argyris and Schön (1996: 280–86) speak about a learning paradox and double-loop learning, and the relationship between the individual member creating his or her theory-in-use and organizational learning. They address the problems of change and knowledge creation, seeing that practice should be the primary context for both research and development of organizational learning (Argyris and Schön, 1996: 285).

Through the dynamics seen here, the role of supervision in promoting organizational learning becomes evident. The ideas of organizational culture and organizational psychology (Schein, 1992; 1994) have set a certain place for supervision, especially in the psychodynamic, classical form of supervision, which still is the main focus for supervision (for example, Hawkins and Shohet, 2000; Kadushin and Harkness, 2002). Although there is also research showing that when the main emphasis of supervision lies on the individual level of coping and support (Bruce and Austin, 2000; Egelund and Kvilhaug, 2001) supervision could be used in a more comprehensive way.

In professional learning, becoming a reflective practitioner (Schön, 1983) or a transformative learner (Mezirow 1981; 1991) – a practitioner who has learned to learn and is capable of developing expertise through practice, and who also is a conscious subject of the activity and able to take alternative actions – has become mainstream in educational (Tynjälä et al., 1997) and even social work research (Fook, Ryan and Hawkins, 2000; Healy, 2001; Karvinen, 1996; Taylor and White, 2000). The idea of transformative learning is central to the theory of supervision as it is perspectives of meaning and the changing of these which, according to Jack Mezirow (1991), are guiding our actions. Meaning perspectives are developed through several processes in human development, many of these processes being of that kind of meta-cognition and emotions that are also the focus of supervision theories (Egelund, 1999; see also Gardiner, 1989), for example, the psychodynamic approach (Hawkins and Shohet, 2000) and systemic supervision (Barnes, Down and McCann, 2000). There seems to be a need to reconstruct not only role and position, but also theoretical understanding of social work supervision for it to contribute to critical practice and the demands of reflexive and open expertise (Egelund and Kvilhaug, 2001; Fook, 1999a; Karvinen, 1996; Phillipson, 2002; see also Gardiner, 1989).

One of the main lines in the discourse on organizational learning, especially in connection to leadership and management in the business field, is based on the work of Senge (1990b) and his idea 'the fifth discipline' in organizational development and 'the change as a dance' (Senge et al., 1999) (see Frydman, Wilson and Wyer, 2000; Juuti, 1997) There is a good portion of idealism in organizational learning approaches, overemphasizing the leadership function in approaching organizational learning as something that individuals share and create, and that can be managed. Argyris and Schön (1996: 180–99, 281–6) criticize both Senge's (1990b) 'Fifth discipline' that 'unites systems thinking with organisational adaptation and with the realisation of human potential in a mixture that has a distinctly Utopian flavor' and Edgar Schein's (1992) idea of managing organizational culture by emphasizing the paradox of learning and opportunities overcoming it. The ideas of paradox of learning and organizational learning developed by Argyris and Schön reflect Kolbian experiential learning, the cornerstone of cyclical models of learning for organizational development and change. New solutions for tackling the problems of the co-operative learning and knowledge generation in organizations, for stretching understanding of organizational relations (see Argyris and Schön, 1996: 190) are ideas of 'communities of practice' (Wenger, 1998) and shared space for knowledge creation (Nonaka, Toyama and Konno, 2000).

Argyris and Schön (1996: 190) are right in stating 'that a theory of learning must take account of the interplay between the actions and interactions of individuals and the actions and interactions of higher-level organizational entities such as departments, divisions or groups' and that the learning problem on the organizational level is 'stretching our ordinary understandings of individual and organization'. This could be interpreted either as a challenge for subjective spheres or as a challenge for contextualization. The risk in forgetting the context has – according to the ideas of material constructivism and actor network theory in the footsteps of Bruno Latour and Steve Woolgar (1979) – a material side, as the social cannot be considered only as the interaction between individuals, but needs to be seen as a network of action, where the material and artefacts for their deal construct social relations. The agency, like the social worker, is not only defined by intentional action, but also by the position of the actor in relation to the network in each case. The dynamic understanding of the actor as a product of the network and a subject of the agency provided by the network, as well as a creator of the network, raises the intermediary elements of the networks as actors on the side of the acting individuals. The actor network approach describes how prevailing understandings, occasions, physical elements and relations between different actors among other things, construct the options and decisions in the network. They start to define the space around them. All this is important to organizational learning as well as for the knowledge formation and processing. The ideas produced in actor networks tend to become facts and construct what would be proper knowledge and in that sense also proper agency (Peltola and Åkerman, 1999). Combined to theories of social construction (Parton and O'Byrne, 2000) and/or to the ideas of structuration

(Giddens, 1984) efforts in promoting organizational learning, supervision, development of expertise or innovative knowledge production necessarily lead to looking for methods of treating the paradox of learning and the creation of intermediate factors and space within the organizational or activity system level.

It seems that to obtain a holistic understanding of the processes of expertise generation one will have to look at the process of knowledge generation from three different perspectives. First, there is expertise as knowledge acquisition for the individual expert. Secondly, there is expertise as social-cultural processes of knowing. In this case the expertise is socially shared and participative. The two mentioned approaches, or metaphors of learning, do not treat the third perspective: the problem of generating new knowledge and overcoming the old solutions. Knowledge generation of progressive problem-solving angles are central to achieving the innovation needed in the complex contexts of agency (Hakkarainen, Paavola and Lipponen, 2002; Hakkarainen et al., 2003). The development of expertise and production of knowledge is a progressive problem-solving process, where people continuously reflect and reframe their work (Tynjälä, 2003: 46–7).

Professional supervision in the changing and contingent context of professional and expert action can be seen as a way of orientation, and gaining deeper understanding of our agency. It is a process of scrutinizing and reconstructing professional orientation. This orientation is constructed in the dialogue of our experiences and the meaning perspectives we hold. The orientation is a process of relating experiences to powerful meanings. In this way we gain more understanding, when we understand 'how our experience is contingent on our meanings' (Eräsaari, 2003).

Social Work Supervision

Social work has long traditions of supervision. Supervision was a central method for early social work teachers, researchers and practitioners in their efforts to construct relevant practices and describe a theory of social work. Reflecting on experience and learning from practical experience were central ways of gaining social work knowledge and constructing practices. Supervision was developed as the forum and method for that reflection (Karvinen, 1993). In the process of professional development, supervision has had different roles, traditions and backgrounds, for example, psychoanalytical and psychodynamic, administrative and competence orientated (Guttman, Eisikowitz and Malucchio, 1988; Karvinen, 1993; Middleman and Rhodes, 1985). Professional supervision seems quite often to be understood either as a professional structure in organizational hierarchies or a specified method for the purposes of ensuring quality and effectiveness of services (Hawkins and Shohet, 2000; Phillipson, 2002). There are also different supervisory cultures in different countries (Salonen, 2003; Stromfors, 2002: 21–5). Though comparative research is lacking (Bruce and Austin, 2000), there are different systems. In the Anglo-American tradition supervision is part of hierarchical line management (for example, Bruce and Austin, 2000; Harris, 1998; Kadushin and Harkness, 2002). In the Scandinavian tradition (Egelund, 1999) professional autonomy is guaranteed by a supervisor who comes from outside the organization (Nordlander and Björn, 2002). In Scandinavia, social workers want to use supervision as their own reflective support both in the daily chaos and in their professional practice. In these traditions supervision has been understood as a forum for knowledge production, professional learning and professional development since the early 1950s and the period of professional expansion in 1980s (Egelund and Kvilhaug, 2001; Karvinen, 1993).

There is also the tradition of attaching the professional development of social work to supervision. The focus here has been on supporting the individual social worker's role as an active and autonomous subject in developing professional practice. Questions include what is guiding the social worker and her choices (Karvinen, 1993; see also Nordlander and Björn, 2002), what makes the social worker do what she does and how can supervision be helpful for the social worker and her choices? How would it be possible for the social worker to keep up with and develop professionally and ethically sustainable practices and expertise in social work? How could discretion become a creative potential for social work practice (Baldwin, 2001) or how could the autonomy of social workers be supported (Karvinen, 1987)? All these questions lead to supervision as a method for supporting developmental potential. The most ambitious aim in these questions would be the theoretical understanding of supervision, and in that sense one has to ask a question about the object of supervision (Karvinen, 1993). Developmental supervision theory must address professional action in a holistic way. Although some critique on social work supervision can be argued in its bias towards individual psychodynamic and emotional issues (Egelund and Kvilhaug, 2001), there are models where supervision is given a wider perspective like the 'seven-eyed model for supervision' (Hawkins and Shohet, 2000: 68) 'a foursome mentality' (Middleman and Rhodes, 1985: 223) or 'developmental supervision' especially in the perspective of action research (Baldwin, 2000b: 137; 2001: 292) and in the ideas of expansive learning as a background theory for supervision (Auvinen and Karvinen, 1993).

A theoretical model grasping the complex and even contradictory contexts that constrain social workers' profession and professional practices in different cultural settings indicate the connections of individual action into wider organizational and social contexts. Also a model that would support the critical, reflexive practitioner is needed (Abbott, 1988; Eräsaari, 2003; Mezirow, 1981; 1991). Each social worker carries some kind of theoretical model about being a social worker in the context of the wider society in her or his mind. This model, which could be called 'the theory or self-understanding of social work' is developing or 'living' and continuously reconstructed and de-constructed in and through professional and organizational practices. This model could also be described as the model of working orientation, a model that provides the contextual setting for different and developing meaning perspectives (Mezirow, 1991) that are guiding choices of human actors such as social workers. Adapting the ideas of the Finnish professor in developmental working studies, Professor Yrjö Engeström, the model of self-understanding can be conceptualized as the model and theory of 'human activity system' (Engeström, 1987).

The construction and transformation of meaning perspectives guiding the actor's orientation in the activity (Mezirow, 1991) are central to the theoretical understanding of supervision. In aiming to develop professional practice, the actions of practitioners and the context of that action, it is the more or less shared meaning perspectives, the shared understandings, which need to be developed, or reconstructed and de-constructed. This is also the object of supervision. According to Jack Mezirow (1991), change or alteration in meaning perspectives opens up ways to take alternative action and for innovative knowledge creation. Change may start in the simple daily routines and end up with new forms and artefacts and ways of organization, new approaches and models of practices (see also, for example, Fook, 2002). By no means is the change only a result of the individual actor's actions, and the issue here is not of voluntarism. In essence, the need for change comes from changes and contradictions in the activity system itself (Engeström, 1987).

Supervision as a forum for reflection allows social workers to reflect their experiences and emotions and through critical reflection to understand them in the wider context of work and thus to look for alternative methods of reaction, action and agency. The individual practical experience as the focus of reflection does not mean the exclusion of education, training, knowledge, research and science, or anything in favour of mere practical knowledge. On the contrary, it is important that social work is seen in all its complexity – as well as in its developmental historical context (see also Fook, 2002: 142–7.) According to activity theory (Engeström, Miettinen and Ounamäki, 1999), human action has to be seen in its contextual development – from historical, present and future perspectives. Human action is also unavoidably complicated including different kinds of emotional, psychological, material, social and cultural dynamics, so social work supervision cannot be reduced either on cognitive or emotional sides.

In order to develop professional expertise in social work, supervision should help social workers to reflect and reconstruct their meaning perspectives, working orientation and 'self-understanding' of social work. The core of meaning perspectives lies in understanding the object of social work, which is the everyday life and action of people in all its complexities. Real understanding of this cannot be achieved without a partnership in reflection and knowledge production with the working community and clients, the people, whom social work concerns (see also Baldwin, 2001). This calls for new kinds of relationships and structures for research, supervision, and developmental social work practices and expertise (Karvinen, 1999). In organizational learning and knowledge generation reflexive and shared forums for communication, like supervision, seem to be of great interest (Hakkarainen et al., 2003; Nonaka, Toyama and Konno, 2000; Wenger, 1998).

It is difficult to define supervision in a theoretically grounded way and definitions remain rather descriptive, general and circular (Hyrkäs, 2002; Karvinen, 1993; 1996). In developmental supervision it is essential to understand the processes whereby the actor is trying to grasp her or his own agency and the constraints of changing this agency in its subjective and societal and developmental contexts. From an activity theoretical point of view, supervision could be defined as the reflection process working on a professional's working orientation or self-understanding and the meaning perspectives constructing it (Karvinen, 1993). This process could make use of ideas of expansive learning (Engeström, 1987) where connection to innovative knowledge production and organizational learning are integral.

The model of expansive learning based on the ideas of the cultural-historical approach in activity theory develops the idea of learning cycles, in which, by deconstructing and scrutinizing existing practices, new models and solutions to solve problems of earlier practices will be developed. New models will in turn be put in place and evaluated in action. As actors of the expansive cycle, participants will reconstruct their understanding and gain new meaning perspectives. The central idea of this approach is to help the organization and working community to reflect on their practice in a systematic way (Engeström, 1987; 1992; Engeström, Engeström and Vähätalo, 1999; Engeström, Miettinen and Ounamäki, 1999).

Reflexive Supervision

Social work is about action (for example, Adams, Dominelli and Payne, 2002: 6). Supervision in its efforts to help practitioners act in the best possible way is about very broad analysis of action . The focus is on the social worker's action, which has its focus on people's action, all unavoidably in complicated contexts. Social work literature on holistic approaches throughout the development of professional education has described this complexity (for example, Mattaini and Meyer, 1995; Payne, 1991; Reamer, 1994). Although systemic eco-psycho-social models are quite comprehensive, only following them in the analysis of professional action would lead to the omission of the developmental perspectives found in the tensions and contradictions of professional action.

In current social work discourse, the concept of critical practice (Adams, Dominelli and Payne, 2002) represents the effort of developing social work according to the ideas of the reflective practitioner and reflexive practice. Although

> critical practice is not social work per se but is integral to social work that makes use of criticality as the route to excellence in performance and advancing expertise ... we cannot claim that critical practice will change the world, but the constant interplay between our actions and the deconstruction and reconstruction that comprise our critical reflection gives us access to advancing our practice. (Ibid.: xxi)

Facing the idea of the shifting complexity and contextual multiplicity is unavoidable when trying to analyse social work practice and development. However, there is an obvious lack of both an inclusive comprehension of this complexity and a theoretically solid tool to analyse this complexity of human action. For example, Adams (Adams, 2002: 84) writes about the reflexive cycle and the 'demanding process of holistic engagement actually involved in practising critically; engaging with contexts, engaging with our-selves; engaging with knowledge, engaging with practice and engaging with paradoxes and dilemmas'. All this is good, but there still remains the difficulty of seeing the relations between these different elements. The difficulties lie especially in the problems of connecting the human action with the non-human structures and developmental processes, and understanding the collective in relation to the subjective.

The concept and model of 'the mediated activity system' developed by Yrjö Engeström (1987; 1992; see for an example Figure 2.1), drawing on the cultural-historical theory of activity, offers tools to understand complicated collaborative human action (Miettinen, 1998: 40). The strength of the model of an activity system is that it provides a conceptual tool addressing and analysing the complexity of human action in its different and changing contexts and relationships between the basic elements. The notion of mediation is of crucial importance as, 'the activity system comprises the individual practitioner, the colleagues and co-workers of workplace community, the conceptual and practical tools, and the shared objects as a unified dynamic whole' (Engeström, 1992: 12–13). The multiple mediations between the different components are decisive features in the activity. The subject and the object, or the actor and the environment, are mediated by instruments, including symbols and representations of various kinds. There are also less visible mediators of activity such as rules, community and division of labour. Between all the components of the activity system, there are continuous transformations and the system thus incessantly reconstructs itself. The system is also 'much more competent and robust than any of its individual expert members' (Engeström, 1992: 12–13). The system does not exist in a vacuum, but is a part of multidimensional networks of activity systems, types of 'neighbourhood activities' producing the components of the 'central activity', the activity in focus. In the network of the neighbourhood activities, systems connected to a given central activity – for example, the socials worker's practice – the exchanges and interpenetrations of the

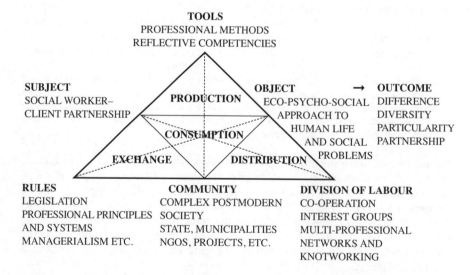

Figure 2.1   The mediated activity system (see Engeström, 1987; 1992) adapted as an outline model for social work self-understanding

different components potentially cause destabilization and change. With the help of the model of mediated activity system and the critical reflection that it facilitates, professional practice can be described, conceptualized and further developed. In supervision the model can be used as an analytical tool for opening the connections from individual reflection to the wider societal and organisational processes (Karvinen, 1993).

The activity system is a concrete and contextual formation, where human and non-human entities have been developed into a historically developing system. This model of the human activity system can also be adapted as a model for professional self-understanding (Figure 2.1). It provides a tool for a comprehensive analysis of professional and human action needed in critical social work. In Figure 2.1 the idea is to describe contemporary social work in very broad terms only in order to give an example of the model.

An activity system is by definition a multi-voiced system, which is evolved through developmental cycles, where the different 'voices', the different viewpoints and approaches of various participants, are re-orchestrated. It is also important to understand the 'historicity' of this development, through which the future re-orchestration can be 'dramatically facilitated, when different voices are seen against their historical background' (Engeström, 1992: 17). The challenge for developing expertise and 'learning what is not yet there' as Engeström (ibid.) points out, is the mastery of qualitative transformations and reorganizations of work activities, the challenge for learning organizations as well. For Engeström and the activity theoretical thinking he is referring to, learning is 'a question of joint creation of a zone of proximal development for the activity system', it is 'a venture of designing, implementing and mastering the next developmental stage of the activity system itself' (Engeström, 1992: 17). Engeström (1987; 1992, 17–18) has developed also a theory and model of expansive learning describing the phases starting from individual experience and the need for change, reaching up to diversification of the initial action model into various applications and modifications. According to Engeström, the developmental cycle has an expansive character and, starting with a few individuals acting as spearheads of change, the cycle can lead to a movement or a bandwagon that involves the entire community.

The developmental tensions in the action system are quite often grasped as problems and disturbances of everyday practices, and interpreted as characteristics of individual practitioners. The solutions to these tensions or contradictions may be studied and drafted by analysing the developmental phase and constructing possible solutions, the zone of proximal development. Change and transformation will be generated through developing or inventing new ways and tools for practice as the steps in proximal field of the new possible action. The theory of expansive learning explains the dynamics in the development of knowing and the creation of new concepts for action. It offers a model for conscious systematization of developmental processes. This model is based on similar ideas of the now widespread notion of reflexive cycle (Adams, Dominelli and Payne, 2002), experiential learning (Kolb, 1984; Schön, 1987), reflective learning (Boud, Keogh and Walker, 1985) or transformative learning (Mezirow, 1981) and organizational learning (Tuomi, 1999). There is no space in this chapter to go any deeper into the methodology of expansive learning, but it is important to note that it often is in supervision where the often tacit 'spearhead ideas' can be made visible and heard from the reflections based on the experiences of the individual practitioners, the supervisees. Getting a grip of the tacit knowledge so central to organizational learning (for example, Nonaka, Toyama and Konno, 2000) is both an issue of listening to the emotional reactions of the practitioners as well as an issue of constructing concepts and models for giving this knowledge a form.

This compact model of mediated action describing the basic elements of human and societal activity in dynamic relations to each other can also be seen to reflect different mental models which guide human action and represent the elements of professional self-understanding or theory-on-action (see Engeström, 1987). The model in itself is a model of the basic elements of action, but by focusing or zooming in on different modes, episodes, developmental processes or even systems of professional practice and thinking, it is a useful tool. The model allows a holistic and dynamic analysis of the descriptions of problems, experiences and ideas brought to supervision by supervisees. The analysis can be focused both on the specific and unique micro contexts of individual work and on the wider contexts of meso- or macro-level phenomena. The model provides tools for the conceptualization and modelling needed for shared understanding and further development of issues under discussion. The holistic use of the activity model also enables understanding professional practices, scientific research-based knowledge and theories in their developmental contexts. In its dynamic understanding of the development of human activity the model also advocates constructionist and contextual awareness (see Parton and O'Byrne, 2000; Payne, 1999) of professional action.

Also the ideas of the innovative learning community developed by Nonaka, Toyama and Konno (2000), where the organization is seen as an entity that creates knowledge continuously through action and interaction with its environment, propose a further developed model of the knowledge-creating process to help us understand the dynamic nature of knowledge creation and to manage such a process effectively – the discipline of knowledge creation. In this model there is a constructive space for the kind of forums for reflection that reflexive supervision can provide and what it also needs in becoming an integrated part of organizational learning and construction of expertise instead of staying 'an autonomous pocket of relief' for social workers or a 'parochial-hierarchical mechanism' of management.

Supervision and Innovative Knowledge Production

Current interest in knowledge creation through learning communities in learning organizations suggests a reinvention of supervision in organizational developmental work and knowledge management. In social work supervision has a long tradition in these processes, but somehow the professional approach has made it either an oasis of the ideal of professional autonomy or the forum for controlling best practices and professional ideals. There are, however, even traditionally, efforts to establish reflective and developmental approaches in supervision. Current trends seem to revive these ideas.

The question of how supervision in social work could contribute to organizational learning and what would be the theoretical grounds for supervision in promoting critical and ethically sustainable professional developments has been approached in this chapter with an interest in new understanding of expertise, innovations and knowledge production. Today the urge to cope with the ever-changing complexity that has to be dealt with even in the everyday practices of social work calls for innovative and open expertise. It calls for learning organizations. In the emerging knowledge society of increasing complexity (Urry, 2003) expertise is created in the processes of learning and practising something that does not even exist yet, something that is in the process of evolution and potential in unrecognized or unrealized options. The challenge for developing expertise and 'learning what is not yet there' as Engeström (1992) points out, is the mastery of qualitative transformations and reorganizations of work activities, a challenge for learning organizations as well. The change and transformation will be generated through developing or inventing new ways and tools for practices as the steps in the proximal field of new possible action. A search can be seen for open and reflexive expertise. Open expertise recognizes uncertainty and, instead of claiming to be the only position from which to possess proper knowledge and professional skills, it will be amenable to questioning, communication and, even, polemics. This connotes a willingness to negotiate and reconstruct expertise according to the different contexts of action instead of merely relying on given good practices.

Social work is becoming ever more context bound and contextual in its approaches, which means that much of professional practice includes inventing new models and methods of working. Innovative knowledge production is embedded in social work in two ways: adapting practical approaches to new and changing situations and innovating new methods is one, but for the second the knowledge learned and produced about people's everyday lives could call for innovations in the wider society. The embryos for these innovative practices quite often can be found in the experiences of social workers and their clients in everyday practices. This makes tacit and experiential knowledge unavoidably important constituents of expertise in addition to more traditional and established scientific knowledge. One of the main challenges for developmental and reflexive supervision in social work lies in supporting these innovative processes.

The model for developing expertise and suiting developmental supervision discussed in this chapter is the model of expansive learning and the mediated action system (Engeström, 1992). It seems that expertise will be created co-operatively in multi-professional co-operation and communities, as traditional profession-centred solutions do not work. Organizations are also changing in their constellation, and new flexible, light and innovative hybrid networks and knotworks are emerging. Reflexive expertise can be seen as a kind of orientation process relating experience to powerful meanings and calling for an epistemological standpoint in contextual and experiential factors of knowledge generation. This kind of knowledge could be called 'orientation knowledge' (Eräsaari, 2003).

Today, there is thus an increasing need for methods like supervision both in the field of organizational leadership as well as in organizational development. The importance of supervision in organizational learning can be seen in the emphases on experiential and tacit knowledge and the opportunity to learn from this knowledge through reflection, but also in the functions of supervision in looking after the well-being of practitioners in stressful work contexts. One could even speak about a new kind of empowering and collaborative leadership. There seem to be emerging several approaches for organizational learning and knowledge creation or innovative developmental work with an emphasis on supervisory methods and mentoring. Here supervision could be used in a more comprehensive way in the creation of knowledge, expertise and innovations. A reflexive and developmental supervision theory must address professional action in a holistic way. There is a need for conceptual tools addressing and analysing the complexity of human action in its different and changing contexts and relationships between the basic elements of the activity system.

The learning problem on the organizational level is 'stretching our ordinary understandings of individual and organization' (Argyris and Schön, 1996: 190). However, there is an obvious lack of both an inclusive comprehension of this understanding and a theoretically solid tool to analyse the complexity of human action. The difficulties lie especially in the problems of connecting the human action with the non-human structures and developmental processes, and understanding the collective in relation to the subjective. It is the difficulty of understanding our agency as acting subjects. A central theme within the discourses in the theory of organizational learning is the search for models of collaborative and innovative learning allowing the search for alternative methods of action and innovation. Many of these models will include moments for research, critical reflection, studying, experimentation and evaluation following the same cyclical ideas that can be found in the Kolbian (Kolb, 1984) model of experiential learning. The idea of transformative learning is central to the theory of supervision as it is the meaning perspectives and the changing of these which, according to Jack Mezirow (1991), are guiding our actions and thus are a key to change them. Meaning perspectives are developed through several processes in human development, many of these processes being of that kind of meta-cognition and emotions that are also the focus of supervision theories. The mediated activity system offers tools for analysing the meaning perspectives.

Professional supervision in the changing and contingent context of professional and expert action can be seen as a way of orientation and gaining deeper understanding of our agency. It is a process of scrutinizing and reconstructing professional orientation. This orientation is constructed in the dialogue of our experiences and the meaning perspectives we hold. Supervision as a forum for reflection allows social workers to reflect their experiences and emotions, and through critical reflection to understand them in the wider context of work and thus to look for alternative methods of reaction, action and agency.

Supervision may, in essence, become a method and forum for critical reflection on experiences gained from professional practice. But for it to face the contradictions of professional expertise, supervision needs to become more analytical and critical. There is also the need to sharpen understanding of the theoretical grounds for supervision and its capacity to develop expertise. A theoretical model grasping the complex and, even, contradictory contexts that constrain social workers' profession and professional practices in different cultural settings indicates also the connections of individual action in wider organisational and social contexts.

Supervision has strengths in meeting the contemporary challenges of developing professional expertise and organizational learning. As this chapter has shown, there are ongoing efforts to develop theoretical bases for developmental and reflexive supervision. Looking at the challenges of today, one may feel tempted to turn back to the solid traditional psychodynamic core of supervision, supporting individual practitioners in their daily stress and in coping with the emotional burdens. However, the speed of change, the 'supercomplexity' and uncertainty of our age may cause both conceptual and emotional insecurity. Reflexive supervision can be qualitatively different compared with its antecedents and, by being able to grasp complexity, uncertainty and the dynamics of ongoing change, can help in coping with the anxiety these can generate.

Chapter 3

Critical Reflection: Opportunities and Threats to Professional Learning and Service Development in Social Work Organizations

Mark Baldwin

Introduction

The merits of critical reflection in the development of social work practice are not universally applauded (Ixer, 1999), so it would help to be positive about what critical reflection is and why it is an important aspect of professional learning and service development. Ixer's critique suggests that it is a slippery notion, hard to identify when it is happening and difficult to evaluate. Nick Gould has already provided a rationale for critical reflection as a fundamental aspect of professional development, and explored the difference between organizational learning and the learning organization (Chapter 1), so this chapter can clarify where critical reflection sits within social work organizations and the opportunities and threats to it as a positive aspect of professional development. I will take a brief look at some of the literature addressing the nature of reflection and critical reflection in the development of professional practice (Boud and Knights, 1996; Fook, 2002; Gould and Taylor, 1996; Schön, 1983), investigate the necessity of critical reflection through the links between individual learning and organizational learning (Argyris, 1999; Argyris and Schön, 1996), before focusing on the dangers of professional discretion in undermining the effectiveness of social work organizations (Lipsky, 1980; Satyamurti, 1981; Baldwin, 2000a) and the promotion of a positive use of discretion within professional learning (Baldwin, 2000a; Ranson and Stewart, 1994). Finally, the lessons from this theoretical and empirical exploration will have something to say about the part that critical reflection plays within the differing usage of the learning organization concept (Argyris, 1999; Argyris and Schön, 1996; Gould, 2000; Pottage and Evans, 1994).

In order to illustrate the ideas in this chapter, I shall use empirical work that I have engaged in with colleagues in a Social Services department and a voluntary organization. This involved a number of co-operative inquiries (Baldwin, 2001; Heron, 1996; Heron and Reason, 2001) in which I was able to facilitate critical reflection for social workers and other professionals in their practice development. I will particularly focus on these groups when exploring the opportunities that collective critical reflection can provide in professional development and organizational learning.

Ultimately this chapter is about effective services for people who habitually experience marginalization and disadvantage, sometimes as a result of services provided by social work organizations. Effective services require social workers who know what they are doing. A key battleground for professional social work practice is the nature of that knowledge, where it comes from, how it is learnt and how it is developed. These are not, then, idle debates, but arguments which are central to ensuring effectiveness in social work services.

What is Critical Reflection for Learning?

The notion of reflection as an aspect of adult learning has been written about widely (Boud and Knights, 1996; Eraut, 1992; Kolb, 1984; Schön, 1983). More recently, reflection has focused upon professional learning within social work (Gould and Taylor, 1996). In some quarters learning is still described as a behavioural process in which the learner learns by receiving knowledge either from their own inquiry, or through didactic teaching from a knowledgeable teacher. I am not persuaded by this linear explanation of learning, and later in this chapter I will note the ways in which this latter approach has influenced some of the key threats to professional learning and organizational effectiveness.

Kolb is perhaps the most quoted proponent of the cycle of learning in which learners pass through a reflective stage in the iterative process of learning from experience (Kolb, 1984). With this model, learning is an active and developmental process, and the responsibility of the individual. What we learn becomes part of our body of knowledge that we draw upon in future reflective observations. Learning is, then, a cumulative process. The difficulty with this model is the focus on the individual and its lack of criticism. It assumes that learning is a lone activity and there is no evaluation of the effectiveness of the learning process built in (Argyris, 1999). Being a neutral model, the danger is that some professional learners might assume that all they have to do is accumulate learning and effective practice will follow.

Schön (1983) has added important aspects to this model of reflection for learning. Schon's concept of 'reflection-in-action' brings theory, what we know, into practice. We reflect while we practice, we think while we do. This persuasive argument undermines the notion that we draw upon a rational body of knowledge separated from action. Reflection-in-action and on action (after the event) are key parts of professional practice in which the process by which we engage with others – colleagues and service users – constructs that practice and those relationships. Schön also argues the uncertainty principle, which, in social work, involves the complex, fragmented and shifting world of social work relationships. Trying to apply a body of knowledge to that uncertainty is not likely to result in effective practice. Using knowledge in action is, then, a process of experimenting with ideas and actions, transferring knowledge from one setting to another, checking out its effectiveness. Formal knowledge has a part to play, but so too does intuition, those tacit ways of understanding and action that become our strategies for making sense of the world.

Boud's model for learning adds an emphasis on the part that feelings can play as catalyst or block to learning (Boud and Knights, 1996). Learning is often about letting go of fond and long held beliefs. This was a painful experience, for example, for many social workers engaging in anti-racism training, as they learnt about their long-held but unconscious prejudices. Learning is personal and potentially threatening. It is particularly anxiety provoking when it happens publicly, for instance, with students on a professional qualification programme or social workers learning new knowledge or skills within their teams and wider organizations.

We need to note that not all learning is necessarily useful learning. In addition, learning is not done by individual learners within a vacuum, but occurs within a social and cultural context. In order to make learning effective, reflection requires a critical edge. This is argued persuasively by Jan Fook (Fook, 2002; Fook, Chapter 4 in this volume). Reflection needs to be critical so that it deconstructs and reconstructs (Fook, 2002) the knowledge that informs practice in order to evaluate its effectiveness, and to ensure that it does not replicate ineffective or discriminatory practices that service users have experienced elsewhere. As an example, we encourage social work students to ask 'naive' questions on their placements. This has resulted in shifts in team practice as they recognize that routine practice based on some unquestioned principle is not an excuse for its continuation if it has negative results.

A broad concept of culture helps us to see the ways of understanding our world which we share with others. People's shared culture enables them to make sense of, or even to construct, their real worlds collectively. There is a huge diversity in these collective ways of understanding the world and they do not all hold equal weight. There are many perspectives or cultures which are marginalized through the processes of disability, racism, sexism, homophobia or ageism, for instance. Through reflecting critically upon what we know in professional practice it is useful to bear this broad concept of culture in mind. To fail to understand another person's culture or way of seeing (for instance, a non-disabled social worker assessing a disabled person's needs) will result in a seriously ineffective assessment. These shared perspectives have a historical, social and political aspect which can shape culture (a 'culture of learning', for instance) in project teams. Critical reflection to identify this culture is, then, a key part of developing effective services.

Why is Critical Reflection Necessary in Organizations?

Individual Learning and Organizational Learning

While we might be persuaded of the part critical reflection plays in an individual's professional development, and agree that professional development is important to organizations, this link requires a more involved analysis. It has been argued that, for an organization to learn and develop, individual learning is a 'necessary but not sufficient' requirement (Gould, 2000: 587). Argyris (1999) has looked at the question of whether organizations, as entities separate from the individuals that incorporate them, are actually capable of learning. While his analysis reminds us of the dangers of treating organizations as if they were animate organisms, it should not negate the notion that organizations as a whole can, through reflecting on experience, adopt new ways of working. This involves the actions of individuals within the organization, so we need to explore the link between individual and organizational learning.

There is here a question of power within organizations (Argyris, 1999; Capra, 2002). Learning by some individuals will not enhance organizational learning, because they do not have the power to influence the whole organization. Even powerful people in organizations sometimes do not have the power to effect change, or feel buffeted by the same processes as their less senior colleagues (Baldwin, 2000; Capra, 2002). Argyris (1999) has noted the mismatch between espoused theory and theory in use at both individual and organizational levels. Where this occurs, individual learning is still unlikely to influence the effectiveness of the organization as a whole. A good example of this is institutional racism, which has persisted in the routine procedures of some organizations despite training and a commitment to social justice by staff.

The link between individual and organizational learning, then, lies at both conceptual and practical levels. Evidence of such organizational learning would be that there was a shift in the culture (Capra, 2002) of the organization and that this would be reflected in the observable practices and procedures within the organization. There need to be practical opportunities and structures to facilitate the process of individual learning and its cumulative effect on organizational learning.

The Negative Effects of Unreflective Discretion

Professional discretion has had a bad press in social welfare organizations such as Social Services departments. Lipsky (1980), in his seminal text, noted the ways in which 'street level bureaucrats' systematically undermine the intended policy and practice of public sector bodies through their discretion. This negative picture of professional discretion has been illustrated in other empirical work by Argyris (1999) and Capra (2002) within business, and, to a lesser extent in social welfare organizations, by Satyamurti (1981) and Baldwin (2000a). Policy rationalists tell us that discretion is a key block to the realization of public policy intentions. The response has been the introduction of policy controls through targets set by government (Baldwin, 2002), bureaucratic and, latterly, managerial techniques to curb variations and aberrations in practice (Clarke, Gertwitz and McLaughlin, 2000; James, 1994) and a search for that practice that 'works' (Macdonald, 2000). But, as Ranson and Stewart argue, 'discretion is inherent in any organisation', and management has to be 'grounded in that reality' (1994: 217). Their democratic answer is not managerial control of discretion, so much as ensuring that discretion achieves 'collective choice' (ibid.: 218). Ranson and Stewart, in exploring discretion in UK social welfare organizations, argue persuasively, as do Capra (2000) and Argyris (1999) from their interest in business, that discretion will achieve this collective choice because it provides the responsiveness that organizations need in the uncertain world of social service provision.

The problem here is that there has been little investigation of the positive use of discretion. It is mostly seen as an unfortunate negative to be managed out of organizations, or an inevitable negative to be accepted. My work within the community care field in the UK, led me to believe that discretion is a potential positive for organizations (Baldwin, 2000a). If individual learning is an important aspect of innovation and responsiveness, then welfare professionals need opportunities to critically reflect upon their use of discretion to ensure that they are not replicating the negative and destructive practices of Lipsky's street level bureaucrats. This encapsulates the link between critical reflection, individual learning and organizational learning.

Promoting Positive Discretion and Practice Development

The empirical work that I engaged in with care managers (Baldwin, 2000a) revealed a widespread belief among social workers that the care management system had managed professional discretion out of their role. When I engaged in two co-operative inquiries with social workers (Baldwin, 2000a; 2001), exploring their practice over a period of time, they learnt that they still held a substantial degree of discretion. This was revealed in the way that they communicated with service users, the emphasis they placed on some questions in the assessment process and whether they asked those questions at all. I will return to this evidence of critical reflection when I look at opportunities below, but, for now I will focus on the need to emphasize the positive use of discretion, not just as an antidote to the negatives identified above, but also for the purpose of effective practice development.

There are aspects of social work where legal and technical knowledge is paramount and practitioners will need to know what to do or what to advise service users. I am also persuaded that there are some models for practice, such as the task-centred approach (Doel and Marsh, 1992; Epstein, 1980) which have proven value in guiding social workers' practice. There is, however, a substantial area of discretion in the use of these methods of intervening. This discretion cannot be managed out of social work practice either by managerialist techniques of control (James, 1994) or through persuading practitioners that the application of rationally tested techniques of practice will yield greater certainty of result (Sheldon and Chilvers, 2000). Discretion is an inevitable and necessary aspect of social work practice for three reasons.

First, it is in the nature of interpersonal relationships within social work that social workers will spend a great deal of time trying to make sense of other people's lives (England, 1986). This process will often occur across cultural divides (Baldwin 1996). Social workers whose unreflective and uncritical discretion results in them making assumptions of understanding, or imposing their own cultural beliefs, across these divides, will be ineffective, whatever the evidence that the method they use works. Making sense of other people's lives requires a process of working towards understanding using a 'constant set of approximations' (England, 1986: 38). The body of knowledge that informs this process will not be purely formal. Intuition, empathy and commitment to values are other important qualities that social workers will bring to these relationships. The problem for social workers wishing to be effective in their practice is that intuition can be based on prejudice, empathy can be experienced by others as patronizing and discriminatory, and values can be based on unchecked assumptions. The use of discretion must, to avoid these negatives, and to maximize effectiveness, be subjected to a rigorous process of critical reflection. The practitioners that I have worked with in Social Services departments and in a large voluntary organization, understand the need for this process of critical reflection, and feel a great deal of anxiety that much of their practice happens 'on the hoof', without opportunity for critical evaluation.

These opportunities for critical reflection and the evaluation of social work practice are also argued as necessary within the uncertainties of our globalized and postmodern world (Dominelli and Hoogvelt, 1996; Pugh and Gould, 2000). There is a great deal of uncertainty inherent in the contemporary context for social work, with an ever-increasing understanding of diversity in the identities of service users as subjects for social work. The rapidly fragmenting service base, with privatization and responsiveness to diverse identities, is another aspect of the context for social work which makes prediction in policy and practice very hard and the need to maximize opportunities for critical reflection at a premium.

These developments come at a time, indeed are largely causal, of a shift in the basis of professionalism within social work (Banks, 2001; Hugman, 1991; Payne, 1997). Traditional views of social work professionalism, based largely on a medical model of expertise, are being challenged by a contemporary view in which the expectation is that professional social workers will engage in partnership with service users and communities, using their expertise in co-operation with these diverse others in making decisions about the nature of need and the services to be made available to meet them. This tendency has come about partly as a result of consumerism within social welfare and partly because of the rise of service user movements. Scrutiny of social work practice can follow the route of managerialist surveillance as well as, more positively, the embracing of systems such as service user involvement, feedback, complaints and representations that could provide service users with opportunities to hold welfare professionals accountable for their practice.

From Individual Learning to the Learning Organization

With critical reflection established as an important aspect of individual learning and professional development, and individual learning as a central aspect of organizational learning, we can now look at the connection between critical reflection in individual learning and the organization that is able to learn, adapt and innovate in an uncertain world. It is the view that people in organizations are interested and able to pursue their own ends as workers (Senge, 1990a), rather than fulfilling functional organizationally determined roles, upon which the concept of the learning organization is built. Another important facet of the learning organization (Capra, 2002; Senge, 1990), is that organizations are constructed through systems, or networks of relationships, and it is these relationships through which staff can potentially effect change. The learning organization of Senge in which 'people are constantly learning to learn together', 'at all levels in the organisation' (1990: 3) is very different to the notion of a static, hierarchical and controlling bureaucracy or managerial organization.

Argyris and Schön (1996) have argued the importance of a match between espoused theory and theory-in-use as a prerequisite for organizational learning. Their empirical work (Argyris, 1999; Argyris and Schön, 1996) has pointed up the way in which organizations fail to learn and adapt where there is a gap between intentions and practice. Routine learning in most organizations is described by Argyris and Schön as single-loop learning, in which organizations and the individuals within them repeat procedures, learning in an uncritical fashion from previous experience. Argyris provides considerable detail of the sort of problems that such an approach leads to – 'defensive routines', 'games of control and deception' and taboos on discussing key issues (1999: 6). It is only by creating an environment in which these routines, games and taboos which construct an organization's culture, are critically evaluated through double-loop learning, that they can be tackled and the organization can more effectively match its espoused theory with its theory-in-use.

So the learning organization is organizationally more flat than hierarchical, it facilitates communication between all parts of the organization, both laterally and vertically, it encourages participation (Capra, 2002) by all staff in the processes of development and learning, it creates opportunities for feedback loops so that double-loop (Argyris and Schön, 1996) or multiple-feedback loop (Capra, 2002) learning can take place. In their analysis of innovation in learning organizations, Tidd, Bessant and Pavitt (1997) argue the need for an incremental rather than rationalist approach to learning and development, equating the cycle of individual learning to organizational learning. Critical reflection, then, is an aspect of the learning organization as it is for individual professional development. It is how and where to facilitate these processes of individual and organizational critical reflection for individual and organizational learning which provide the practical context for discussion in the remainder of this chapter. What are the opportunities and threats to critical reflection within organizations?

Threats to Critical Reflection

I will highlight four threats to critical reflection and therefore to organizational learning and development within social welfare organizations. Although I am separating these out, there is a distinct overlap between the first three of them, and each of these holds the potential to become more opportunity than threat through critical reflection and organizational learning. These initial three areas of focus are managerialism, evidence of what works, and scrutiny of policy implementation. The fourth threat, which is failure of critical reflection, follows on from the above three where they are built around a narrow rationalist approach to policy implementation, management and evidence for practice.

Managerialism

Managerialism has developed, in health and social welfare organizations, as a response to the perceived inefficiencies of pre-1980s' public services. The key facets of what has become known as managerialism are favouring of managers and management control over welfare professionals such as social workers (Clarke, Gerwitz and McLaughlin, 2000; James, 1994) and the introduction of quasi-markets (Le Grand and Bartlett, 1993) within organizations to encourage competition and the discipline of 'functional units' (James, 1994: 46) or cost centres. More specifically, this has meant that work is determined by objectives denoted as targets or performance indicators set by managers, role specialization, hierarchical line management and some devolution of decision-making to managers down this line of control.

Managerialism poses two threats to critical reflection. First, there is the concept of the right to manage, in which it is managerial knowledge that outweighs the understanding of others such as professional staff and service users. This is not to deny the argument that managers are accountable through the implementation of policies sanctioned in the wider political arena. In this case I am referring to the ideology of managerialism, which would appear to override the democratic concept of collective choice (Ranson and Stewart, 1994), mentioned above. If one of the requirements of organizational learning is that all stakeholders should contribute to the body of organizational knowledge, then this favouring of an elite is a serious threat.

Secondly, there is the rationalist reliance on managerialist practices – notably the use of resource management techniques such as eligibility criteria and staff and service control techniques such as targets and performance indicators – to overcome the inherent uncertainties of social welfare provision. One of the tenets of effective organizational learning is that it is there to manage the uncertainties of organizational life and, indeed, to use them as a positive force for change and development. To attempt to manage out uncertainty is to destroy the potential opportunities for dynamic creativity present in managing uncertainty.

What is Meant by 'Evidence'?

'Evidence' of what works has become a battleground of meaning within social work (Baldwin, 2000a; Hudson, 2000; Jordan, 2000). The problem is that there are different meanings attached to the concept of evidence, with the Centre for Evidence Based Social Services (CEBSS) at Exeter University (Sheldon and Chilvers, 2000) arguing that evidence of what works in social care must come as a result of evidence produced through natural scientific method. The result has been preference for specific methods of intervention, such as cognitive behaviourism. This version of evidence is at odds with a more reflective and pragmatic approach to the development of effective practice through co-operative, inclusive methods developed as a result of an incremental process of critically reflective evaluation. The similar pursuit of certainty should make clear the connection between managerialism and CEBSS-type evidence.

Rational Policy Implementation

These rationalist expectations with regard to management and practice are mirrored in the continuing government approach to policy implementation, characterized by a plethora of targets and performance indicators for social care (www.doh.gov.uk). The belief that outcomes can be determined by such rationalist means is still influential at different levels in social work organizations. If these organizations are to be responsive and flexible in the face of change and uncertainty, as has been argued, then threats to a critically reflective approach are likely to reduce effectiveness in the long run. Indeed, Argyris has argued that organizations that fail to institute the double-loop learning that provides critical reflection at an organizational level are never likely to realize their espoused aims (Argyris 1999).

Failures of Critical Analysis

The last of the threats is that evaluation by individuals and organizations fails to be critical and analytical. In Argyris's terms this means that the organization will fail to pick up on those 'second order errors' (1999: 6) such as defensive routines, games of control and deception, and taboos on discussing issues that seriously undermine learning and organizational responsiveness. Argyris and Capra speak of the organizational culture that prevails when these failures of critical reflection occur. Argyris mentions the 'frames' or perspectives which provide the context for interpretation of events in organizational processes. These frames reflect organizational culture and are seldom (in the ineffective organization) held up to scrutiny. Argyris (1999) and Capra (2002), much as Lipsky (1980) did before them, talk of control systems that are constructed to try and ensure people follow rules. There is a mismatch between the business of the organization and the network of relationships that constructs it, with organizations habitually trying to impose change upon these networks of relationship. As Capra argues, and Lipsky demonstrated 20 years ago, people tend to 'resist having change imposed upon them' (Capra, 2002: 87). Most proponents of the learning organization argue that participation by all members of the organization is necessary if proposed change is to have meaning for them, and if they are to own that change. So what are the opportunities for critical reflective approaches in organizations, and how might they affect organizational learning?

Opportunities for Critical Reflection

There is recent evidence that practitioners in social welfare organizations have little time for reflection upon the work that they do in systematic ways (Sheldon and Chilvers, 2000). This is backed up by the empirical work that I have carried out in both a Social Services department (Baldwin, 2000a; 2001) and a large national voluntary organization. In both cases I engaged with groups of workers in co-operative inquiry to investigate certain aspects of their work which we were agreed was important to explore. In the case of the two groups that I worked with in the

Social Services department this was primarily an investigation of how they used their discretion to link their social work knowledge to the practice of care management in a way that was both effective, from their own professional evaluation, and within organizational (that is managerial) boundaries. The three project teams that I engaged with in the national children's charity were all engaged in investigating the nature and development of innovative practice. All five groups that I engaged with were agreed that the opportunity provided by the co-operative inquiry replicated the critical reflection that was missing in the everyday preoccupations of their organizational lives.

What I want to do now is to describe the process of co-operative critical reflection for some of the work done with these groups. This will provide evidence of the possibilities for critical reflection within organizations. It also reveals considerable gaps in organizational processes. For effective organizational learning to take place, it is not even sufficient to facilitate team or group learning, if that learning is not incorporated within the broader organizational processes.

In working with the two groups of social workers in the Social Services department, it became immediately apparent, somewhat ambiguously, that they were both convinced that there was little scope for discretion in their practice, but at the same time they were anxious that they were not working within the prescribed processes of the organization. This anxiety was enhanced by a disciplinary culture within the organization. The three projects that I worked with in the children's charity had volunteered to investigate the development of innovative practice, following a complaint from a young person that she had been oppressed by the imposition of an innovative approach in a separate project. All three project teams admitted that they had not engaged in a critically reflective approach to their work in the way they would have liked and that this unreflective approach to their work could result in repetition of routine and ineffective work, ill-considered and potentially discriminatory practice or, like the Social Services department workers, in practice that fell outside organizational procedures and thus laid them open to criticism.

Method for Exploration

Investigation of a sophisticated professional practice such as social work requires a methodology that can reflect that complexity. The process of making sense of other people's lives across cultural divides requires a particular approach if investigation is to be able to make sense of relationships. Enabling people who have perhaps considerable problems of communication to have their voice heard in decisions about their future is not a skill that can be looked up in a book, demonstrated and then 'captured' by interview or questionnaire. A research method that enables practitioners to enter into a process of action and reflection is more likely to result in learning through and about the process of practice. Co-operative inquiry (Heron, 1996; Heron and Reason, 2001) provides such an approach.

Co-operative inquiry was selected in both cases as a form of action research that replicates the kind of critical and reflective cyclical process of learning described above. If workers such as those I engaged with use their professional discretion in often ill-considered ways to construct their practice, despite the managerial systems in place to reduce the scope for such practice, then it was a useful experiment to use a system that allowed them actively to track the development of their practice in a mutually supportive environment over a period of time. It was, with my facilitation, their inquiry, so it was far more difficult for them to distance themselves from the learning that took place. The opportunity that the co-operative inquiries provided was to engage in a critically reflective approach to their practice which could enhance individual and team effectiveness. In that it might also reduce anxiety, it enhanced the learning opportunities if we recall David Boud's belief that feelings can seriously undermine the learning process.

Social Workers and Managing Professional Discretion

With the social work groups, I was investigating the process through which social workers, at the bottom end of the policy implementation hierarchy, implemented and, therefore, influenced policy. We have seen how Lipsky (1980) describes 'street level bureaucrats' using their practice to undermine policy intentions. There is some evidence (Baldwin, 2000a) that participative approaches which engage street level bureaucrats in the process of implementation are more likely to avoid these negative consequences. If the argument is that professional practitioners construct policy through the use of professional discretion, then there needs to be a methodology which engages with participants over time, if this process is to be explored with any degree of validity.

In our inquiries we chose a focus of investigation, made decisions on how it was to be explored and how the exploration was to be recorded. After a period of time we met together to reflect upon what had been learnt, noting how it informed understanding of that practice. This new knowledge was then used when practitioners engaged again with their practice. We went through a number of cycles of action and reflection, and a great deal of understanding was gained about the way in which practice develops and the part that mutual critical reflection plays in such development. The inquiries, then, replicated to some degree, and in a small part of the organization, the notion of double-loop learning. Participants were not just learning how to replicate habitual practice but engaged in a process of critically evaluating the basis of that practice.

In order to illustrate this I will offer a couple of examples. One of the social work groups investigated their approach to a small aspect of the bureaucratic process they are required to engage with. When someone is in hospital and a social worker is assessing their needs, the social worker is required to get written permission from the service user to contact third parties, such as their doctor, to glean relevant information. The social workers in this group often did not seek permission because they were concerned that asking a vulnerable person in a hospital bed might add to their feeling of marginalization, even though they also knew, from their knowledge of best practice in social work, that getting permission was important. It was practices such as this that raised anxiety, and was clearly undermining part of the intended policy of the organization.

They engaged in several cycles of action and reflection in which they recorded the occasions that they should have received permission, and the reasons why they did, or did not, get a signature on the appropriate document. This provided an opportunity to investigate in a critical and mutually supportive way the process of their discretion. With my facilitation, they analysed the process of decision-making that they entered into, gaining increasing clarity, as we went through cycles of action and critical reflection, about the nature of the knowledge that informed their practice. It was a fascinating and important investigation of the ways in which professional workers use a range of knowledge in making decisions. This is a mixture of formal, theoretical, methodological, legal and organizational knowledge, alongside a whole range of intuitive and tacit knowledge that makes up their day-to-day practice wisdom, but so often is not critically reflected upon. Learning about this largely unconsidered process of knowledge-in-action was both liberating and frightening for these participants, and they learnt that they needed opportunities for critical reflection to continue if they were to maintain an effective critical edge to their developing practice.

Managing the Development of Innovation in Complex Practice

One of the project teams in the children's charity investigated the development of their practice in outreach work. This was a drug education project that spent some of their time on the streets with young people responding to their requests for information and advice. This was, by any standards, sophisticated practice. They never knew what was likely to come up or what was necessarily the best response to that eventuality. It was a good example of the 'swampy lowlands' of Schön's world of professional practice (Schön, 1983: 42). As someone from a different project team said to me, 'you can't go to a book that tells you what to do in these circumstances'. They had developed a range of responses, relying heavily upon teamwork in these difficult circumstances. Through the co-operative inquiry, they recorded what happened on each occasion, what they did and how they knew that was the best thing to do at the time, and were then able to return to reflect upon the practice in a mutually supportive and critically reflective environment later. What these practitioners learnt was the range of knowledge that they adopted in these circumstances, the degree to which much of it was tacit rather than formal, and the degree to which they had built up ways of working without critically evaluating their effectiveness. Practice seemed to work on a day-to-day basis, but if they were committed to the development of innovation, then evaluation needed to be endemic within their practice and based upon this process of critical reflection and learning.

Opportunities for Replicating Co-operative Inquiry in Organizations

These are just two examples from a wealth of detail that these co-operative inquiry groups developed over the six months that I worked with each of them. The learning is important because it provides evidence, in a small way, of the kind of opportunities that could be provided within social work organizations for the use of critical reflection as a part of individual and organizational learning.

The collaborative, participative, nature of co-operative inquiry has a number of advantages for investigators wanting to engage in a change process. These can be closely associated with our understanding of organizational learning and the learning organization. In traditional research a researcher captures knowledge and information from the objects of research. What was owned by the practitioner, becomes the property of the researcher, as they take away and analyse their data. Then through data analysis, it takes on the meaning bestowed upon it by the researcher rather than the meaning of those objects of the research. For change in behaviour to occur, it is important that what is to be changed, and what the change is to consist of, has some meaning within the experience of those who are expected to change. It is only when potential change has such meaning that it is likely to be owned by those involved and result in desired change. This is a crucial part of organizational learning, that requires opportunities such as those that were tested out in these experiments.

Teamwork

In working with groups of social workers and related professionals it was necessary to recognize the importance to them of a supportive team (Payne, 2000) to maximize opportunities for the development of effective service. These experiments replicated that supportive environment, providing a context to explore complex and contested ideas, and the feelings generated by engaging with stressful and challenging situations. All the groups discussed ways in which they could replicate these benefits after I had withdrawn from their teams. It is important to note that such a supportive context is another key aspect of the learning organization, which most of these participants did not experience habitually within their workplaces.

The Value of Facilitating Participation in Organizations

The value base for social work practice involves a recognition of the potentially negative effects of power within professional relationships. All the inquiry groups worked with people who were marginalized because of social forces such as age, disability, mental health, learning difficulty, racism and sexism. Working within democratic work groups and a wider organization in which their voice was being heard in the development of practice and service provision was important for them, but not necessarily within their experience. Having unethical practices imposed upon them in contradiction to their espoused values was a real fear for these professionals. There was a feeling that group processes must mirror practice with people using their services.

Some group members felt that policy, procedures and practices had been imposed upon them by national government and their employing organizations. It is this sort of imposition that Lipsky's street level bureaucrats were resisting, and which leads to potential undermining of intended policy. Exponents of the learning organization, such as Argyris (1999) and Capra (2002), argue strenuously for the democratic and participative processes of practice development that we replicated in our inquiries. Sadly, in both organizations, some participants came up against considerable resistance to their developing practice from managers at first-line level, or higher up the organization. These managers viewed important opportunities for critical reflection such as supervision, team discussion, training and conference attendance, more as managerial tools than chances for individuals, teams and, therefore, the organization, to learn.

Threats to Organizational Learning

This is where the limits of this experiment lie. Authors such as Argyris and Capra have argued persuasively that these organizational processes are essential *throughout* organizations if the necessary opportunities for organizational learning are to be maintained. Even in the children's charity, which had an expressed commitment to becoming a learning organization, staff experienced threats from paternalism or managerialism that sought to control their practice even in its day-to-day minutiae, rather than provide organizational opportunities to develop innovative practice through the critical reflective process described above. These particular social work organizations were, in their own ways, still too wedded to the notion of inspection for quality control rather than understanding that managing a process of change and innovation (Tidd, Bessant and Pavitt, 1997) requires letting go some of the control of the processes of learning and discretionary behaviour which will, we have noted, occur anyway. Staff in one project said that they had learnt not to be interested in their practice because they felt so marginalized from the service. Their commitment actually belied this statement, but even to be saying it seems to be an indictment of organizational processes that fail to use the learning of individuals to the greater learning and development of effective practice across the whole organization.

Conclusion

This chapter has argued the links between critical reflection and learning for professional practice development. It has also argued that individual and group (that is, team) learning is a crucial aspect of organizational learning. There is powerful evidence from the literature on organizational learning and the learning organization that, unless organizations can maximise these aspects of organizational learning, social welfare organizations will not be in a position to deal with the necessities of responding effectively to the rapidly changing demands of social welfare in the global context.

The opportunities for replicating organizational learning through critical reflection in teams has been explored in this chapter, but the threats still exist, even where I engaged with organizations that were keen and interested to see how such opportunities could be explored in their organization. The blocks to organizational learning seem largely to flow from processes that are described in great detail by Argyris in his studies of organizational learning. These processes are all too easily mediated through fear of uncertainty located in middle and senior management in organizations, and a consequent desire to hold on to control of the processes through which practice is mediated and services are delivered. This desperation to control uncertainty, manifested in policy and managerial practices, reflects a philosophical and practical error, in which it is assumed that rational organizational procedures can be imposed upon staff in organizations and outcomes controlled. These managerial processes create anxieties for staff and stifle innovation and development. Working with the inevitability of uncertainty is the only method of ensuring that an organization will be able to be creatively responsive to the eventualities that uncertainty throws into its path.

Chapter 4

Critical Reflection and Organizational Learning and Change: A Case Study

Jan Fook[1]

The concepts of reflective practice and the learning organization are frequently coupled, from the earlier writings of Argyris and Schön (1978) to increased interest in the present day. However, in social work, while there has been burgeoning practice and research using reflective approaches, there has been less work which examines the relevance of the idea of the learning organization (Gould, 2000). In addition, there is a need to differentiate the notions of reflective, and *critical* reflective practice.

In this chapter, I aim to further our discussion of these three areas by highlighting some of the issues involved in teaching a critical reflective approach within a human service organization, and some possible ways in which it relates to organizational learning, and change to bring about that learning. I do this by presenting a case study of a training programme in critical reflection within a large statutory human services organization. In the first part of the chapter I set the context for the training programme by reviewing briefly the current thinking about critical reflection and some of its uses within social work. Then, after a description of the organizational background to the training programme, and its content and format, I also summarize the main findings of the evaluations undertaken.

In the second part of the chapter I discuss the major issues which arose from this experience, especially in respect of their implications for the development of organizational learning. In particular I discuss the type of learning which occurred and its relevance to organizational learning, some of the factors involved in the setting up of a partnership between two organizations to undertake the training, process and implementation issues which were not predicted and, finally, ongoing issues regarding organizational learning. I should acknowledge that although this programme was undertaken in a partnership and with a number of colleagues, this chapter represents my own perspective.

Critical Reflection in Social Work

Interest in reflection, as an approach to teaching and learning in social work, has increased markedly in recent times (Gould and Taylor, 1996; Hess and Mullen, 1995; Yelloly and Henkel, 1995). The values of reflective practice are touted as manifold: the possible improvement of practice by closing the gap between espoused theory and enacted practice; the learning of knowledge generating capacities; the potential for ongoing evaluation of practice; and the integration of theory, practice and research (Fook, 1996). More recently, the critical possibilities of reflective social work practice in challenging dominant power structures and relations have received attention (Fook, 1999; Issit, 1999).

The idea of reflection is discussed in many traditions, including the learning, professional practice, political and identity politics (and the related idea of reflexivity), all of which show a surprising overlap (Boud, 1999). I have developed it from the professional practice tradition, that is, the basic reflective process, as developed by Argyris and Schön (1976) and Schön (1983), as the simple examination of practice to uncover hidden assumptions which are implicit in the activity. In this way the gaps between espoused theory and enacted practice are highlighted, enabling practitioners to scrutinize, evaluate and change their practice, while at the same time developing and articulating the theory which is implicit in their actions. Quite a lot has been written about this reflective process in educational literature (for example, Brookfield, 1995), although there is relatively little in social work literature which actually describes a reflective process used by social workers. However, there are a few notable examples (Evans, 1999; Fook, 1996; Fook, Ryan and Hawkins, 2000; Moffat, 1996; Napier and Fook, 2000; Yelloly and Henkel, 1995).

In my own work I have taken care to link a reflective approach with a critical analysis (Agger, 1998), to develop a process and theory of critical reflection (Fook, 1999; 2002). Thus it is possible to differentiate reflection from critical reflection, in that critical reflection shares commonalities with critical social work (Fook, 2002), and thus places emphasis on the transformative potential of a reflective approach. This shares similarities with the 'political-social' tradition developed by Kemmis (1985) and Smyth (1996). In simple terms this involves the use of a reflective process to unearth assumptions which relate to power relations and structures. These assumptions are then examined for their role in constructing dominant power relations and structures, and a theory of power is reconstructed to upset this domination. This theory is also reconstructed to include the development and naming of practical strategies which are suggested by the reconstructed theory (Fook, 2002). The process of critical reflection thus involves a deconstruction and reconstruction of a person's own theory of power, and of their practice theory about power. In this way, people are enabled to create transformative ways of practising by using a critical reflective process. I find, in practice, that many assumptions about many issues involve an aspect of assumptions about power. I understand the concept of power to involve many different types of power, encompassing personal, interpersonal, structural and formal and informal aspects. In this way, a theory and process of critical reflection manages to cover most aspects of a practitioner's working life.

Critical reflection which examines power relationships can be relevant in organizational life, since much of an organization's workings can be analysed and explained in terms of many different aspects of power and its enactment. Once a worker understands how their position, practice and role within an organization is affected by power relations and their own ability to act upon these, there is also potential for organizational change.

One of the perceived disadvantages of the reflective process is that it can appear to be a 'practice in search of a theory', in that a reflective process can potentially unearth *any* assumptions about *anything*, without necessarily indicating which specific ideas require more focus for change. However, this can be a potential advantage, in that without preconceived ideas about what to unearth, some crucial but hitherto deeply hidden assumptions may be uncovered. This is another reason that a reflective process can take many different forms, and have many different outcomes, depending on the theoretical perspectives of participants and their propensity to delve deeply for important assumptions.

There are other dissenting voices as well. Some have argued that reflection is a highly individualized activity, its outcomes difficult to generalize to other people and situations. It is also a highly diversified activity, its processes can lack clarity of detail and its outcomes are difficult to measure, so it seems impossible to assess its success (Ixer, 1999). Of concern is that the reflective approach and its practice seem to fly in the face of current managerial and cost-cutting trends. It can be argued that reflection takes too much time in a climate of maximum efficiency; its outcomes are often open-ended and unpredictable in regimes which value concrete forward planning and budgeting; it encourages self-examination and the disclosure of vulnerabilities and limitations (Hess, 1995) which can undermine the competitive edge of services; it fosters holistic and contextual ways of knowing in economic contexts requiring scientific proofs of effectiveness and 'evidence'.

Proponents of the learning organization ideal might, however, argue that a learning organization would value this sort of expertise developed from reflective practice, because there is a need for the organization to adapt to changes, given that the contexts in which they operate are continually changing. However, there still needs to be more work done on how and whether this more prescriptive ideal of the learning organization can actually be implemented, and the outcomes which might be achieved (Gould, 2000; Tsang, 1997).

In summary then, several aspects of critical reflective practice need to be further addressed: more details of what the training and learning entail; whether and how a critical reflective perspective can be learnt; and whether and how this is of value in terms of developing a learning organization. These are the issues addressed in this chapter.

Context and Background of the Training Programme

The training programme was commissioned as part of a broader move to introduce a framework for Quality Improvement and Peer Review within a protective services section of a statutory human services department. There had been a series of crises in the organization when its work had undergone some external review, and the framework was being introduced as a response to these reviews. The critical reflective approach was seen as congruent with the peer review training in this framework, since the format of the training involved interactive small group workshops, and both self-reflection and group reflection on practice. There was seen to be a need to bring about a change in the way workers learnt about and improved their practice, and it was hoped that the peer review process learnt through a critical reflective approach would play a part in these changes.

It was planned that the entire section (involving approximately 65 staff at three levels – worker, team leader and unit manager) would participate in the training programme during a similar time period, in order to maximize the effects of the learning, and to maximize possible changes to the learning culture in the section. These 65 staff were located in a regional area, in several different offices, up to four hours drive apart.

The commissioning of the training took place within the broader context of a partnership agreement between the human services department and a local university, which conducted several different practice and research projects. A pilot critical reflection training programme had been run through this partnership a couple of years earlier, and the interest in this had contributed to the commissioning of broader training.

In addition, there were current policy initiatives within the human service organization in support of strengthening staff skills through enhancing training and support, and to increase service quality and an evidence base for practice. Overall, the climate was strongly conducive to running a programme of this kind.

The Training Programme

Planning

A considerable period of time (six months) was spent in writing a proposal for the programme, negotiating details of programme delivery, and organizing the logistics of group membership and timetabling. Several meetings were held between the co-ordinator of the programme (myself) and key people within the organization who were responsible for different aspects of training and management. Several evaluation instruments were designed for this programme, and these were developed by the co-ordinator in consultation with key organization and university staff.

In addition, the five group trainers/facilitators (myself and four others who were all social work educators from the local university) engaged in extensive planning and preparation. This involved several sessions in which curriculum materials were chosen, format discussed and a pilot critical reflection session was held. Although all group facilitators had their own experience in teaching various forms of reflective practice, the particular model being used had been specifically developed by the co-ordinator as a critical reflection model, so there was a need to ensure that all facilitators were familiar with the particular approach and model being used.

The stated aims of the critical reflective training programme related both to the general aims of critical reflective training as well as the specific aims of the peer review programme. They were:

- Aims of critical reflective practice training:
  - to link theory and practice;
  - practice evaluation;
  - practice improvement;
  - the undertaking of ongoing research on practice;
  - development of best practice models;
  - the development of alternative, more collaborative, systems of practice review and supervision;
  - the development of a more collaborative learning culture within the organization.
- Specific aims of this programme:
  - to introduce the reflective practice approach to workers, team leaders and unit managers;
  - to train workers, team leaders and managers in the basic process of critical reflection;
  - to assist workers, team leaders and managers to use critical reflection as a personal process in evaluating their everyday work practices;
  - to begin to develop, in a collaborative way, and from actual practice experience, personal and departmental models for best practice with clients in different case contexts;
  - to provide the basis for developing an organizational model for the use of critical reflection as a peer review process;
  - to provide a basis for models of ongoing learning with the organization.

Content and Format

The original proposed format was for five groups of approximately 12–13 participants in each, which were to be held for two-hourly blocks over a period of 13 weeks. This represented the 'ideal' organization of the programme, to allow maximum time for ongoing and developing reflective abilities, but also to allow longer for a group culture to develop around critical reflection. After two introductory sessions providing didactic material on critical reflection and modelling the process, it was planned that participants would have two separate opportunities to present their own practice (through a description of a critical incident) and use peer reflection to assist in self-reflection: the first would be a presentation of the incident; the second, following at least a month later, would be their reworked practice theory, based on ongoing critical reflection on their incident.

Unfortunately this format was regarded by the organization as too intrusive on workers' time, and would have created access difficulties for staff situated in long-distance offices. In addition, it was decided to structure training so that the interests of specific target groups could be met, that is, that workers, team leaders and unit managers could separately focus on the specific practice demands of their roles.

With these imperatives in mind, the format was renegotiated. In total seven groups were organized as follows:

- one for unit managers situated in the local office (seven members) meeting a total of three times (4 hours each);
- two for team leaders from both local and distant offices (six members each) meeting a total of three times (4 hours each);
- one for child protection practitioners in an office two and a half hours distant (10 members) meeting a total of three times (one half day, then two full days);
- three for child protection practitioners in local office (average 12 members each) meeting a total of five times (four hours each).

The format (number of hours and number of group meetings) was planned to maximize accessibility for members (especially long-distance participants), as well as to allow sufficient time for individual member presentations. In general, the sessions for each group were spread over a period of 6–12 weeks. The composition of the groups was organized so that whole teams or offices would not be left unattended for the period of the workshops. This was often impossible to co-ordinate. The logistics of organizing the groups and timetabling their commitments among other training requirements was a difficult and huge task which itself spanned about four months, and involved several specific meetings between the co-ordinator and different representatives of the organization.

The curriculum of the programme was based on the principle of a continual focus on establishing a collegiate learning culture, one in which it was 'safe' to present doubts about practice. The second ongoing principle was to focus on how doubts about practice could be used to construct new ways of practising, so that changed thinking could be linked to changed practising.

Actual sessions involved the following:

- an initial introduction to the reflective approach presented by the co-ordinator and in which participants were provided with a set of basic readings. Topics covered included the theory of critical reflection, basic critical reflective questions, 'rules' of critical reflection (including group norms such as confidentiality) and the critical incident technique;
- a follow-up introductory session in which the group facilitator modelled the critical reflective process by presenting their own critical incident and inviting reflective peer feedback and questioning;
- a series of small group sessions in which each participant presented his or her own critical incident (this was defined as a specific practice which encapsulated a current practice dilemma for them) and the reflective group process was facilitated and structured by the group facilitator;
- a second series of small group sessions in which each participant made a second presentation of their practice incorporating their ongoing reflections and changed thinking and practices. The group process was again facilitated by a group facilitator structured to ensure further learning.

While the content of the discussions in each of the small group sessions was to some extent determined by the content of the critical incidents which were described, the broad brief was to focus on protective work in the groups for child protection practitioners, and to focus on supervisory or management practice in the groups for team leaders and unit managers.

Elsewhere I have documented in some detail the use of the critical incident technique in critical reflection (Fook, 1996; Fook, Ryan and Hawkins, 2000). It is a reasonably widely used tool (for example, Davies and Kinloch, 2000). However, particularly in my later work, I have placed emphasis on using it in conjunction with a critical deconstructive and reconstructive framework which provides a much more explicit theoretical framework for the types of reflective questions asked, and the analysis which guides the meaning made.

Evaluations

A package of five evaluation instruments was designed to identify the learning of participants as follows:

- an analysis of a scenario (administered as a pre- and post-test to enable comparison and identify changes in relation to the conceptualization of practice options – participants were presented with a typical protective services practice scenario involving some inter-professional and inter-agency conflict and asked to respond to broad questions regarding the main factors, their options and responses to the conflict;
- a self-rating (completed at the end of the workshop series, designed to elicit opinions about change in relation to personal and professional matters and skills – these were based on themes which had arisen from the evaluation conducted on the earlier training programme, and on claims from the literature about the advantages of critical reflection);
- a programme evaluation (administered at the beginning and end of the workshop series) – designed to elicit the opinions of the participants on the value of the programme, but also to identify changes in their conceptualization of practice dilemmas.

In addition, each group facilitator conducted some focus group discussions with each group about their perceptions of the workshop programme. The individual group facilitators themselves also engaged in several group discussions with each other for debriefing of learning experiences and for analysis of evaluation results. Themes arising from these discussions were included in formal evaluations. The results of all evaluations were collated and presented in written form to the director of the organization.

The results are presented in highly summarized form here for several reasons:

- attendance at the workshops was sporadic and unpredictable. What is presented here are largely the results from participants who attended all sessions. But since a large proportion of participants only attended some sessions, the results do not therefore represent the bulk of participants;

- there is far too much detail to be reported accurately for our purposes in this chapter;
- not all the results are relevant to the focus of this chapter, that is, the relevance to organizational learning.

For the purposes of this chapter, I will focus more particularly on the results which are pertinent to the issue of organizational learning.

Scenario analysis indicated a broad movement from a more 'forensic' orientation (a preoccupation with finding the 'truth' about 'child safety' and a 'fear' of getting it wrong, with a hierarchical attitude to authority) to a more 'relational' orientation (more emphasis on being collaborative and minimizing conflict). In respect to supervisory options, this 'relational' orientation expressed itself as seeing more, different and complex ways of relating to supervisors and providing supervision.

Analysis of the self-rating scale yielded the following results. The 16 factors below were all rated as involving some change. They were rated on a five-point scale ranging from 1 ('no change') to 5 ('extensive change'). The list below is graded between 3.5 at the top and 2.6 at the bottom.

- 'awareness of new and different perspectives';
- 'personal growth and development';
- 'more open to learning and exposing practice to scrutiny';
- 'ability to see complexities in making decisions';
- 'awareness of new options and ability to create options';
- 'new and improved ways of using supervision/providing supervision';
- 'more collaborative ways of working with colleagues';
- 'ability to evaluate practice';
- 'strengthened sense of my own professionalism/professional identity';
- 'willingness and ability to reflect on practice';
- 'different and more positive view of my practice dilemmas';
- 'ability to make decisions';
- 'more and different ways of working with the system';
- 'building my own practice theory';
- 'sense of my own career directions';
- 'awareness of the number of factors involved in cases'.

In terms of programme evaluations, I focus on the practice dilemmas identified by participants, and the changes in these.

In terms of dilemmas and what had been learnt, the major themes which emerged were:

- participants generally felt that they had an increased ability for self-analysis and awareness, and had developed personally and professionally because of this. They generally saw more possibilities for the use of critical reflection in their work;
- they spoke of themselves as more 'reflective' and less 'robotic' or 'reactive', able to respond in more humane ways;

- a sense of connectedness with colleagues was reinforced, an increased sense of what each worker had in common with each other. Perhaps related to this, participants felt that their work with their colleagues had improved;
- workers felt that overall they had learnt more practice strategies, and had gained more insight into decision-making;
- although the content of the main dilemmas raised at the beginning of the workshop series (for example, tensions between professional and bureaucratic ways of working, and lack of resourcing and support in undertaking difficult roles) does not appear to have changed, workers were more explicit about organizational dilemmas, and in some cases were in danger of being overwhelmed by them, possibly 'stuck' because of an inability to connect their broad structural understanding of dilemmas with personal experience and an ability to act;
- the theme of 'time' as a metaphor for the culture of their work and how it is organized was pervasive. Some saw the problem of time as equated with a procedural or outcome-based orientation to work, and therefore were inclined to speak about the limitations of their jobs as limitations of time (for example, not having enough time to critically reflect), and not necessarily as limitations of prioritization or structure. This seems to indicate that if the workplace culture is to be changed, workers need to feel that a 'time' space has been carved out to undertake new or different duties.

The following are themes which emerged from focus group discussions, both with participants and between group facilitators:

- a belief in the overall value of the process as being effective in training workers in a reflective process, although there is uncertainty about how critical it is;
- while attendance was sporadic, and logistics difficult, there was a clear commitment and interest from a large number of workers. Several made an effort to attend (even while on leave) and others travelled a great distance, and were prepared to finish other work outside hours, so that they could attend. They were also prepared to take risks in exposing their practice so that they could learn to maximum benefit;
- often there was a need to maintain a balance between debriefing workers in relation to upsetting or traumatic incidents which had just occurred with service users or colleagues, and building a more focused and constructive process of reflection;
- in relation to the above, there needs to be more focus on constructing positive directions, in moving on from traumatic and critical incidents and their analysis. In many cases there was not the time to do this in workshops, as some only spanned three sessions. Many workers moved well through a first reflective stage which also functioned as a type of 'debriefing', but were still stuck at this stage in the second part of the series, although it focused on the rebuilding of theory into new practice options;
- the sporadic attendance perhaps contributed to this difficulty in moving on, as not all group members were necessarily at the same stage;

- the need for (and appreciation of) an opportunity to discuss, share, debrief and reflect in a safe environment, and with a group leader from outside the organization, was invaluable for participants and perhaps helped model a collegiate atmosphere;
- the need for participants to be informed of the purpose of the workshops, and to feel supported by the organization in attending.

Discussion

In this second part of the chapter I discuss selected aspects of the training programme, and the experience in running it, which have a bearing on the development of a learning organization. I begin with a closer examination of what the systematic evaluations reveal about the learning of participants, and then move on to discuss aspects of partnership development and process and implementation issues. I finish with a discussion of some ongoing issues for organizational learning which arise from this case study.

The Learning of Participants and Organizational Learning

How much did the formal evaluation instruments identify about organizational learning? In responding to this question, I analysed both the instruments, and the participants' responses, in respect to learning which related directly to organizational concerns, or to the participants' view of the organization or other people within it. This is not the same definition of organizational learning as developed by Argyris and Schön (1996) in their classic work. Organizational learning, in their classic sense, is about the ways the organization as a whole gains new knowledge (Argyris and Schön, 1996: xxi). However, because the whole organization was not the focus of the training programme, but rather specific people within it, I modified the focus accordingly.

An analysis of the evaluation instruments themselves reveals several important points in relation to this question. First, in the structured aspects of the instruments (for example, the self-rating scale) there is a stronger emphasis on individual learning than organizational learning. Only two of the factors ('ways of using supervision' and 'ways of working with the system') might be said to have an explicitly organizational focus. Other aspects of the factors identified relate to more individualized aspects, such as personal/professional development, self-evaluation and improved practice. Of course, these factors will also have a bearing on the capacity of the organization to learn if many individuals show improvement on these scores, but it is significant to note that the way in which these factors are constructed implies an emphasis on individual change rather than change in relation to aspects of the organization.

This bias perhaps reflects some assumptions about learning held by all partners in the programme – that organizational change would automatically occur if individual change occurred. While this might be true to some extent, there is of course a wealth of theorizing and literature which runs counter to this idea. As is often argued, the organization itself is an entity, which has a life over and above its individual elements (Argyris and Schön, 1978; 1996). In order to bring about organizational learning, specific aspects of the organization need to be worked with.

Perhaps there is also an automatic 'blind spot' in some social work thinking about organizations. It is relevant to note that in some research I undertook with colleagues on professional expertise, organizational and contextual awareness is something which tends to develop only after a more individualized awareness (Fook, Ryan and Hawkins, 2000), and therefore is more likely to characterize the work of more experienced professionals. The focus on individual learning might also be indicative of a 'blame the victim' type of assumption. As I reflect on my own practice in relation to designing and implementing this training programme, it is crucial learning for me that some of my own espoused ideals about critical reflection (relating to worker empowerment and an analysis of all levels of power analysis) are not necessarily evident, for example, in the way I designed the evaluation instruments. I could have included more questions, for instance, which focused on the ways in which workers' thinking about power changed in relation to their organization and their place within it.

An analysis of the responses to the less structured aspects of the instruments reveals a slightly more complex picture. In some ways there were similar assumptions about the importance of individual learning inherent in the responses to less structured aspects of the instruments. For instance, although I have not summarized all the responses in relation to learning expectations in the previous section, suffice it to say that participants tended to speak of their learning goals in more individualized terms, such as the need for more specialized knowledge, to improve practice, or to use critical reflection in their work. Only a small number of the responses could be categorized as learning goals relating to the need to develop a better understanding about working in and with the organization, or a need for better learning conditions.

In relation to perceived dilemmas, however, the picture is a little different. These fell into six major categories: workers' commitment, lack of time and resources, work and life balance, organizational context, casework politics and supervision. It is possible to trace in these responses a greater awareness of the influence of the organization on practice, perhaps through an emphasis on bureaucratic concerns, internal/external politics, lack of organizational support or supervision issues. This possible discrepancy between perception of dilemmas and goals for learning may indicate again that workers do not make a link between the possibilties of how/what they can learn, and possibilities for organizational change. For instance, it is interesting to note that while the theme of lack of organizational support and organizational tensions dominated the workers' descriptions of their practice, there was not a corresponding expectation that workers could learn how to change these situations reflected in their statements about their learning goals. This, of course, may also reflect that workers simply felt disempowered about making such changes, although there did not appear to be any significant differences between how front-line workers responded and how team leaders and unit managers responded to these questions. Therefore, this discrepancy may say something about how we construct separately the worlds of 'learning' and the worlds of 'organizational change'.

However, on a more positive note, although there may be a tendency for participants and trainers not to link learning explicitly with organizational learning and change, it is still possible to make connections between individual learning and the potential for organizational change. For example, the theme of increased collegiality, a reinforcement of connectedness with colleagues and a resultant improvement of work with colleagues, was a strong thread running through responses to both the more and less structured aspects of the evaluation instruments. In addition, the theme of being able to find more and different ways of both supervising and working with supervisors was also encouraging from an organizational learning point of view, since supervision appeared to be perceived as one of the first and systematic points of learning.

Running perhaps counter to this though, there was the idea that workers' sense of practice dilemmas brought about by the organizational context did not change. The critical reflection learning process had perhaps succeeded only in raising awareness of these, but not in increasing their learning about how to address them. In some cases it is possible that the learning process might have heightened the sense of disempowerment, because increased awareness did not necessarily lead to an increased ability to act upon them. This may have been in part due to the collapsed time frame of the programme, or to the sporadic attendance of some workers (not having enough time to turn their 'deconstructions' into 'reconstructions').

Time limitations were a major factor in terms of the limitations of the groups. First, the planned time span of the groups was collapsed at the request of the organization, as it was felt that too many sessions would not be practicable for workers' attendance. Second, attendance was sporadic and unpredictable, meaning that many participants did not attend all sessions, so did not benefit from sustained reflection over a period of time. In many cases, work pressures took precedence over attendance and there was also high levels of leave taken during the period, both forseen and unforseen. In other instances, staff were directed not to attend, because of work deadlines and sometimes possible threats from immediate managers.

Overall however, one clear outcome of the learning process, which needs further work in subsequent programmes, is how to move participants from broader awareness and analysis to an ability to create and implement new practice options at an organizational level. This bears on perhaps the most important issue for myself, as the co-ordinator of the programme, as it relates to the issue of whether participants learnt about *critical* reflection as opposed to simply learning to be reflective. Did they gain a sense of how they theorized the idea of power, and how this affected their practice, and were they able to devise new ways of practising which used power in more effective ways?

In the view of many of the group facilitators, there was some doubt about this. In addition, the evaluation instruments did not focus specifically on changed perceptions of power, although these notions were, of course, implicit in much of the material. Participants did talk about learning new ways of practising and learning new perspectives, but whether or not they explicitly linked these with their understandings of power, and their ability to act in and upon situations, may be another matter entirely. The learning from this case study indicates that there needs to be a more explicit focus upon, and naming of, theories of power and that the process also needs to focus on developing this new thinking into explicit ideas about practice, in order for the critical reflective learning process to be effective.

Partnership, Process and Implementation

Given that a formal partnership already existed to provide for the training programme, the superficial formalities of contractual arrangements were relatively problem-free. However, there were several factors which made it a much more complex venture.

First, neither partners in the project were unified entities. Gonczi and Hager (1998) make much of this point of the idea of diversity in discussing the development of a corporatist policy. There are diverse interests and diverse ends sought, even though there might be espoused unified agreement. They note (ibid.: 57) at least three dimensions which may be complex: diversity of ends; diversity of motivations; and diversity of the process itself. In the case of the critical reflection training programme there were differences on at least these three dimensions. While there was commonality about some of the ends sought (for example, a changed learning culture within the organization to incorporate peer review), there were varying levels of commitment to this, both between the two partner organizations and between different workers and management levels within the human service organization. The highest commitment came from the directorate level, and, possibly because of this, lower levels of management were not explicit about their own lesser levels of commitment. However, these varying degrees of commitment became more apparent in the actual implementation of the programme. From the university's perspective, because of the imperative to establish industry links, success in some ways was as much in the negotiation of the contract as it was in the effective implementation of it.

In terms of the process itself, given the large number of participants and group facilitators of various designations, there was a high degree of diversity. For instance, group facilitators, while all experienced with teaching critical reflection and in agreement about the broad philosophy, had all come to it from various perspectives. They also ranged in amount of experience, personal teaching style and specific theoretical orientation. Therefore, group experiences could not be completely standardized, nor was this the intention. In fact, diversity of style was to some extent valued. However, this can be problematic in running critical reflection groups, when the group climate and culture in establishing trust and new ways of learning are just as important as the content discussed. This aspect of the diversity of the training was the subject of an independent research study (Askeland, forthcoming). While we do not have data which correlates these differences with the effectiveness of specific groups, it is possible to surmise that the critical reflection learning experience might have been quite different for different participants, even though many identifiable outcomes might have been similar. While this in itself is not necessarily problematic in terms of the success of a programme, it is an issue in negotiating contractual arrangements, as the necessarily open-ended nature of critical reflective teaching means that it is difficult to completely standardize offerings and predict all the desirable outcomes as experienced by all participants.

In terms of contractual arrangements, Morrison (1997: 24–5) quoting Hay (1992), notes three types of problems which can occur: organizations and trainers team up (against participants); trainers and participants team up (against the organization); or organization and participants team up (against trainers). In some ways, the original contract might have been seen as the first type of problem – that the trainers and organization were colluding to target problematic or below standard participants. When I as the co-ordinator became aware that not all participants (or even middle-level managers) were aware of what the programme entailed, I attempted to provide more information at all levels both formally and informally, through written material and through face-to-face discussions. I felt, that in order to maximize the learning opportunity for all participants it was important that not only were they informed of the motivations for the programme, but that they could participate to some extent in planning its design and implementation. This was achieved with some participants and some managers. Others chose not to be involved. Others initially agreed to assist and then simply did not deliver agreed input. It proved extremely difficult to engage with different management levels of the organization in productive ways.

There was also a danger, in this period, of the second problem-type arising, which is that trainers could be seen to be colluding with participants against the organization. For instance, in introductory group sessions, when it was important to engage participants in the learning process, much resentment and anger was expressed about why the organization had not informed participants of the nature of the training. To complicate matters, attendance was compulsory, and workers resented this, when no alternative arrangements had been made to relieve them of equivalent duties for each workshop session. Individual workers felt blamed for the bad practice of the organization, yet unsupported in efforts to improve the situation. Repeatedly this type of thinking was reflected in the critical incidents they described. Often the critical incident reported would have just occurred in the office, and was often related to the fact that they had to attend the workshop. It was difficult for group facilitators to treat these concerns with respect, to move workers to a point where they could see and analyse these incidents in broader perspective and to enable workers to devise constructive practices to address these situations, while also maintaining an impartial stance. There was almost a need for participants themselves to be heard, accepted and supported in their feelings of anger towards the organization before they could move to see the situation from a different perspective. Again, time was a factor here, as with a greater span of time it would have been possible to move participants through these changed stages of thinking in a more effective manner.

In terms of the third problem-type, where organization and participants team up against trainers, it was difficult from our position as trainers, to know whether this happened. However, we were aware that there was a significant proportion of participants who never attended any workshops. Some of these people never made any contact with the facilitators, so it is possible to assume that there may have been some in this group who were simply alienated from the trainers or the idea of the training. However, they may also have been alienated from the organization, and their non-participation could be seen as a statement of protest against the authority of the organization.

It is also interesting to speculate about the meaning of this significant degree of non-involvement and non-attendance contrasted with the high degree of commitment and interest demonstrated by a significant number of participants at all levels. Perhaps critical reflection as an approach and process polarizes opinion because of its non-traditional and potentially threatening perspectives on knowledge hierarchies and, hence, forms of authority.

As alluded to earlier, there were many pragmatic problems in the implementation of the programme. This is, of course, old news. Hinks (2000) discusses the issue in relation to trying to develop a reflective culture in an organization when the imperative has come from the top down, and needing to know more about the concrete realities of how workers actually do learn before this can be implemented successfully. Hough (1996) talks about the practical ways in which his ethnographic study of a child protection agency was undermined once the study was under way, despite the initial formal agreement to participate. What these, and the present case study indicate, I think, is not that we can always avoid these problems, but that often the specific and practical issues cannot always be pre-empted. In the case of the critical reflection training programme, meetings with different middle managers to organize the logistics of the programme (for example, timetabling, group composition) often yielded contrary opinions. In any case, there did not seem to be any timetable in the end which could accommodate all interests and needs. Also, the longer the programme ran, the more apparent it became as to which specific workers and managers actually supported it or undermined it. There was no way of identifying these definitively beforehand.

Related to what might appear merely 'practical' problems was the issue of 'time' which was a theme emerging from the formal evaluations. Many workers either did not attend the training, or felt they could not engage in reflecting on practice because of 'lack of time'. This, however, may also have been a metaphor for 'lack of support' or 'lack of resources'. That is, one way in which the organization is perceived to give support for an activity is to give time. What was operating was a type of organizational culture, a value on the 'commodification of time', the idea that things are only important if accorded time. Argyris and Schön's concept of 'double-loop learning' (1996: 20–21) may be important in relation to this idea. Double-loop learning is learning which results in a change in the values of theory-in-use (as well as assumptions and strategies). And if organizations wish to address the actual *desirability* of values which govern their theories in use, double-loop learning is essential (ibid.: 22). For double-loop learning to occur in relation to this critical reflection training programme, there perhaps needs to be an examination of this issue of 'time'. How are issues like support, resourcing, and so on communicated in the organization, and how are these best communicated in relation to desired forms of learning?

Ongoing Issues?

There are several ongoing issues which arise out of this case study of critical reflection training for peer review within a large human services organization. First, is the question of how to relate individual learning to organizational learning. Argyris and Schön (1996: 200) discuss this issue as related to the problem of 'levels of aggregation' – at what levels (individual, team, section, and so on) can we make sense of organizational learning and how do we relate different levels of learning to each other? This case study indicates that one of the ways to do this might be to address any tendencies to construct individual and organizational learning as separate processes or issues. There is also a need for a more explicit focus on how individual learning can become applied in organizational ways. This is particularly the case if the training is for *critical* reflection – to develop personal practice theory and action in empowering ways so that the organizational context can be worked with in an empowering way, rather than merely perceived as restrictive of practice.

Argyris and Schön also note the issue of 'productive learning' (1996: 200–201), and the importance of distinguishing between two types of 'double-loop' learning: one which changes the values inherent in the organization's instrumental theory-in-action; and the other which changes the values inherent in the organization's theory-in-use of the process of inquiry. What this case study reveals is a need to recognize and re-examine the values around activities which are supported, and what is the communicated organizational culture about some forms of learning. The commodity of 'time' is a possible starting point – a learning activity is valued if it is accorded appropriate time.

Argyris and Schön (1996: 201) also speak of 'the impediments to productive organisational learning that arise in real world organisations'. In particular they note the subversive effects of organizational politics. These issues became major considerations in the implementation of the critical reflection training programme, and indeed will continue to be major considerations for any further organizational development. They presented as issues of diversity, the need to recognize the politics involved because of a diversity of interests, and how new practical issues may emerge and change during the course of implementation rather than being predictable beforehand. What is a welcome challenge to some will be a threat to others; what is experienced as empowering for workers may be seen as disempowering for managers. For example, many participants spoke of gaining an increased feeling of connectedness with colleagues, within an initial climate of distrust. How will such learning be turned into productive organizational learning if there are those within the organization for whom the distrust serves an important function?

To what extent, then, can a critical reflection training programme address these ongoing issues? How can such training hope to contribute to empowering workers to act in more empowering and empowered ways with and within their organizations? The answer to this may be related to how we construct the purpose and focus of the learning. In closing, I again refer to Argyris and Schön (1996) who provide, I believe, a clear way of framing this learning. If we see organizational learning as learning about 'the political conditions under which individuals can function as agents of organisational action' (ibid.: xxii) we immediately have a framework which allows us to link personal and individual learning with organizational practice. Critical reflection can become organizational learning by increasing awareness of the individual worker's theory about their own place within the organization, and therefore their ability to act with and within the organization. By guiding reflective analysis and discussion to focus on how workers construct and understand their place, position, purpose, role, practice and power within and in relation to the organization, the critical reflective process can also help workers transform the ways they act within and in relation to their organizations. If workers think and act in more organizationally aware ways, this should have the potential to transform the ways in which workers act as organizational agents.

Note

1   With acknowledgements to Heather D'Cruz, Charles Gibson, Martyn Jones, Jane Maidment and Christine Morley.

Chapter 5

Multi-professional Teams and the Learning Organization

Imogen Taylor

Introduction

In the field of health and social care in England, New Labour's Modernization agenda has resulted in far-reaching change with new legislation and unprecedented numbers of new policies and associated guidance. Traditional health and social care structures are fast disappearing and are being replaced by new organizational forms including a confusing array of different kinds of Health and Social Care Trusts. Of significance for this chapter is that whereas in social care in the past there has been a patchwork of multi-professional practice operating in a somewhat ad hoc fashion, often depending on individual champions, there is now an increasing government requirement for services to be multi-professional. Furthermore, in multi-professional teamwork, there is a concurrent drive bottom up from service user groups and top down from government to involve service users as stakeholders in service planning, delivery and review. These changes are occurring in the context of an emphasis in public policy discourse on the 'learning organization'.

My focus in this chapter is on exploring the possible implications of multi-professional work, including service user involvement, for learning in and by organizations. The learning organization in the public service sector is itself undertheorized and underresearched. Similarly, multi-professional teamwork is undertheorized and underresearched. This chapter is an attempt to draw together existing relevant theory and research and identify the issues for future empirical study. My argument is that if we build knowledge about learning in and by the organization, we will contribute to strategies to develop the 'learning architecture' of such organizations (Wenger, 1998).

I begin by highlighting three sets of policy drivers relevant to this discussion: those that emphasize the learning organization; those that emphasize multi-professional work; and those that emphasize service user involvement. In the interests of clarity and not becoming lost in the multiplicity of policy initiatives across the entire public sector, I focus on mental health services policy as an exemplar for both multi-professional work and service user involvement. I then briefly examine the literature about the learning organization for its relevance to our discussion in this chapter. Following a discussion about organizational structures and learning, and in particular the structure of the team, I go on to examine theory and research about multi-professional teams, including service user involvement on teams. I particularly refer to a recent small-scale empirical study by Caroline Miller and her colleagues (2001) of multi-professional teamwork that touches on implications of the latter for learning. Based on this analysis, I go on to suggest that we need to know more about the interaction of power, trust and confidentiality with multi-professional learning to enable the design of learning organizations.

Relevant Policy Drivers

An interview by the *Times Higher Education Supplement* with Maggie Pearson, the Deputy Director of Human Resources for the Department of Health, revealed the priority given by New Labour to the learning organization:

> It is her job to turn the National Health Service into a learning organisation. Delivering a workforce fit for the future is a key part of the delivery contract signed between the Department of Health and No. 10 Downing Street. 'The commitment to creating a learning organisation comes right from the top,' she says. (Sanders, 2002)

The above statement by Maggie Pearson introduces the policy drivers which explicitly refer to learning and the learning organization. The concept of the learning organization first appeared in UK organizational literature in the early 1990s (Senge, 1990a), but it did not significantly appear in public sector discourse until the late 1990s when it appeared embedded in the New Labour Modernization agenda. The latter is primarily concerned to improve public services and the government clearly views developing knowledge and skills, and thus building the capacity of the workforce as integral to such improvement.

The Modernization agenda draws on the discourse of lifelong learning prioritized by the European Commission White Paper, *Towards The Learning Society* (1995: 2–3). This was endorsed in the UK, as demonstrated by this statement from the White Paper, *The Learning Age: A Renaissance for New Britain*: 'The skills of the workforce are vital to our national competitiveness. Rapid technological and organisational change means that, however good initial education and training is, it must be continuously reinforced by further learning throughout working life' (Department of Education and Employment, 1998: 3–4). Policies assume that lifelong learning is delivered by the learning organization. According to Alan Milburn, the Minister of Health in his introduction to the later White Paper, *Working Together, Learning Together: A Framework for Lifelong Learning for the National Health Service* (Department of Health, 2001a):

> Learning and development are key to delivering the Government vision of patient centred care in the National Health Service [NHS]. Lifelong learning is about growth and opportunity, about making sure that our staff, the teams and the organisations they relate to, and work in, can acquire new knowledge and skills, both to realise their potential and to help shape and change things for the better. (Ibid.: 1)

The White Paper identifies eight characteristics of the successful learning organization which include: a well-resourced learning strategy; a regularly reviewed system of appraisal and personal development planning; non-discriminatory and flexible access to education and training; provision of a learning infrastructure that is accessible in terms of time and location; demonstration of strong links between education, training and development and career progression and reward; a variety of development methods to enable staff to build on skills and expertise; and, regular evaluation and monitoring of learning activity.

Working Together, Learning Together (Department of Health, 2001a) also addresses 'work–life balance' issues. It emphasizes government commitment to ensuring that all NHS organizations are accredited for implementing the Improving Working Lives (IWL) standard. This standard is about modern employment practices, valuing and supporting staff, understanding that staff work best for patients when they can strike a healthy balance between work and life outside and balancing the needs of patients, staff and services.

The discourse of the learning organization is embedded in mental health policy and guidance. For example, the Workforce Action Team was established to enable mental health services to ensure that their workforce 'is sufficient and skilled, well led and supported to deliver high quality mental health care' (Department of Health, 2001b: 2), and recommends that to do this mental health services must 'develop a learning organisation and culture' (Department of Health, 2001b: 4). Furthermore, 'The employing Boards of NHS Trusts, Committees of Local Authorities and governing bodies of independent sector organisations must promote and demonstrate a culture of a learning organisation' (Department of Health, 2001c: 55). Employers must have in place frameworks for delivering and monitoring supervision, supportive mentoring and appraisal, and continuing professional development (CPD). Local councils are inspected for success in delivering this agenda.

The second set of policy drivers selected for discussion focus on multi-professional work. Alan Milburn, in his speech to the National Social Services Conference in 2002 clearly articulates the government view that, 'The old style, public service monoliths cannot meet modern challenges. They need to be broken up. In their place we can forge new local partnerships that specialise in tackling particular problems local communities face' (Milburn, 2002: 3). He had already provided the basis for newly forming Health and Social Care trusts with the Health Act (1999) which imposes a duty of collaboration. This Act required general practitioners to join together to form primary care groups (PCGs) to provide a wider range of primary care services. New partnership working relationships were forged between PCGs and community-based NHS Trusts and some took up the option of forming primary care trusts (PCTs). The Health and Social Care Act (2001) allows these PCTs (and NHS Trusts), if they choose, to form care trusts to jointly commission, purchase and provide services previously covered by local authorities, acute hospital trusts, mental health trusts and community NHS trusts (George, 2002). The result of this fast-changing landscape is a mosaic of different kinds of providers of health and social care services.

New organizational structures do not necessarily equate with improved multi-professional working. One recent inspection of how councils are managing the modernizing agenda in social care found although there was 'considerable evidence that partnership working had developed substantially in recent years ... there was little evidence of the Berlin Wall of five years ago ... Today, if a wall remains at all it appears largely redundant, breached in many places and now the scene of only border skirmishes (Department of Health and Social Services Inspectorate, 2002a: 19). However, an inspection of mental health services in the same year reports that in pursuing joint services insufficient attention had been paid to conditions of services; organizational and cultural issues; working practices; and supervision. 'Mental health services were a long way from being able to demonstrate that they were engaged in a process of continuing improvement' (Department of Health and Social Services Inspectorate, 2002b: 5).

The third set of drivers feature service user involvement in the design, delivery and review of services, a development also commented on by Milburn in his speech to the National Social Services Conference:

> It is all about putting users centre stage. You can already teach the health service a thing or two about that. But today I want you to go further. If social services are genuinely going to put users first then users have got to have more power. And that means more choice. Choice is not just a question of consulting users or promising to take their views into account. Nor is it just about making advocacy services more widely available. It is all these things – and it is more. Choice means opening up a broader span of services so that care can be tailored to fit the needs of the individual rather than assuming the individual will simply fit the off-the peg service. (Milburn, 2002: 5)

Whereas user involvement is not in itself a new challenge to social care or health, it is now taking centre stage in government policy and, significantly, Milburn refers to the central feature that users must have more power. In health settings this is exemplified by the concept of the 'expert patient' (Department of Health, 2001d).

Suzy Braye (2000), in her discussion about user participation and involvement in social care, highlights the range of possibilities for user choice and participation. These include: participation by a service user in his/her own use of service; participation in strategic planning for service provision and development; participation through the development of user-led services; participation in research into social care provision; participation in education and training of staff in social care; and, finally, participation in the community as citizens rather than service users. However, Braye notes that this is a contested arena of differing perspectives. On the one hand there is the notion of consumerism where in theory consumers choose from a range of services, influencing price and quality through their purchasing power. Braye notes that consumerism does not sit well with services where there are profound inequalities in the distribution of resources or where there is actual or implied coercion in the provision of service, as is often the case in mental health. On the other hand, there is the democratic model of participation with the purpose of achieving greater influence and control, which may relate to service provision and also operates at the level of policy-making, resource allocation, organization and management. Furthermore democratic participation 'is likely to work to a wider agenda, seeking improvements not just in service provision but in all aspects of social experience' (ibid.: 19). In mental health, Peck and Barker

(1997) trace the development of the mental health user movement and distinguish between users as consumers who seek more participation in decision-making and users as 'survivors' of mental health services who seek fundamentally to change the dominant paradigms upon which service is based. The latter inevitably involves a transfer of power from service providers to service users, the theme which as we have seen was picked up by Milburn five years later.

The Learning Organization

In this part of the chapter, I select four themes that recur in the learning organization literature and are relevant to our discussion here. First, is the notion that the learning organization is responsive to change, important in the context of the degree of policy and organizational change discussed earlier. Senge's (1990a) work flowed from a conviction that in a global economy, maintaining a competitive edge depends on the process of continuous improvement, and the most effective insurance against being left behind by the rapid pace of change is to embed within the organization processes which facilitate learning. Dovey (1997) highlights the learning organization's ability to see things in new ways, gain new understandings and produce new patterns of behaviour, on a continuing basis and in a way that engages the organization as a whole. As discussed earlier, in health and social care, public service organizations are engaged in fundamental structural change. However, the learning organization literature tends to discuss organizations as if they themselves are structures with a stable core, albeit engaged in a process of change. For example, although Wenger (1998) warns that learning involves a close interaction between order and chaos where learning communities reorganize their histories around destabilizing events, he appears to make an assumption about sufficient continuity for communities to provide a basis for engaging in a process of restructuring.

The second theme is that learning is a way of life rather than an episodic event (Senge, 1991). Handy suggests that learning organizations are those 'which encourage the wheel of learning, which relish curiosity, questions and ideas, which allow space for experiment and reflection, which forgive mistakes and promote self-confidence' (1989: 199). Wenger (1998), and others, emphasize that learning in the workplace is a social process (Lave and Wenger, 1991). Wenger (1998) refers to the organization as a 'Social design directed at practice ... . It is through the practices they bring together that organisations can do what they can do, know what they know, and learn what they learn' (ibid.: 241). The evidence is that most workplace learning is non-formal and unplanned (Eraut et al., 1998; 1999) where learning occurs continually but employees do not think about their jobs as learning because what they learn is their practice. 'Learning is the engine of practice and practice is the history of that learning' (Wenger, 1998: 96).

It will have been noted that much of the policy discourse about the learning organization referred to earlier is about formal planned learning rather than informal unplanned learning. Eraut notes that formal planned learning does have an important role in organizations in 'providing concepts and theories ... to make sense of ... experience and understand issues and alternative perspectives more clearly'

(Eraut et al., 1998: 8). An Economic and Social Research Council funded study by Davies and Bynner (1999) of credit-based systems and their impact on the learning culture generated some key findings. They found that certification of learning was important for a sense of achievement and as proof for family, friends and employers, and that learners believed that the assessment regime associated with accreditation had improved the quality of work produced, increased the shelf-life of learning and made them more conscientious about learning. Eraut et al. (1998) found that qualifications are important at particular stages, for example, initial training and mid-career management, and that the timing of courses is very important. Linked with timing is the importance of follow-up and the role of work-based learning in facilitating knowledge acquired on courses.

Third, is the theme that learning 'is a collective undertaking which involves people making choices' (Senge, 1991: 38). This notion of choice and participation is picked up by Eraut in his discussion of 'learning communities' that 'maximise participation through a culture imbued with inclusive, interdependent views of human relationships and democratic values' (Eraut, 2002: 2). Longworth and Davies (1996) suggest that learning organizations are concerned with empowerment of the workforce. As we have seen in the discussion about policy, service user and carer participation implies choice, control and a shift of power. Interestingly, participation by practitioners who are members of the social care and health workforce is a neglected topic.

Fourth, picking up on the theme of work–life balance endorsed in *Working Together, Learning Together* (Department of Health, 2001a), is the issue of whether we work to live or live to work? Do organizations exist for economic purposes first, and individual second? Or should the focus be on human beings first? Fielding criticizes Senge for omitting discussion about work–life balance, 'ultimately any debate about the nature of the learning organisation has to confront hard choices about whether work is seen as the raison d'etre of human activity or whether work is subservient to wider notions of human fulfilment (2001: 25).

Organizational Structures and Learning

Cayley suggests that 'an organisation bent on encouraging learning needs to focus not just on the circumstances which make learning necessary, but its own systems and structures to support learning, and the culture within which learning is embedded' (2000: 39). However, the learning organization literature tends to focus on learning in, rather than by, the organization and does not satisfactorily address what it means for a group or organization to know or to learn, or the linkages between different levels in the organization and how one level learns from another. In this next section of the chapter, I examine what we know about organizational structures and learning. I then introduce a model for linking individual and collective learning.

Given the extent of organizational change in health and social care, it is worth taking a few minutes to consider the nature of the organization itself rather than assuming we share a common understanding about how it is defined. To return again to Alan Milburn who stated: 'today over half of all councils have broken away from the old monolithic, single social services departmental structures towards greater specialisation and more integration with other service providers' (2002: 3). Trusts of various kinds are forming with new governance arrangements, new mandates and new structures, and the overall impression is of a network of loosely connected groupings where staff are forming into new multi-professional groupings. Such fundamental changes raise questions about the nature and shape of organizations themselves. Schein's definition of an organization is helpful because it emphasizes the key elements that are transferable from old to new organizational models. 'The planned co-ordination of the activities of a number of people for the achievement of some common, explicit purpose or goal, through division of labour and function and through a hierarchy of authority and responsibility' (Schein, 1989: 15). In the learning organization, how does learning occur horizontally across the division of labour and vertically through the hierarchy when different professions are involved? What impact does the participation of users and carers have?

There is some evidence that formal and informal team roles are significant in team learning. Organizational attempts to increase knowledge creation and use and promote learning have to begin with managers whose primary task is the management of knowledge and support and Eraut (2001) suggests that their interpersonal skills, knowledge and learning orientation is significant. He further suggests (ibid.) that managers are in a pivotal role as they allocate work, and the consequent lack of variation and lack of challenge lower the rate of learning whereas changes in role or new assignments promote new learning. Wenger (1998) does not specifically address multi-professional working or learning but he does introduce the notion of the informal role of 'broker' which it would seem might be significant in a multi-professional context. Brokers introduce elements of one practice into another, make connections across communities, enable co-ordination and open up new possibilities. They must have enough legitimacy to influence the development of practice, mobilize attention and address conflicting interests. Wenger suggests this often entails managing the complexities of multi-membership, a feature central to multi-professional work.

Dutch academics, Simons and Ruijters (2001), have developed a model of work-related learning which allows for the linkage between individual and collective learning. The core of work-related learning is that it includes both implicit and explicit processes that lead to changes in knowledge, skills or attitudes of individuals, groups or organizations and under some conditions these may lead to changes in work processes or outcomes. They identify three stages in the process of learning: elaboration where competencies are elaborated on by learning from and in practice; expansion where theoretical knowledge and insight are expanded by learning from research; and externalizing where building on practical and theoretical insights contributes to the development of the organization. They suggest that individual outcomes become collective when groups reflect on common implicit outcomes, reflect on or plan common learning outcomes and define common plans for externalization. They also theorize organizational collective learning where people share a common interest in the organization and professional collective learning where people share an interest in learning but not necessarily in one organization.

Learning in and by the Multi-professional Team

The team is a 'cellular organisation' (Alvesson, 1998: 6) and in the public services, the team is a commonly found collective or group. Senge, in his early work on the learning organization, emphasized the significance of teams: 'Team learning is vital because teams, not individuals, are the fundamental learning unit in modern organisations' and 'unless a team can learn, the organisation cannot learn' (Senge, 1990: 10). Teams are a way of sharing objectives and understanding. However, as commented earlier, Senge did not expand on the nature of the links between vertical levels of learning, neither did he examine horizontal multi-professional learning. As indicated above, Wenger (1998), in his seminal study of the learning organization and claims processors, does not explicitly address multi-professional learning either. However, he does refer to the value of negotiating alignments across 'discontinuities' where 'we can be forced to perceive our own positions in new ways, to have new questions, to see things we had not seen before, and to derive new criteria of competence that reflect the alignment of practice' (ibid.: 218). This process would seem to be transferable to different professionals who come together in a team and learn new ways of seeing things and new criteria of competence. Eraut suggests an alternative view, that multiple professions also imply multiple perspectives and multiple practices, and issues of differing power and status and different allegiances constrain co-operation (2002: 11).

There is a growing literature about multi-professional teamwork in health and social care (for example, Leathard, 1994; Ovretveit, 1993; Pritchard and Pritchard, 1994). Mandy (1996), reviewing characteristics of successful interdisciplinary teams, selects five main attributes: goal directedness, disciplinary articulation, communication, flexibility and conflict resolution. However, there is little discussion in this literature about team learning. The exception is a three-year study of multi-professional working and shared learning by Carolyn Miller, Marnie Freeman and Nick Ross, commissioned by the English National Board for Nursing, Midwifery and Health Visiting (Miller, Ross and Freeman, 2001). They used a case study approach to research six multi-professional teams from the following specialisms: neuro-rehabilitation, medicine, child development assessment, diabetes, general practice and community mental health.

Miller, Ross and Freeman (2001) identified three types of multi-professional work. First, integrated multi-professional work which is characterized by a stable and predictable organizational context where team members serve the same population of patients, records are jointly kept, communication is open and professional differences are raised, and members develop an allegiance to each other. It is a safe learning environment and the norm is to challenge the status quo. Second, the fragmented type is one where many aspects of patient management, problem-solving and decision-making relate to a single professional group. Communication between groups is relatively brief and focused on sharing information rather than sharing different professional perspectives. There is a superficial understanding of each other's roles and role boundaries are actively protected. The fragmented team does not discuss the process of teamwork. The community mental health team in their study fell into this category. Third, the core and periphery team combines aspects of the integrated and fragmented teams.

One focus for Miller and her colleagues was how individual understandings of teamwork affect multi-professional interactions (Miller, Ross and Freeman, 2002). They identified that individual beliefs about teamwork may be bounded by each team member's professional culture and each member will bring a different professional identity to the team, and that identity will have status and power through organizational recognition of a knowledge hierarchy. They suggest that when members from different professions are part of a multi-professional team, professional allegiances need to shift from a position where professional group membership is paramount, towards seeing the team also as an important reference point. They identified three interpretations of multi-professional working that they frame as three different philosophies, as they were to a large extent bounded by individual professions. They then relate each philosophy to willingness to engage in multi-professional learning.

First, the directive philosophy was most frequently held by members of the medical profession. It was based on an assumption of hierarchy where one person takes the lead because of status and power, and directs the actions of others. This generates assumptions about the what, when and how of communication, and to whom. It also assumes that where roles were lower in the hierarchy they were valued for their service to the powerful role. 'Learning from others was apparently defined by status, with those in positions of power believing that they *could only learn from their (same profession) peers or superiors*' (Miller, Ross and Freeman, 2002: 3, original italics). Second, the integrative philosophy where there is commitment to being a team player and to collaborative care. There is recognition of different levels of role understanding and role boundaries are negotiated. Each member's contribution to both the patient's progress and to the professional's development is equally valued. There was an acknowledgement of the complexity of communication and a belief that there should be discussion and negotiation in order to develop a team understanding of the patient. 'It was assumed that professionals would *learn both knowledge and skills from each other*' (ibid.: 3, original italics). Third, the elective philosophy was 'essentially a system of liaison' (ibid.: 3) where professionals preferred to operate autonomously and refer to others when they perceived a need. Communication is brief to inform others. Role clarity and distinctness is emphasized. Learning is valued from those of equal or higher status only. This philosophy was held most often by those working in mental health services.

Power, Trust and Communication

Miller's (2002) study alerts us to factors that shape multi-professional learning that the learning organization literature largely ignores. In the final section of this chapter I will examine power, trust and communication, and hypothesize that they each have an impact on multi-professional learning.

Fielding (2001) has criticized learning organization theorists, particularly Senge, for omitting an analysis of power. Fielding suggests that advocates of the learning organization more often than not retain a traditional grip on levers of power. Dovey (1997) argues that the learning organization does introduce a potentially radically different strategic option for an organization provided that those in control are also committed to change that implies power-sharing. Miller (2002) alerts us to the interaction of a hierarchy of roles, power and status in multi-professional teams and their implications for learning in multi-professional teams. However, Miller's analysis is limited and in particular she does not address the interaction of informal attributes of gender and ethnicity with power and knowledge which other theorists indicate might be significant factors. Clarke and Newman (1997), in their analysis of the 'managerial state', theorize the implications for men and women of the restructuring of the welfare state. Harlow (2000) draws our attention to the consequences of managerialism for social work and the relationship between gender and managerial aspirations and opportunities. She suggests that while men may experience enhanced opportunities in the new public sector management, women may be less attracted to posts concerned mainly with managing budgets and achieving performance targets. However, we lack a detailed empirical study of gender, power and multi-professional work.

Closely linked to the theme of power is that of trust, a topic focused on by Onora O'Neill (2002) in the BBC Reith Lectures. Miller (2000) notes that a 'safe' learning environment was one of the characteristics of an integrated team but she does not develop this theme. Eraut (2001) implies acknowledgement of the importance of trust in his discussion of the importance of the micro-climate of a blame free culture that encourages talking about learning, provides mutual support, learning from positive and negative experiences, and making full use of knowledge resources of members. These dynamics suggest the possibility for learning from mistakes, yet the increasing risk of litigation, together with today's public sector context of league tables, naming and shaming, rewarding high-achieving councils with stars, financial rewards and light-touch inspections mitigates against acknowledging mistakes. Increasing control, regulation, monitoring and enforcement have made the work of professionals more demanding because of relentless demands to record and report. 'The pursuit of ever more perfect accountability provides citizens and consumers, patients and parents with more information, more comparisons, more complaints systems; but it also builds a culture of suspicion, low morale, and may ultimately lead to professional cynicism, and then we would have grounds for public mistrust' (O'Neill, 2002: 57). A recent study of Joint Reviews of Social Service Departments identifies three different kinds of accountability: financial, performative and political. 'The claims of each stakeholder are absolutely legitimate and irrefutable, but to honour some claims is to violate others' (Humphrey, 2002: 474). Humphrey found that reviews are far more painful than traditional audits and are characterized by 'nakedness, exhaustion, bombardment, and inquisition' (ibid.: 472).

Communication is the third cross-cutting factor that would appear to be significant in multi-professional learning. Miller (2002) refers to the role of communication in learning in multi-professional teams. She found, for example, that the integrated team kept joint records, whereas the fragmented team kept separate many aspects of patient management. Clearly, learning in the workplace requires a flow of information, yet the sharing of information by practitioners is becoming increasingly complex. On the one hand, is the government enthusiasm for openness and transparency and, on the other hand, a requirement for confidentiality and protection of personal data (O'Neill, 2002). The rapidly increasing use of information and communication technology (ICT) to generate, store and retrieve information has given rise to the discourse of knowledge management. It is now being recognized that, rather than the development of ICT itself that is crucial, it is the interaction of ICT with individuals or teams and their willingness to share and use information which is significant to learning and to practice (Gould, 2003). There is also a concern that health will be the driver of information technology developments in the health and social care sector because it is relatively more generously resourced compared with social care (Watson, 2003).

Service User Involvement and Multi-professional Teams

How do the themes of power, trust and communication interact with service user and carer involvement and multi-professional learning? As we saw earlier, the learning organization does not address service user or carer participation, although today there are significant top-down and bottom-up pressures towards increasing this. Models of teamwork construct the service user as the pivot around which the team revolves but do not discuss the service user or carer as a team member (Ovretveit, 1993). More recently, the user or carer has been constructed as part of a network of relations within which teams operate (Payne, 2000). However, the literature on multi-professional teamwork, by and large, does not address the implications of participation of service users for the teams themselves. As already indicated, Miller, Ross and Freeman (2000) do not refer to this issue in their study in spite of the increasing emphasis on the expert patient (Department of Health, 2001d).

A recent evaluation of integrated working between health and social services for the joint commissioning and provision of mental health services in Somerset was not encouraging on the issue of user and carer participation. It showed that users felt less involved in care planning than previously, although both users and carers had been included as non-voting members of the commissioning board. Furthermore, although some helpful initiatives had taken place to support user and carer participation, there had been no shift in power towards users (Peck, Gulliver and Towell, 2002). In contrast in a uniprofessional context, Turner and Balloch (2001) show how the Wiltshire and Swindon Users Network developed an organization of service users to become involved in the planning, delivery and evaluation of services and to facilitate direct links between service users and Social Services.

Earlier in the chapter we saw that Alan Milburn, in his address to a Social Services audience suggested that they are 'further ahead' on service user involvement than their health colleagues (Milburn, 2002). Yet, a conference presentation by Christine Sealey and Jane Cowl (2002) from the National Institute for Clinical Excellence about the development of NHS clinical guidelines for schizophrenia described rigorous processes to establish and support participation by patients and their carers in development of the guidelines. We know that there are activities to support service user and carer participation but we do not know what impact they are having on the service users or carers, or on other team members. We do not know what practitioners are learning from service users and carers, how such learning may vary according to the profession of the practitioner or, crucially, how this is changing practice, or not as the case may be.

Conclusion

In this chapter, my focus has been on learning in and by the organization, particularly multi-professional learning and learning from service users and carers. My argument is that we need to undertake research to better understand about how people learn from each other in organizations, individually and collectively, and horizontally and vertically. In particular, in today's practice context, we need to know more about the implications of multi-professional learning and the implications of learning from service users and carers. Once we have that knowledge, then we are in a position to develop the architecture of learning organizations to integrate the evidence and properly respond to the policy directives that emphasize development of the learning organization. If we do not invest in acquiring this knowledge and do not structure learning based on our findings, then the discourse of the learning organization risks remaining at the level of rhetoric and, as Gould (2000) comments, becomes nothing more than a slogan for justifying top-down change.

Finally, I end this chapter by introducing a new factor that may be significant but has not yet been mentioned. Geraldine Macdonald (2002), a Canadian nursing educator, presents a convincing argument that organizational learning must be balanced with 'unlearning'. She discusses the emotional and intellectual work of unlearning by nurses and suggests that the work of unlearning is 'conceptualised within a transformative education paradigm, one whose primary orientation is discernment, a personal growth process involving the activities of receptivity, recognition and grieving' (ibid.: 170). Receptivity refers to being open to new evidence, to the practitioner's response to the evidence. Recognition refers to seeing that the evidence is strongly in support of new practices. Grieving refers to the loss and confusion that may accompany new information that touches the core of professional identity. She suggests that practitioners must unlearn before they can be effectively open to new practices, and this process must be undertaken in a safe environment with 'informed, trusted and engaged colleagues; it is a process undertaken at a time of vulnerability, a process that challenges the nurse's professional identity' (ibid.). Macdonald concludes that her professional identity must include a new identity as a 'knowledge worker'. Her analysis of unlearning and the resulting impact on professional identity may be useful in the process of developing learning in and by organizations to enable the integration of multi-professional learning and learning from users and carers.

Chapter 6

Sustaining Reflective Practice in the Workplace

Hilary Sage and Mary Allan

Introduction

A partnership developed from 1999 between the Diploma in Social Work programme at the University of Bristol and Stonham Housing Association (SHA) in the south-west of the UK, as a consequence of developing practice placement opportunities for students. At that time SHA were undertaking the implementation of the *Care Practice Standards Manual* (*CPM*) with their staff and this implementation exercise led to a shared interest and inquiry into how self-assessment and reflective learning approaches could be used and justified not only for preparing students, but also as a way of sustaining workers in professional practice and enhancing their decision-making skills. The aim of this chapter is to analyse the particular influence of social work courses and the outcomes of and issues raised by the implementation programme, as an example of an organization changing its approach to staff learning. The discussion is set in the policy context of the 1996 Housing Act establishment of Registered Social Landlords (RSL), the UK Department of the Environment, Transport and the Region's implementation of care practice standards and the Supporting People programme by 2003, and of the UK Department of Health's (2000) A Quality Strategy for Social Care. Key issues arising from these policy documents which this chapter will help to illustrate are:

- dissemination of knowledge through creative partnerships;
- commitment to lifelong learning;
- better trained workforce;
- focus on fieldwork experience in social work training;
- focus on planning and decision-making in management training;
- new roles and skill development for workers.

Examples of *creative partnerships* between education establishments and social care organizations are looked at in the first section as a framework for understanding different ways in which learning can be exchanged and become part of the culture of the organization. The use of *portfolios* as part of *lifelong learning* and professional development for individuals and their potential use by organizations such as SHA as a tool to demonstrate their own progress as a learning organization is explored in the second section. The third section evaluates how the reflective approaches used in the implementation of the *CPM* at SHA can lead to a *better trained workforce*, but recognizes the tensions created where the approach conflicts with a more management-led procedural style to training. The discussion draws on the literature on professional autonomy, risk assessment and decision-making in health, housing and social services, and recent empirical research into self-assessment and professional development. The findings are presented in the context of workers' capacity to deal with complex situations, dilemmas and conflicts, and the outcomes and benefits for service users. The chapter concludes with suggestions for strategies which will encourage students, workers and organizations to maintain the reflective learning process.

Creative Partnerships

Underlying the concept of creative partnerships in government policies since the NHS and Community Care (NHSCC) Act 1990 has been a belief in not only innovative projects and choice in service delivery, but also in economies of scale and efficiency through interagency work. The Griffiths Report highlighted the need for housing agencies to become partners in community care arrangements: 'Social Services Authorities will need to work closely with Housing Authorities and Housing Associations and other providers of housing of all types, in developing a full and flexible range of housing' (Department of Health, 1989: 25).

The implementation of the NHSCC Act 1990 and subsequent policy developments and reviews have tended to focus on difficulties over the health/social services boundaries and responsibilities (Lewis and Glennester, 1996). Wistow (1999) has also pointed out the increasing complexity of community care arrangements with the contracting out of local authority services and the growth of the independent sector, particularly in the provision of accommodation. Stonham Housing Association (SHA), for instance, had been providing tenancies with additional support since the 1960s and expanded their work in the 1980s and 1990s in response to the Government Housing Corporation's allocation of grants for 'special needs' housing. The SHA is now one of the largest providers of supported housing in England. Organizations which provided supported housing to marginalized groups such as the single homeless, drug users, women escaping violence and young people have barely been recognized as partners in community care in the social work literature, although Means and Smith (1994) drew attention to their role in discussion of housing policy and joint working between the local authority departments of housing, health and social services. A work book for inter-agency training on partnership working was subsequently produced and used for management courses (Means, Brenton and Harrison, 1997). Reid (2001) has highlighted the importance of housing associations as stakeholders in partnership working with their knowledge of the needs of service users but also recognized that new roles for workers and organizations have implications for staff training.

The 1996 Housing Act led housing providers to become registered as 'social landlords', and the proposed separation of financial support for rent and funding for support under the Supporting People (DETR, 1999) legislative framework obliges organizations to train staff to meet care practice standards. The Supporting People programme identifies the need for a consistent and professional approach to support. The *CPM* was developed through collaboration between the Housing Corporation and the National Institute for Social Work, and sets out standards for practice in all key aspects of supported housing work. Comparisons between these standards and practice requirements for trainee social workers can be made and will be discussed in the second section.

The authors' view is that there are strong reasons for supported housing agencies to be considered as major partners in care in the community programmes as well as in the education and training of social work, health and social care professionals, but that there are inequalities in these relationships due to the power of different professions and the organizational structures within which they are employed (Balloch and Taylor, 2001). The core training programme operated by Stonham Housing Association, for instance, does not lead to a professional qualification. Workers can feel undervalued by housing, health and social services professionals, although supported housing straddles the disciplines of housing management, mental health and social work. This will be discussed further in the third section as part of the evaluation of the *CPM* implementation programme.

There are several ways in which creative partnerships between social work courses and social care organizations can be developed and influence learning and structural change in the way services are delivered. Five main areas are outlined below and set the context for the authors' own evaluation projects.

- *Social policy development.* A historical perspective establishes the connection between universities as promoters of learning and teaching and the evolution of social housing, that is, affordable housing, for those on low incomes. Housing organizations have been responding to public concerns and government initiatives since the nineteenth century when social reform programmes aimed at health, poverty and childcare problems were often centred on housing settlements set up by charitable trusts. Links were established with universities and students who were often from more privileged backgrounds were encouraged to carry out voluntary work. In the early twentieth century the work of Octavia Hill could be said to have led the way in developing the focus on the individual and family, developing the social work perspective and the rights of tenants to have a say in how housing estates were run (Malpass and Murie, 1999). Although a history of social policies including poverty and homelessness is included briefly in most social work courses, it is marginal compared to other teaching on law in the field of adult care and work with children and families. Manthorpe (2002) has reviewed the history of settlements and their links with universities, the exchange of learning and influence on social policy reform. Her research identified six social work courses which still use settlements for practice placements although these projects are mainly city based advice and resource centres. Housing projects for vulnerable people now come under different organizational arrangements as described earlier. The curriculum of new social work courses may need to reflect more closely the variety of agencies in which social care workers will be employed or trained beyond the traditional Social Services Departments (GSCC, 2002).

- *Joint research*. The exchange of learning between organizations has been recognized through joint research programmes between universities and social work agencies elsewhere in this book. Kemp (2001) also explores the participant observer research method in relation to observation of students and workers in practice, and the involvement of service users. The benefits for service users and staff of work-based and practitioner research programmes are also described by Heywood (2001). Workers who were involved as research interviewers with service users said that they had gained greater insight into differences in the way assessments and the allocation of services were carried out by practitioners, leading to improvements in service delivery. Evidence-based practice and critical appraisal skills for understanding and applying research are currently being promoted by academic and health and social care agencies.
- *Work-based training*. Elsewhere in this book definitions of the meanings attributed to 'learning organizations' have been discussed, involving the notion of 'embedding' learning into organizational structures. The General Social Care Council (GSCC, 2002) also prescribes its view of the outcomes to be achieved in terms of continuous learning by staff and the welcoming of students into a work-based learning culture. This environment ideally develops because practitioners are updating their training regularly on internal courses, and undertaking post-qualification awards and, hopefully, being allowed time to read research findings or participate in practice evaluations. Titterton (1999) evaluates the effectiveness of risk management training, although changes to practice and outcome for service users are difficult to measure. Practitioners in this study and in another following the Post Qualification Child Care Award are asked to rate how their practice has changed (Cooper and Rixon, 2001). The responses are mainly positive and practitioners value the time and space that attendance on a course allows them to reflect on their work. However, course participants also report the demands and conflicts experienced in meeting time pressures of the job and operational priorities of managers and organizations while also finding the time needed to consolidate and reflect on learning. Where courses are delivered in partnership universities and social services are also reviewing their collaborative and joint assessment processes giving useful indicators of the difficulties and benefits of consortium working in education and training particularly where employers are taking a leading role (Mitchell, 2001). The *CPM* implementation by the SHA can also be considered an internal training programme driven by a government agenda and prescribed criteria. However, the opportunity to try different methods of delivery in their five regions and encourage each service to be involved in the development and design of their own local policies and practice, enabled further evaluation of the effectiveness of the approaches in terms of ownership of learning and improvement in service delivery, and these outcomes will be discussed later in the chapter.

- *Staff supervision.* This is usually provided on a one-to-one basis, and in Social Services departments has followed the practice teacher/student model established by social work qualifying courses. The importance of dialogue between practice teacher and student as a way of exploring and recognizing changes in attitudes, values and problem-solving is emphasized in the social work literature (Dick, Headrick and Scott, 2002; Taylor, Thomas and Sage, 1999). However, the pressures of the workplace have often meant that this once-a-month session is used mainly for managing individual workloads rather than any teaching, with an annual staff development review being the only chance to agree individual learning needs and a place on a course. It can therefore be difficult for social work courses to feel confident that students in some organizations will be allocated the mandatory time for supervision each week to enable feedback, teaching and reflection. The new role of Practice Development Adviser (PDA) that was created in Stonham Housing Association to assist with the implementation of the *CPM* was also intended to consolidate learning within the organization, formatted on a regional basis but with strong links to the centre. The PDA had the role of encouraging reflection but, with five service areas in the south-west region and 250 operational staff, individual supervision was impractical. The idea of reflective groups for staff developed and involving students in these groups enabled further exchange of learning and a move away from reliance on a one-to-one approach and more recognition by the organization of the importance of practice discussions.
- *Peer review.* Educational institutes are now favouring peer review methods as a way of developing practice. However, when this practice becomes established in universities, some elements of performance monitoring and quality assurance reviews by management are soon incorporated. Direct observations of social work students on practice placements by a trained practice teacher, who has also been observed by a mentor during the course of their training programme, has been found to be a valuable way of developing learning for students and practitioners and could be counted as a form of peer review as well as assessment of practice (Kemp, 2001). Peer collaboration is also the theme of a Canadian study which describes and analyses the support programme set up for field instructors of social work students (Barlow, Coleman and Rogers, 2000). A significant point from this study which also arises from feedback from participants of other training programmes (Titterton, 1999) is the degree to which individuals' employers support their professional development and whether practice teaching or field instruction is marginal or well integrated into the organization's activities. Response to the programme set up by Calgary University from field instructors was that they had felt isolated as agency workers but valued when the university provided opportunities for peer discussion of the supervisors' role (Barlow, Coleman and Rogers, 2000).

Creative partnerships can therefore extend learning for some individuals but not have a lasting influence on organizations in which they work, so that further monitoring of the effectiveness of training is required.

The use of portfolios to chart progress and change with social work students is a key feature of the development work carried out by the authors and transferring their use to the organizational context could offer a way of learning permeating practice more thoroughly.

Portfolios and lifelong learning

The employment patterns that have evolved in recent years indicate that individuals will not spend more than a few years in one organization and that they will need constantly to repackage and sell themselves in the marketplace of social care, as in the commercial sector of the economy. The creation of Skills Councils and National Occupational Standards for all the caring professions further emphasizes this trend (GSCC, 2002). Portfolios showing personal development of knowledge and skills as well as curriculum vitae may provide essential documents for social care job applications in future. However, the portfolio system as a learning and assessment tool in the fields of education, health and social care needs further evaluation since its introduction to social work education in the 1990s. At its best a portfolio can provide an autobiography of professional growth and increase the sense of ownership of learning (Jarvinen and Kohnonen, 1995). Evaluations of the introduction of portfolios for presentation of practice evidence were carried out in 1998–99 at the University of Bristol as part of the Self Assessment in Professional and Higher Education (SAPHE) joint universities project in the south-west of England (Taylor, Thomas and Sage, 1999). Feedback from students showed that the portfolio structure and the opportunity to evaluate their own skill and knowledge development were welcomed. At the same time, findings also indicated that the process could become too bureaucratic and the amount of written work required tended to discriminate against some disabled students. Much consideration is given in the social work literature to the development of the reflective practitioner (Eby, 2000; Gould and Taylor, 1996). However, as Ixer (1999) points out, it is not easy to measure reflection or to explain why a student has not reached the expected standards of competence. Crisp and Green Lister (2002) have also reviewed the literature on methods of assessment in social work education but concluded that evidence of effectiveness is lacking.

The concerns that prompted the authors to continue the evaluation of practice manuals and portfolios as assessment and learning tools in the workplace were:

- students who were failing on practice placements and struggling with the concept of 'developing professional competence' (CCETSW, 1995);
- workers' lack of depth and ownership of learning when faced with new procedures;
- questions about the erosion of professional autonomy and decision-making skills in a managerial, procedure-led environment.

Criticism of the competence based approach to social work assessment has focused on fears that it would lead to technical knowledge and skill without the ability to cope with complex situations or find creative solutions (Crisp and Green Lister, 2002). Similar concerns were felt by the Practice Development Adviser for Stonham at the start of the implementation of the *CPM*. The section which discussed values in the manual was a separate module and not integrated into all units, creating a potential for the values to be disembodied from practice. The Diploma in Social Work practice requirements have been more explicit about the need to link evidence of practice with reflection on values and professional development (CCETSW, 1995). It seems pertinent to consider how professional competence is developed and assessed before the new Degree in Social Work gets under way and students are required under the new curriculum to demonstrate skills in inter-professional work, a requirement of the *CPM* as well. The approach of the *CPM* which sets a series of questions on current staff responsibilities in the workplace, is to 'professionalize' the practice into a discrete body of knowledge and skills. The example of social work student portfolios with collections of work-based evidence influenced the West Region Practice Development Adviser to look at how this method of assessment might be adapted so that the organization can present its own evidence of effective service delivery and professional development of staff when seeking contracts and funding. Although the requirement for portfolios of services was already present in the *CPM* from the outset, there was not much staff or organizational enthusiasm for this model of evidencing, seeing it as more work and bureaucracy, rather than an effective means of demonstrating the quality and range of practice in the service.

In order to gain further knowledge about whether social work education was relevant to the changing world of housing and social care practice, and to provide some answers to the concerns set out above, written evidence for selected practice requirements was tracked through a sample of student portfolios. Themes arising from this analysis highlighted four main areas where students had experienced difficulties and dilemmas, and had complex decisions to make:

- personal /professional boundaries and roles;
- resolving differences with families and groups;
- operating with conflicting policy directives;
- confidentiality and the exchange of information.

Although all areas appeared in both first- and second-year practice portfolios, the second and third points were highlighted more often for second-year students, indicating their need to develop greater interpersonal and negotiating skills with families and others, and to understand and resolve conflicts around needs-led assessments and limited resources. Learning about organizations and management decisions brought home the reality of the workplace and the re-examination of values when coming to decisions. Difficulties in understanding and coping with the complexity of tasks and decisions were often shown to be the reason for students failing placements and justified the use of portfolios in collecting detailed evidence and determining where the problems lay. In terms of practice teachers and Practice Assessment Panels, determining what is positive evidence of learning and demonstration of professional development examples from students placed in housing associations such as Stonham and drug support agencies illuminated the dilemmas faced. Written accounts by students described how they had explained choices and outcomes to service users who faced the possibility of eviction, homelessness, prison or a health treatment programme and how they had examined legal, ethical and power issues in trying to also enter into some degree of partnership in decision-making. Where these interviews had also been observed by the practice teacher and feedback given by them and perhaps also the service users, the evidence for the development of professional skills was further acknowledged and verified.

The experience of observing students working directly with service users encouraged Stonham's West Region PDA to try this as a way of auditing how staff were putting their learning from core training sessions on the *CPM* into practice. Verbal acceptance of standards did not necessarily mean that staff were able to translate a change of attitudes and language into practice. As with student social workers, opportunities to try out changes and receive feedback were found to ensure greater confidence and skill.

The portfolio assessment system highlighted the need for social workers to gain the capacity to cope with conflict and complexity. By providing the opportunity to analyse and reflect on practice, permission was given to voice feelings of confusion and anger as well as to find ways of challenging and constructively resolve issues. The foundation for coping with constant change in the social work profession and to undertaking post-qualification awards is thus laid down. Social workers and many care staff and housing support workers without professional qualifications are still on the front line between service users and care agencies interpreting policies, needs, risks and rights to services. The extent to which workers are able to develop skills in risk assessment and decision-making, and move from being competent, following standardized procedures to being proficient or autonomous experts with analytical, creative problem-solving skills, has been discussed by Eraut (1994) in studies of social care and health professionals. Questions are raised about the level of skill organizations expect of professionals and allow through organizational structures and management systems (Aleszowski, Harrison and Manthorpe, 1998). As the following section indicates, it is not easy for care staff in local projects to continue to question their own practice and the policies and procedures of the management of their organization.

Equipping the workforce with the necessary skills and providing a broader education is the subject of current UK General Social Care Council planning (GSCC, 2002). Providing practice placements is just one way in which agencies and educators can share ideas and influence standards of practice.

Better Trained Workforce

The *CPM* sets out a standard for support practice in all Stonham services and consists of nine modules including values and principles, risk assessment, support planning and linkworking. As part of its commitment to ensuring high standards of practice in its services, Stonham appointed a Practice Development Adviser in each of the five regions, initially for three years and subsequently permanently, whose task was to work with operational staff to develop good practice and policy, implement the care practice manual and identify further training and learning needs. The Practice Development Adviser role is designed to co-ordinate the learning for the organization and act as conduit to ensure knowledge and new information reaches the appropriate staff delivering support in the services.

The manual contains standards and principles for developing local policies and procedures, but does not directly provide them, as it is predicated upon notions of reflective practice and requires that project staff be involved in the development of their own local policy and procedures. In the five regions in Stonham, some regions have decided upon a regional approach and have designed a common assessment format for all services, others have stayed with the concept of local design and each service has developed its own paperwork. In the West region, the decision to adopt an individual service approach was made to ensure that all staff were involved in the development and design of their own local policies and practices, although some service areas (subdivisions of the region into mainly county boundaries) have developed their formats across a range of services. Theoretically, then, each service has thought about what service they offer and how they can best risk-assess referrals and service users for that service and, subsequently, how they plan support and linkwork (the supported housing word for keywork).

Development of Reflective Practice Groups

When considering how the *CPM* would best be implemented there were differing perspectives within the organization that would be likely to have an impact on the outcome of practice standards. Some managers, whose experience of practice was either some time ago or had never been involved in working directly with service users, saw the manual in functional and simple technical rational terms; practice merely had to comply with the *CPM* in a consistent and routine manner and practice would then be good. Others recognized the dangers of this approach and the need first for relationship-building with service users in order to work in partnership and properly risk assess, plan support and linkwork. While there was a good deal in the *CPM* about relationship-building, the length and depth of it more or less guaranteed that busy project workers and managers would hastily seek the section which referred directly to standards or organizational requirements. Additionally, the separation of values and principles into a discrete module offered the potential disconnection of values from practice, as well as seemingly adding to the workload.

Awareness of the possibility for different interpretations, informed the choice of approach. Since individual services were required to develop and design both their own policies and procedures, interpretations were inevitably varied and, in order to attempt some congruence between essentially different services, the concept of reflective practice groups was proposed. Initially there were some difficulties in establishing these groups, partly due to other competing demands such as restructuring and low staffing levels during a transitional period.

The PDA was committed to ensuring that practice in services did not become routine and inflexible, which would have hardly differed from what was believed to be the existing case and the situation the *CPM* was attempting to displace, hence the setting up of reflective practice (Schön, 1987) groups. These groups, initiated and supported by the PDA, enabled staff to spend protected time discussing, sharing practice and problems, challenging and analysing their practice, developing their local policy and agreeing standards at a local level. Whenever students were on placement, they also attended to contribute to the debate on practice. Throughout the three-year period, the groups' membership has fluctuated between project workers (staff directly involved in working with service users) along with team managers to project managers alone. While this was not ideal, as the original purpose and intention was to ensure that the people who were working with service users had the opportunity to discuss practice in this forum, in reality project workers often did not feel they had sufficient authority to take new developments back to their teams and, subsequently, initiatives were getting lost. However, the groups were formally adopted into regional structure giving them an authority, which has helped to establish them and staff use them constructively for a wide range of practice discussion and policy development. The value of these groups ultimately, however, is in the flexibility they offer. They provide opportunities constantly to review and adapt practice to ensure that the 'way we always do it' approach is challenged and staff are required to think and reflect on their practice and develop the ability to constructively criticize their own practice and to challenge the potential for rigidity of a top-down practice.

Evaluation of the effectiveness of these groups has been mixed. Although mostly positive about the groups themselves, concerns focus around the time available to staff to leave the service and meet. Competing demands from government initiatives and management monitoring can also sometimes crowd out the ability to spend time in quality interactions with service users, which presents problems for committed staff. All staff reported that the groups helped keep a focus on practice, which in the busy environment of the modern workplace is often difficult to sustain. Over time the groups have become more focused and, while service area approaches differ, they are increasingly seen as an important element in the learning of the organization.

Staff Backgrounds

Importantly in supported housing, there are no particular qualifications that staff routinely hold. Staff come from a wide range of professional backgrounds and therefore the knowledge, skills and values can be widely different. Some staff do come from social work backgrounds and some may have mental health or nursing backgrounds, but more often at service level there are no specific qualifications required and just as many staff may have no formal qualifications. Interestingly, the approach of the *CPM* is concerned with professionalizing the practice into a coherent and discrete body of knowledge and skills, however, the parallel process for staff, the core training, does not lead to a professional qualification. Training has been the subject of much discussion and some staff have taken the initiative to organize their own professional qualifications. Stonham does have a fund to which staff can apply for either a grant or loan to further their professional education. Nevertheless at present there is no organizational route to professional qualification, although a post has been created to develop a route to professional qualification. There is still, however, the dilemma of what that qualification might be. Since supported housing straddles two distinct disciplines, those of housing management and social work, there are issues to be resolved in where exactly the knowledge skills and values base would sit before any accredited qualification could be provided in-house or indeed in an academic institution.

A further complication to the standardization of care and support practice is the different levels of care and support offered in different services. Services offer varying levels and degrees of support, as opposed to personal care. However, within that spectrum there is a very wide range of support levels, measured in a variety of different ways, for example, time spent on support ranging from floating support at an hour per week all the way to 24-hour cover with intensive support, which has raised concern about how the standards could be applied to such differing environments. Over the three-year period, nevertheless, the perceived disparity of practice in different services, has largely disappeared and almost all staff recognize that there is a body of practice which is consistent and coherent, and applies to all services which offer support regardless of the extent to which it is offered.

One of the major difficulties in implementing the *CPM* was realized in the conflict between the acceptance of the *CPM* as a management-monitoring tool and the potential for delivering a service that service users actually want and would benefit from. There was also recognition of the tensions created by organizational necessity for meeting legislative changes and monitoring of what is essentially a one-to-one human interaction, the quality of which is determined not so much by what is said but how it is experienced by the participants in the interaction. Anecdotally there have been instances where the service to the service user has been compromised by staff belief that a bureaucratic and officious approach to practice was required by the organization. While generally the understanding and commitment to social work values and good practice prevails, in the interpretation anomalies can and do appear. This can be potentially linked to the separation of the values module from the main body of practice. Feedback from staff about the *CPM* has been varied. Without exception staff say that it has led to a greater awareness of a coherent body of practice, while opinions on whether it has significantly improved practice remain divided. Newer staff tend to think that it provides a sound foundation for their practice, while older more established staff can find it repetitive and condescending. A perhaps unsurprising point to note is that staff who have struggled with practice in the past still appear to struggle, in spite of the *CPM*.

One of the authors' original concerns about the depth of practice (Howe, 1996) and the potential for technically correct but humanly unconnected interactions with service users has to some extent been realized and picked up through direct observations of practice. Inevitably, the very fact that the *CPM* came from the top impacted upon the way in which it was seen. Rather than the belief that practice should be good because the service user is being valued, some staff felt they were being forced to change their practice and did not realize that what was really changing was the language – in other words the perception of the manual was not always that it was about good practice. Also, services where good practice was evident in the past perceived the arrival of the *CPM* as a criticism of their practice. In the three years, however, that misconception has largely been replaced by the belief that the *CPM* is about good practice and this has, to some extent, resulted from the reflective practice groups. This has helped give credibility to the notion of reflective practice and promoted discussion about practice at all levels of operational staff meetings. The value of this reflective space in the organization has been demonstrated in the sharing of practice and the solving of practice dilemmas, and has assisted in the process of identifying learning needs, understanding staff issues and concerns, and promoting the role of the organization in learning.

Another area of practice that was strongly influenced by the work done with students on placements involved the compilation of a portfolio in each service. Although a requirement of the *CPM*, there had been little progress achieved in the first two years of the PDA role. While the PDA promoted this means of presentation and linked it to the notion of the learning organization, staff found it difficult to understand and believed that they did not have the time to compile such a document. However, services where student placements took place were more comfortable with the notion and coupled with a brief illustration of an index for the portfolio staff were inspired, and the idea took off. Currently, since this work has been shared with PDAs from other regions, it is becoming a national approach. The concept of the portfolio for services is a demonstration of the practice in that service and, for ease of use as a marketing tool in the new environment of Supporting People we have just entered, best value reviews are included in the portfolios. The portfolio approach has a number of benefits: first, the portfolio acts as a portable market stall for the service and reports coming in from some services indicate that local authority Supporting People teams have been impressed by the quality of the work; secondly, staff can become skilled in compiling portfolios which will be useful for undertaking professional qualifications; thirdly, a systematic and methodical approach to practice within the service – regular reviews of portfolio and updating of policies – ensures that there is always a current version of how practice is carried out in that service. This develops the notion of portfolios from the demonstration of an individual's practice to a showcase for the whole service, which, rather than being assessed, becomes a selling point. In the next year, portfolios are likely to be developed for individuals learning to achieve National Vocational Qualification (NVQ)-type qualifications.

The last area in which the influence of work with students can be clearly seen arises out of work done by the PDA in auditing practice in services. The original audit of practice against the *CPM* was a self-assessment exercise by staff and signed off by the Operations Manager. Subsequently the PDA role included a programme of audits to ensure that the paperwork practice was in place. Reflection upon this programme identified the possibility that, although the practice looked good on paper, the actual interactions between service users and staff might not necessarily be so effective. From the experience of practice teaching and direct observations, the idea of extending this to staff arose. While it would be clearly impossible to devise a programme of direct observations extensive enough to be meaningful, the idea of peer observations was developed. Adapting the requirements of the Diploma in Social Work – communicate and engage, promote and enable, assess and plan, intervene and provide services, working in organizations and developing professional practice, for the supported housing environment – a format was designed and training delivered to enable a pilot to take place to see if this could be a way forward to more critically constructive and open discussion about practice. This peer observation pilot in a women's refuge in Dorset successfully promoted the concept of reflective practice and has led to a range of practice development initiatives, including challenge of many accepted practices.

Conclusions

'Retaining a reflective space' (Preston-Shoot, 1996) in the workplace should be the aim of all social care organizations and should go beyond individual workload management and supervision or an annual team-building day. This chapter has discussed the various ways creative partnerships between social work education and social care agencies can develop mutual learning opportunities which benefit individual workers and the organizations' delivery of services. It has also illustrated, through the case study of Stonham Housing Association's implementation of the *CPM*, how reflective practice groups can be established and regularly sustain the process of reflection within the organization's structures. The building up of practice knowledge through the use of individual and agency portfolios also maintains the commitment to lifelong learning and the idea of the learning organization. Further monitoring of the outcomes for service users with the achievement of a better trained workforce will be needed as the Supporting People programme becomes fully operational.

Chapter 7

Using 'Critical Incident Analysis' to Promote Critical Reflection and Holistic Assessment

Judith Thomas

Introduction

In the UK recently the learning agenda has placed more emphasis in social work on learning in, from and through work. For some people this may be in the traditional role of being a 'student' on placement. Staff increasingly are expected consciously to carry the dual roles of worker and learner and be assessed through the National Vocational Qualification (NVQ) system, work-based and part-time qualifying programmes, and post-qualifying awards. However, the notion of the worker who, in his or her daily practice, embraces the triad of critical thinking, self-awareness and reflection to be a 'reflective practitioner' is still a long way from the reality. Mission and policy statements may promote work-based learning but for many the pressures of everyday work and the lack of opportunity to engage in meaningful dialogue with themselves and others means that the learning from significant experiences is lost.

This chapter draws on my experiences as a practice-based teacher and a university-based tutor involved in the design, implementation and evaluation of learning and assessment processes. The 'students' I have worked with are located in practice settings, undertaking study and working for qualifications alongside their 'normal' work. They are mainly the practice teachers of social work students working towards qualifying awards. These practice teachers play a crucial role in paving the way for students to be reflective practitioners.

The aim of this chapter is to look at the way practice teachers are encouraged to develop as reflective practitioners and as reflective educators. One of the tools I have used to do this is a critical incident analysis so, after a brief introduction to some literature on reflection, the chapter explores ways of critically analysing incidents from everyday practice and considers how these have been used on training courses for practice teachers. I then look at how critical incidents can be used in competency-based assessment.

A range of methods has been used to inform the ideas presented. These are founded on a detailed evaluation of the critical incident analysis undertaken by 18 practice teachers in 1996, the quotes in italics are taken from this study. Since this study the exercise has been used on over 50 courses for new practice teachers. Of these over 120 of the practice teachers have subsequently applied for the Practice Teaching Award (PTA), a nationally recognized qualification approved by the UK General Social Care Council (GSCC). Submission of the critical incident analysis has formed part of the PTA selection process, so I have had the privilege of reading and discussing these incidents in detail with many practice teachers. The 'sample' has included male, female, black, white and disabled practitioners working in the statutory local authority sector, voluntary and private settings. A detailed study of similarities or difference between these groups has not been undertaken, but I have made specific reference to these groupings where relevant. My thinking is also informed by course evaluations and other relevant research.

A short chapter does not offer the scope to provide a detailed discussion of all the data collection, sources of evidence and relevant experiences. This illustrates the complexity of determining how knowledge is created and the difficulty of containing this within formally constructed research processes. The purpose of this book is to explore critical reflection, and so here I present my critical reflections on this subject and the practice wisdom I have developed through the medium of using and studying the critical incident analysis.

Critical Reflection

Morrison argues that 'reflective practice has become a conceptual and methodological portmanteau, catch all term' (1996: 317). Ixer (1999) questions whether there is such a thing as reflection, arguing that more research, clarity and consensus is needed before we can justify its place in the curriculum let alone know what we are assessing. As the notion of reflective practice is problematic, I start by exploring some of the models and frameworks I use in teaching to assist course participants in the process of developing a conceptual understanding of critical reflection.

Kolb's (1984) learning cycle of going through the process of action, reflection, abstract conceptualization and planning provides a useful starting point for theorizing about reflection. Eby (2000) identifies interconnected circles of critical thinking, reflection and self-awareness as essential components of reflective practice. However, as reflective practitioners build on their experiences and are actively engaged in developing theories that they can use in practice, it is more useful to conceptualize the circle as a spiral. The concept of transforming the circle into a spiral is articulated by Ruch (2002) who brings out the different dimensions of thinking, doing and feeling. Marshall and McLean (1988) look at the spiral within the paradigm of collaborative research identifying how the collective process of sharing knowledge creates a new understanding that then informs the next stage of action and enquiry.

Morrison (1996) draws on the work of various writers to identify two models of reflection: reflection in and on action; and reflection, development and empowerment.

Reflection in and on action is based on the work of Schön (1983; 1987) where reflection-in-action is critiqued as being short term and concerned with technical efficiency, drawing on tacit knowledge to reframe a situation. Reflection-on-action is a more distant, structured, logical analysis where the practitioner 'is empowered, through clarification, understanding and articulation of principles and theory, to develop greater professional autonomy through the conscious exercise of judgement' (Morrison, 1996: 319). The criticism of Schön's work and of this model of reflective practice is that, among other things, it does not explicitly look at power and the political context within which the practitioner may be constrained and/or trying to change (Kincheloe, 1991; Smyth, 1991).

The second model, reflection, development and empowerment, looks to reflective practice to bring about 'individual and social empowerment' (Morrison, 1996: 319) or what Masschelein describes as 'individual autonomy within a just society' (1991: 97). It moves beyond the focus on individuals within their immediate practice environment to examine wider structures of society and to question underpinning ideologies. Like feminist and collaborative approaches to research (Reason, 1994; Stanley, 1990), it sets out 'to change the world, not only to study it' (Stanley, 1990: 15). Morrison connects this model of reflective practice to the work of Habermas and his concept of emancipatory knowledge which is socially transformative and 'promotes individual and collective political freedoms and equality' (Morrison, 1996: 319).

This latter model is more akin to the sort of critical reflection we expect social workers to achieve in qualifying training. Morrison's research also identifies the difficulties practitioners have in achieving the second model, but this construction is essential to avoid Wright's (1993) criticism that reflective practice is about making people work harder rather than challenging constraining policies and structures. It also moves beyond seeing learning as isolated individualistic activity to a process that is enhanced by a more collaborative approach. The models are also useful in helping to conceptualize the difference between reflection and *critical* reflection. Later in this chapter I will explore how practice can be analysed in different ways, and link this to Habermas's theory that knowledge is constructed in technical, practical or emancipatory ways.

The extent of writing on reflective practice leaves all but the most dedicated researcher in this field with a plethora of constructions, and it is well beyond the scope of this chapter to provide a full literature review. Useful summaries and critiques of various models of reflection are provided by Ghaye and Lillyman (1997), Brockbank and McGill (1998) and Evans (1999). These summaries, together with more recent publications, lead me to question whether it is possible to have a fixed definition of reflective practice or, by its nature, does it need to be flexible as new ideas and thinking are incorporated? Speaking of values, Elliot considers:

> Values are infinitely open to reinterpretation through reflective practice; they cannot be defined in terms of fixed and unchanging benchmarks against which to measure improvements in practice. The reflective practitioner's understanding of the values s/he attempts to realise in practice are continually transformed in the process of reflecting about such attempts. (Elliott, 1991: 50)

Critically reflective practice is similar; a definition cannot adequately encompass all the ideas that can usefully be incorporated into the notion of critical reflection. However, as educators, the least we can do, particularly if we are intending to assess it, is to be able to articulate the concept in terms of the processes we would expect, and to debate these with 'students', peers, mentors and managers.

My expectations of critically reflective practitioners are that they are willing to look at events in their practice. Looking at these involves some description of the immediate effects on the people involved and the feelings of the person reflecting would feature. The reflector draws on his or her existing knowledge to make sense of the experience and also seeks new perspectives to ensure critical thinking. These new perspective could come from challenging questioning and discussion with others, and would include an examination of relevant theory and research. The critically reflective practitioner would be able to articulate his or her new understanding in terms of the learning process and as a rationale for action that is then demonstrated in future practice.

Developments in the UK in the 1990s, such as the Centre for Evidence Based Practice (CEBSS), have encouraged social workers to draw more on research in their practice. Sackett et al. (1996: 71) describes evidence-based practice as 'the conscientious, explicit, judicious use of current best evidence in making decisions'. However, by constructing this 'best evidence' in terms of quantitative scientific methods, as proposed by Sheldon and Chilvers (2000), we are in danger of subjugating qualitative studies and the practice wisdom that has emerged from specialist services, often where service users have played a key role in creating that knowledge.

Within the expectations of a critically reflective practitioner, articulated earlier, are a host of complex processes and ideas that can be explored further by looking in more detail at the framework of the critical incident analysis and considering how these are used on practice teaching courses.

What is a Critical Incident Analysis and How is it Useful?

Critical incidents are reflections based on an analysis of a practice where the individual has taken some action and whatever he or she does has important consequences either for him or herself, the service user, others involved or all of the players. Brookfield outlines such occasions as 'an incident ... that for some reason was of particular significance ... the emphasis is on specific situations, events, and people' (1987: 97). He identifies that analysing incidents is a useful a way of promoting reflection and critical thinking. It has also been used extensively on post-qualifying social work programmes to develop professional competence (Winter, 1990). Critical incidents are the times where we have to take some action and whatever we do has important consequences.

As part of their training practice, teachers analyse a 'critical incident' from their work as a social work practitioner, later in the programme they go on to analyse an incident from their work as educators and assessors. These critical incidents act as a trigger to reflection. I often describe them as the sorts of situations that come into our thoughts when we are doing something else, we may have 'flashbacks' while watching a film of a 'moment' in an interview or meeting when something unexpected happened or was said. This prompts us to go over the incident in our minds, and re-examining it can lead to critical reflection of our existing knowledge, understanding, practice and values. Experience may lead to all sorts of learning, such as avoidance of difficult situations, being more controlling or circumspect, re-enforcing prejudices or developing a greater understanding of oppression. The challenge for learners and educators is to capture these incidents and make best use of them for learning. My research (Thomas, 1997) and experience suggests that analysing experiences in a structured way with critical colleagues enables us to make good use of the potential learning for ourselves, service users and the agency.

Using Critical Incident Analysis to Promote Different Types of Reflection

There are various formats for analysing 'critical incidents' see for example, Benner (1984), Butler and Elliot (1985), Ghaye and Lillyman (1997), Evans (1999), Fook, Ryan and Hawkins (2002) and Taylor (2000). Looking at reflective practice in nursing, Taylor considers that: 'Daily work incidents are the focus of emancipatory reflection and they are interactions in which you are active and central to what is happening. This means that practice incidents have within them all you need to construct, confront, deconstruct and reconstruct your practice' (Taylor, 2000:197). She looks in detail at questions that will prompt analysis of different types of learning. Using Habermas's (1972) knowledge-constitutive interests of *technical*, *practical* or *communicative* and *emancipatory*, Taylor argues that each has its place and offers formats for looking at incidents from each of these perspectives.

Technical reflection is useful for looking at particular procedures or treatments (in the case of health care), where the worker analyses the practices they undertake and examines the evidence base for this so clearly making the case that evidence-based practice and reflection are linked (Taylor, 2000: 172–3). Technical reflection is analysed under the headings of assessing and planning, implementing and evaluating.

Practical reflection focuses on 'developing interpersonal understanding through attention to people's lived experience, context and subjectivity' (Taylor, 2000: 175). The prompts for analysis encourage the worker to return to the event and focus on senses and feelings as well as the content to build up a 'thick description'. The interaction between the learner and other players is considered along with social norms and expectations before going on to look at learning that has occurred. Prompts under the headings of experiencing, interpreting and learning are used. The difference between the first two types of reflection is that in technical reflection much of the knowledge examined is external to the person, such as that derived from research. However, in practical reflection the focus is more on internalized knowledge, feeling and intuition, and the re-examination of this is triggered by the incident.

Emancipatory reflection involves looking more at structures and power within situations. Taylor emphasizes the challenges for the worker in this sort of reflection where the practitioner works through the process, of starting with a detailed construction of the event and then going on to deconstructing, which leads on to confronting and reconstructing. In this type of reflection the learner is encouraged to look at the constraints on their practice and how to challenge them. Doing this can make the practitioner vulnerable as the action they need to take may involve challenging well-established practices or confronting more senior people. The timescale for this process will extend well beyond that of a short training course.

Taylor is concerned that practitioners should not fight 'big battles for small gains' (2000: 198). She advises working with a critical friend or colleague who will be supportive by telling the truth and giving honest responses, be willing to challenge attitudes and behaviour, and who concentrates on enabling the person reflecting to be the main 'sense maker' of the situation. Critical friends need to listen more than they talk, avoid making early foreclosures, point out inconsistencies and ask questions for their rhetorical value (Taylor, 2000: 74–5). I would also add to Taylor's list the value of critical friends who can raise questions about power – looking at where it lies, help reflectors explore their own power in the situation or lack of it and explore what strategies can be used most effectively to question established practices. There are links here with theories of anti-oppressive social work, for example, Dalrymple and Burke (1995) who identify that when we move from recognizing oppression to taking action we are often daunted by the size of the task and need the support of others to keep challenging.

Many social workers come from agencies that ascribe to the principles of being a learning organization but making this a consistent reality in the face of resource constraints or entrenched working practices is difficult. Research by Gould (2000) indicates that students are perceived as supporting learning within organizations. However, practice teachers struggle to have their work with students seen as part of the mainstream work of the agency. This is highlighted by the well-documented problems of workload relief, for example, Bell and Webb talked about the 'old chestnut' of workload relief in 1992 and this was still identified as being highly problematic by Lindsey (1998). The practice teachers I work with are still struggling to have realistic workload relief for practice teaching activities. These constraints mean that those on practice teaching courses really value the opportunity to engage in systematic reflection on practice teacher training courses and the 'learning organization' created to support this, as discussed in the next sections.

How the Critical Incident Analysis is Used on Practice Teaching Courses

This section outlines a format for analysing incidents (Box 7.1). It is based on a model used successfully on introductory courses for practice teachers (Thomas, 1997) and a similar structure has also been used with students on qualifying courses. The way in which critical incidents are used is explained, this is followed by an analysis of the practice teachers' responses and a discussion of some of the challenges for the trainers on the course.

Process

The starting point is to introduce participants to the concept of reflective practice by outlining some of the theoretical concepts outlined earlier in this chapter. Participants are then asked to prepare for a future session, a week or two later, by working through a series of prompts similar to those in Box 7.1.

Box 7.1

In preparation for this exercise you are asked to bring along an outline of a piece of work you have undertaken, preferably within the last six months. Please change any names and identifying details. Choose a piece of work that might be the sort of thing that a student would undertake, and *pick out one incident, event or situation*, for example, a telephone call, taking a referral or discussing concerns, a group work session, a family interview, a key-working session, a review or planning meeting, a drop-in session, and so on. Do not attempt to describe a whole piece of work undertaken over a period of time.

Then:

- Give a brief outline of the situation, what happened, who was involved, where it took place. Include any relevant issues of oppression or discrimination that you were aware of.
- Describe what you did or said, what action you took and what the response was from others?
- How were you feeling at the time and how do you think others were feeling?
- What were the main challenges for you?
- What went well and what did you do to enable this?
- What underpinning knowledge and theories did you use? What methods of intervention did you use? How were these informed by research and evidence-based practice?
- What values underpinned the work and how did you demonstrate or convey these?
- What value conflicts were you aware of and how did you deal with these?
- If you were undertaking a similar piece of work again is there any thing you would do differently? If so, what? If not, why not?
- What do you think you learnt from the work?
- What have you learnt from reviewing the situation and your practice with in it? (This question is posed after the incident has been discussed in small groups.)

The initial reflection of choosing an incident and working through the question is usually done individually between workshop days. Undertaking the first stage as an individual activity allows learners to work at their own pace, to acknowledge their role within the situation, be active in starting to make their own meaning and begin to develop their understanding of the incident. Placing this responsibility with learners immediately gives them some power and control in the learning process, rather than the agenda being determined by the course trainers.

At the next session participants work, where possible, in groups of three. Opportunities can be offered for groups to work together on the basis of choices around gender, 'race', sexuality, being disabled or other combinations pertinent to the people attending. Each person has the opportunity to present his or her incident, act as consultant to the presenter and be the note-taker. The consultant asks questions to clarify or draw out issues in more detail and keeps the emphasis on what the worker was doing, what skills he or she was using and what the challenges were rather than having a detailed 'case discussion'. In questioning and commenting, other group members draw on their own practice experience and theoretical frameworks so offering a range of different perspectives, understandings and also, importantly expressions of empathy and support. The notes that are given to the presenter, should provide a brief record of the discussion and the further insights the group have developed during the discussion.

The group members then consider the assessment framework they will use with students and whether the presenter has demonstrated any of the competences or outcomes and, if so, which ones have been covered in the incident analysed. The exercise is completed by the presenter, either during the group session or later, reflecting and recording what he or she has learnt from the incident, his or her initial analysis, the discussion, and by assessing the competences the work may have met. Each person has a turn in each role, the group work normally takes most of the morning and finishes with one of the trainers asking for feedback and clarifying the main learning points.

To summarize, the stages of using the exercise can be structured as follows:

- Introduction to reflective practice.
- Participants identify and start to reflect individually on an 'incident'.
- Work in groups of three to continue the process of reflection, moving into more detailed critical thinking and theorizing.
- Continue to work in small groups linking the 'incidents' and learning to a competency framework.
- Review the process and learning in small groups.
- Review with trainers in the large group.

What are the Questions Designed to Do?

The questions focus the learner on aspects to consider but are sufficiently open to allow them to bring in important aspects; these will vary according to the individual, the situation and the context. The questions draw out an exploration of value conflicts and issues of oppression so giving the message that these aspects need to be fully integrated in any analysis of work. Boud and Knights (1996) identify critical incident analysis as a useful strategy for reflection, however, Boud and Walker (1998) argue against providing recipes or placing inappropriate boundaries on reflection. In her powerful critique of adult learning theories, Humphries (1988) challenges some of the laissez-faire, non-directive philosophies of learning and emphasizes the necessity of providing structures to support learners. So the questions provide a structure to guide people to the sorts of areas to consider but should be seen as prompts rather than a definitive list or questions that will have easy answers. One important area that participants are guided to consider is that of values.

The opportunity to analyse the values underpinning practice, to articulate these by individually capturing the essence of the principles underpinning their practice and then to explore these further through discussion with peers is a crucial aspect of the learning that arises through critical incident analysis. This is because practice teachers often express their frustration at how 'political correctness' and the pressure to 'get it right' can block a more authentic exploration of value conflicts and dilemmas, with similar concerns being expressed by others, for example Sing (1994) and Taylor, Thomas and Sage (1999). One practice teacher talked of the *'stress of value conflicts'* and then went on to discuss how practice teachers *'need to question (their) own values'*. Another felt that *'value base must be an inherent part of students' practice'* and that it is *'important to allow time to explore values, prejudices and enable them (students) to work with these'*.

Training courses can offer a safe environment in which to explore doubts and uncertainties about ethical dilemmas and value conflicts. To create a safe learning community facilitators need to negotiate group working agreements and encourage debates about terminology, for example, what being 'anti-oppressive' or 'anti-racist' means. Definitions such as those provided by Phillipson (1992) and concrete suggestions of the activities practice teachers can consider, such as Baldwin (1996), can be helpful, but uncertainty is part of the reflective process and leads to internal questioning. Trainers need to encourage group members to be 'critical friends' supporting the process of exploration by questioning or by making connections with similar dilemmas from their own experience. Before the groups start work it is useful to remind people not to rescue each other but, as Fook, Ryan and Hawkins (2000) suggest, work to create a climate of 'critical acceptance' where each person is focused on their own learning. Trainers can support this openness by articulating their own dilemmas, highlighting complexities, being open to challenges about their own practice and articulating what they are learning as facilitators in the process.

One of the criticisms of reflective practice that has emerged from discussions with colleagues who assess reflective accounts of practice is the tendency to use theory to justify action taken rather than adopting a more critical approach. Relating this back to Kolb's (1984) learning circle it is important to stress that abstract conceptualization needs to include considering incidents from different theoretical perspectives. Here it is useful to explore the critical challenge theories and debates about anti-oppressive practice have offered to social work theory and practice. The format for analysis (Box 7.1) can also be amended to encourage deeper thinking on oppression. Possibly by asking practice teachers to compare incidents where they have enabled students to actively value difference or to challenge structural oppression with ones where they felt uncomfortable, were paying lip-service or felt unable to find ways of challenging.

How They are Received/What Happens

The incidents people choose include what one person describes as *'routine work'*. Others choose to look at high-risk situations where the service user's life is in danger, while some concentrate on incidents that connect with their own life issues. Sometimes learners find it is difficult to separate out a specific 'incident' so have looked at their work over time with an individual, family or group, despite encouragement to start by looking at a something more manageable. Reasons for this can vary but discussions with these participants suggest that operational factors, such as the need to take action quickly to protect service users, the focus on assessing the situation or understanding the user, inevitably take priority over enabling the practitioner's learning. These factors combined with very limited time for supervision, a managerial style of supervision or the competence of the supervisor all play a part in meaning that practitioners may have little structured opportunity or permission to evaluate their practice.

Writers on supervision and practice teaching (for example, Doel et al., 1996; Evans, 1999; Fisher, 1990) argue that it needs to encompass various functions, which include the educative, supportive, accountability and assessment functions. When considering these models, practice teachers comment on how the accountability function can dominate their own supervision where the focus is on checking records and procedural issues to ensure that the service is not vulnerable during inspections or investigations. The emphasis is also on understanding the service users, debating the involvement of other professionals or looking at how to use limited resources most effectively. These aspects are important and we cannot leave service users and ourselves vulnerable by not paying attention to procedural issues. However, it does need to be balanced with other functions so that practitioners are encouraged to make sense of their experiences. What seems to be missing is the opportunity for social workers to look at the impact the work is having on them and what they have learnt from the experience about themselves, practice or theory. We seem to have moved a long way from the model of supervision promoted by Hawkins and Shohet (1989) where the practitioner's feelings are an important part of the analysis of work. They argue that while it is important to return to what the implications are for the service user and the service provided, looking at the impact on the worker should also be part of the process.

Peer groups can form a safe place to explore feelings of guilt around inadequacies in our practice that it may not feel safe to explore within managerial settings. This does not mean in any way that we should encourage collusion with poor practice, but do need to recognize that social workers may carry unfinished business and that unresolved feelings that come to the forefront when the opportunity to reflect is presented.

On short courses trainers need to encourage participants to look at work that can be contained within the time available, however, it is also important to recognize that imposing rigid boundaries is impossible. In asking someone to critically reflect we are asking him or her to engage in a process of discovery and exploration that is open and learner centred. We need to accept that part of the function of training courses for social workers is to enable them opportunities away from the immediate workplace where they can feel safe to return to difficult situations that have not been fully resolved.

Boud, Cohen and Walker (1993) identify the many challenges of turning reflection into learning, and one of the principles that underpins Boud's work is that: 'ideas are not separate from experience, learning is not unrelated to relationships and personal interests, and emotions and feelings have a vital role to play in what we may later come to identify as intellectual learning' (ibid.: 2). Intellectual learning does not just happen through formal teaching, understanding theory or examining evidence, it is a more sophisticated process – analysing and reflecting on practice, exploring feelings, articulating dilemmas, teasing out the underpinning theory and considering the research base we have been drawing on, or highlighting where our knowledge base is limited, using the medium of critical incident analysis – assists the process of intellectual learning. One of the problems in developing learning organizations is that the knowledge that is favoured or given highest status tends to be that which is created externally, or what Fook, Ryan and Hawkins describe as 'scientific textbook descriptions of practitioners' practices' (2000: 13). Gould (2000) also notes this phenomenon where reports written by external researchers are given more credibility than the knowledge generated by its own practitioners, despite well-established practices of using action research to evaluate initiatives.

The experience of trainers using the exercise has enabled us to develop strategies to manage the situations where the work brought is complex. Usually the learners themselves manage this by deciding to work through a break or contact each other between sessions to finish off. Trainers may also need to offer support at the end of the day and ensure that the participant has access to other support systems. Looking at the sorts of systems available offers the opportunity to transfer some of the learning back to the organization such as exploring with participants how they can raise issues in supervision sessions, team meetings or informal discussions. Often in the situations they describe there will have been other significant players; revisiting incidents with them and articulating the insights gained can help to consolidate their own learning and initiating a dialogue with others involved, offering the potential to further promote learning for all involved. Another possibility is to set up buddying systems among course participants to maintain contact after a short training course. A more effective way of transferring learning from training courses back into the organization is to encourage participants to identify a colleague from within their team who would act as a critical friend.

Feedback from participants indicates that the process of revisiting situations that may have been '*demanding and emotionally painful*' can result in '*increased confidence in own practice*'. Course evaluations suggest that the opportunity to turn experiences that may have been painful and distressing into learning is invaluable for the development of participants' practice as social workers and practice teachers. The comment '*stimulating and thought provoking, enjoyed doing exercise*' is the typical response.

Linking Critical Incident Analysis to Assessment and Competency Frameworks

Once course participants have critically analysed the incident, they then link it to the assessment format that they will use with students. The examples in this chapter relate to the British professional qualifying award, the Diploma in Social Work (DipSW). Social work in the UK, at pre-qualifying, qualifying and post-qualifying levels is assessed using a competency framework in which candidates identify work they have undertaken and outline how this demonstrates they have met the competence. This usually is then verified by an assessor, in the case of DipSW the practice teacher, who may agree or question the participant's view. Competence-based assessment has been criticized for being a reductionist model (Gould, 1996; Preston-Shoot and Jackson, 1996) as statements of competence are presented as unproblematic, self-explanatory and generalizable hurdles to jump. While a lot of work has been undertaken to retain more holistic and creative assessment methods (see examples in Hinett and Thomas, 1999), even at the level of qualifying and post-qualifying training some assessment documentation relies on a tick-box approach. This can create the impression that, for example, a value requirement where students are asked to demonstrate that they 'identify and question their own values and prejudices, and their implications for practice' has a finite end rather than being part of a lifelong learning process. Yelloly argues that 'Defining competences, specifying the work to be done, measuring performance against specified criteria (and paying accordingly), combined with opening up the professional market place has further eroded professional autonomy' (1995: 19–20).

However, relating the analysis to competency statements, such as the DipSW requirements or the National Occupational Standards, is a useful way of promoting learning about assessment and showing how competency-based assessment can be used in a more holistic way. One participant selected an example of '*routine work not specifically undertaken to achieve competences*' who then went on to make the point Ward (1995) also makes, that evidence of competence should evolve naturally from everyday work. Critical incident analysis is a useful way of examining how competency statements or assessment criteria can be interpreted and applied in different settings and situations. Practice teachers see how their everyday practice links more closely with the requirements than they had initially anticipated. This is particularly helpful for social workers in day, residential, community action and voluntary settings, as they often feel that the way requirements are written make them easier to apply in the statutory local authority sector. It is particularly important to make the requirements accessible to people who often feel marginalized as practice teachers, many of whom work in small specialized settings with people who are oppressed because, for example, of their 'race', sexuality, gender, disability, HIV status or age. The consistent feedback from these staff is that approaching requirements in this way makes them much more accessible and user friendly than trying to interpret the requirements and then think of evidence. Practice teachers report that working in this way '*increased my confidence and familiarity with DipSW core competences*' and gave '*insight into how to identify specific competences*'.

One of the implications of recent trends in social work is that services will be delivered by a greater range of agencies (Platt, 2001). This means that competency and benchmark statements will need to be interpreted in a wider variety of settings. Services are moving further away from local authorities to voluntary agencies, the private and the 'not for profit' sector and a broader range of services will be involved (Platt, 2001). Hopefully, these services will be more flexible and responsive and it will be designed with and for service users who will be 'at the heart of the enterprise' (Platt, 2001: 6). Practice teachers will need to be able to interpret and discuss assessment requirements in a language that is accessible and clearly linked to practice with service users and other professionals whose contribution to the education and assessment of social workers is likely to become increasingly important.

Looking at the situations participants choose to explore also leads to thinking about expectations of students and whether the examples they have looked at would be appropriate for students on placement and, if so, at what level. It also prompts other questions, such as, 'How do we work with students who bring extensive practice experience?' Or, 'How do we enable further learning and development rather than just go through the routine of providing evidence of practice competence?'

Sometimes all the boxes are ticked, so promoting questions about the danger of a 'tick-box approach'. Questions can be asked here about the quantity and quality of evidence and the need for skills, knowledge and values to be demonstrated over time for competence to be confirmed, rather than just in relation to one situation. Issues relating to the range of evidence can also be explored as the incident brought may have concentrated exclusively, for example, on working with a white, heterosexual, working-class male service user.

The competency statements looked at can be replaced by whatever assessment requirements are relevant to course participants. Starting with a critical incident is also a good way of familiarizing assessors with changes to assessment requirements. Examining practice and then relating it to assessment requirements is a more active and engaging way of bringing these to life than trying to develop detailed, all-encompassing lists of performance indicators.

The Value of Self-assessment and Peer Assessment

Assessing their own practice prompts practice teachers to consider how to use these insights from self-assessment and peer assessment in subsequent work with students. One practice teacher recognized that analysing practice was '*much harder than I thought*' and also '*the value of and the need to provide an empowering assessment experience for students*'. The level of anxiety different people feel over assessment will, of course, be influenced by previous experiences. Also, as it is where the power differential is inescapable previous experiences of oppression need to be actively considered and acted upon. The research conducted by people such as DeSouza (1991) and DeGale (1991) with black students, clearly articulates the discrimination students experienced, many of whom are now the practice teachers of today. These comments from those who undertake the exercise show the anxiety they felt and remind us of the continual need to address and acknowledge power differentials between learners and assessors: '*reminded of the feelings of anxiety and uncertainty that assessment provokes*', '*It brought home to me how stressful it must be for students to have to do such pieces of work and be assessed on them*'; and '*reminded of 'fear' (lack of confidence)'*.

The arguments for self-assessment practices to be used to challenge structural power differences are not new, see, for example Cowan (1981), Heron (1981) and, more recently, Boud (1995) and Stefani (1998). Brew (1999) clearly sees the learner as being an active participant moving towards a position of power-sharing with the assessor. Like Morrison (1996) and Taylor (2000), in their work on reflective practice, Brew (1999) uses the framework of Habermas's (1987) knowledge constructive interests to argue that self-assessment can operate within the domains of technical, communicative and emancipatory knowledge. She suggests the more we can move towards self-assessment, the greater the potential for creating 'emancipatory' knowledge where meta-analysis skills such as critical reflection are part of the process of creating knowledge.

Conclusions

This chapter has identified the potential for learning from everyday practice that is not being used to its full potential at an individual or at an organizational level. It has considered some of the reasons for this, such as the operational pressure on organizations to deliver services and the way in which the educative function of supervision loses out to the more administrative and bureaucratic functions. Boud and Walker (1998) explore the dilemmas in promoting reflection and conclude that reflection is about uncertainty; similar assertions are made by Gould and Taylor (1996) and Napier and Fook (2000). However, current expectations of service agencies to work to codes of practice, government guidelines and performance indicators means that clearly defined outcomes are required and the place for the uncertainty that is integral to critical reflection is difficult to sustain.

Writing this chapter has given me the opportunity to critically reflect on my practice of working with practice teachers using critical incident analysis. I have highlighted the need for the safe environment, a climate of 'critical acceptance' and the need for 'critical friend'. However, I realize that I need to work more actively with practice teachers to help them transfer more learning back into their organizations, using tools like the critical incident analysis. As facilitators we need to look at how practitioners can develop realistic and manageable ways of promoting critical reflection within the structures they have, such as supervision with their managers and team meetings. We also need to explore how to use other forums more actively, such as informal discussions and critical friends, to move from just expressing frustration to articulating learning and its implications for practice.

Gould notes the 'sometimes current sterile oppositions between "evidence-based" practice and reflective learning' (2000: 595). In writing this chapter I have been struck with the way that developing practice relies on critical reflection using the lenses of practitioner experience, a range of personal perspectives as well as being able to critically evaluate research and theory. The challenge now is to integrate these 'sterile oppositions' into dynamic tensions to develop practice wisdom and theoretical frameworks that are grounded and that can be applied in our specific contexts with integrity and confidence.

Chapter 8

Evaluation for a Learning Organization?

Ian Shaw

At first glance evaluation and the idea of a learning organization do not seem to fit comfortably. Evaluation, so it may be said, is about outcomes, effectiveness, bottom lines and evidence-based practice – in sum, accountability. Learning organizations, on the other hand, are about systems, interaction, process, feedback and improvement.[1]

The doubts are not easily dismissed. 'In essence, accountability is evaluation, and evaluation is accountability', remarked one senior manager in the National Science Foundation (House, Haug and Norris, 1996: 142).[2] The push-pull tension between evaluation purposes of accountability and learning are real. 'Although administrators and funders may state that they believe in organisational learning, the way evaluations sometimes are used is as a win-lose, "gotcha" game' (Stockdill, Baizerman and Compton, 2002: 19). 'Accountability-hungry funders and legislators who continue to demand outcomes within short periods of time' present one of the several challenges to evaluators and organizations interested in an organizational learning approach (Torres and Preskill, 2001: 389). Indeed, a plausible case can be made out for arguing that evaluation capacity building – 'the intentional work to continuously create and sustain overall organisational processes that make quality evaluations and their uses routine' – requires art, craft and skill that are very distinct from programme or project evaluation (Compton, Baizerman and Stockdill, 2002: 1).

I do not wish to overstate the tensions. On the one hand, proponents of learning organizations might bear in mind that lessons learned must be evidentially based, albeit in a variety of ways, and not simply unfalsifiable insights. In addition, in practice, if not in rhetoric, most evaluation is about incremental change and improvement.

> It is a distinctly Washington idea that those in the center of government can discover mechanisms to effect change in the periphery of the country. The search for discrete mechanisms of change has rarely been successful, probably because change is more complex, the result of many interacting factors in the local setting rather than the presence or absence of a few common elements. (House, Haug and Norris, 1996: 144)

Further grounds for not over-playing the tensions between accountability and learning models emerges from a recent discussion in which Kirk and Reid, in their critical appraisal of social work and science, have favoured arguments that implicitly narrow the gap between accountability, evaluation and organizational learning. Accountability, they suggest, 'is not just a question of determining the effectiveness of whatever methods have been tested ... . It involves showing that the practitioner has used the best possible methods for the case at hand in the most suitable way – that he or she has engaged in "appropriate practice"'. This larger and fuzzier concept should, they believe, 'replace the one track idea of accountability as measurement of change' (Kirk and Reid, 2001: 91). They also back the approach that accountability be seen as an organizational responsibility, rather than that of individual practitioners.

This line of response to our initial doubts will, however, only take us so far. We should not only loosen the concept of accountability, but recognize that evaluation is not *only* about accountability, but is a fairly loose coalition of purposes and practices.[3] In particular, evaluation is often about learning and perhaps always about persuasion. Several writers have made this point. Owen and Lambert, in an early discussion, regard enlightenment as a 'first order use' of evaluation, and sometimes the prime motivation for commissioning an evaluation (Owen and Lambert, 1995).[4] Greene has more recently concluded that 'We must not just proclaim goodness or badness, but we must also offer conceptual, programmatic and theoretical insights relevant to that particular context *and* to others' (Greene, 2001: 398).

Michael Patton engaged in some fairly unflinching exchanges with Carol Weiss a quarter of a century ago, defending an instrumental, pragmatic position on evaluation purposes and uses, against her argument for enlightenment as the political reality of evaluation use. Yet he now acknowledges the use of evaluations to offer illumination and 'influence thinking and deepen understanding by increased knowledge' (Patton, 2001: 332).[5]

Preskill and Torres present all this as a principle and 'see evaluative inquiry as a kind of public philosophy whereby organisation members engage in dialogue with clients and other stakeholders about the meaning of what they do and how they do it' (Preskill and Torres, 1999a: 44). Ernest House long ago argued that evaluations never yield certain knowledge: 'Subjected to serious scrutiny, evaluations always appear equivocal'; the aspiration after certain knowledge 'results from confusing rationality with logic. They are not identical ... Evaluations can be no more than acts of persuasion' (House, 1980: 72). They are acts of argumentation, not demonstration. The requirement is for, as van der Knaap (1995) suggests, feedback and enlightenment, but also for argumentation. In summary, 'Evaluation persuades rather than convinces, argues rather than demonstrates, is credible rather than certain, is variably accepted rather than compelling' (House, 1980: 73; cf. House and Howe, 1999).

I risk digressing before even beginning. There *is* tension between evaluation and the development of learning organizations, which cannot neatly be resolved. We should not exaggerate the differences, but nor should we see them as simply negative factors.

By way of final preamble, it is worth emphasizing that the current interest in evaluation and learning organizations in social work is not some stand-alone development. The fields of health and education have both seen corresponding developments.[6] In all three fields there is a cluster of associated developments. Ideas about *best practice* can be read as an argument for practice that is less tied to a trust in the possibility of linear applications of research findings. *Reflective learning*, despite its more individualized approach, is a direct predecessor of the learning organization literature and still has something of value to contribute to organizational learning, as, for example, through the emphasis on cycles of action and learning. One reaction to arguments for evidence-based practice has been to make a case for *knowledge-based practice* – a process that suggests professional interaction, exchange and judgement, closely akin to the brief discussion of learning-based practice below. I have already mentioned in passing the emerging literature on *evaluation capacity building*. This in turn owes a debt to the development literature and arguments for *sustainable development*. It is also linked to efforts to *mainstream evaluation*, which is argued to have occurred when evaluation is institutionalized as the ordinary way we do things in an organization. Finally, there are frequent references in the learning organization literature to the importance of *systems thinking*. The potential for reactivating links with the social work literature from the 1970s onwards, on intervention guided by systems approaches, is an obvious association of ideas, despite the characteristically thin treatment of evaluation issues in the majority of that literature. These links imply that we will gain far more from the interest in learning organizations if we avoid treating it as a *de novo* phenomenon, and hold it in dialogue with this family of cognate ideas, principles and practices.

In the following paragraphs I briefly outline the core requirements for the evaluative dimension of a learning organization. I then raise two potentially difficult questions, first, about insider/outsider relations in a learning organization and, second, regarding the underlying political thrust of pleas for a learning organization. I partly acknowledge these criticisms, but also respond to them through an outline of evaluating as a direct practice competence, and through a re-visioned practitioner research with a potential for organizational critique. I illustrate these points from recent projects in which I have been involved. I conclude with some cautionary comments about what we might hope for from embedding evaluation and evaluation capacity in a learning organization.

Evaluative Requirements for a Learning Organization

There are four basic characteristics required if evaluation is to be embedded in a learning organization, namely an evaluation culture, an organizational focus for evaluation, a conscious attention to evaluation capacity building, and learning-based practice.

Evaluation Culture

There has been little empirical work on the production of evaluation, and this hampers efforts to assess the characteristics of an evaluation culture in an agency. We can accept House's definition of an evaluation culture as 'those social arrangements and practices that sustain honest evaluative inquiry and utilization of findings' (House, Haug and Norris, 1996: 139). The work of House and his colleagues provides as good an indicator as we can find on the makings of an evaluative culture. Much hard, unseen work went into developing a culture in the National Science Foundation (NSF) whereby evaluation was accepted. This work was often described as 'building trust', and some staff seemed more adept and spent more time doing it than others. On the contrary, bad evaluations create a 'hang-over' effect. 'If you want to talk about one word – it's trust. And they felt that their trust had been damaged. Our trust, their trust in us had been damaged' (Research, Evaluation and Dissemination staff in NSF, cited in House, Haug and Norris, 1996: 141).

Evaluation cultures cannot exist in isolation from organizational structures. Birleson describes the application of a learning organization to child and adolescent mental health services in Victoria (Australia), and emphasizes the need to align structure and culture for learning. Existing structures tend to emphasize the roles of individual professional groups, and thus 'both structural and cultural change is usually required, although culture is less tangible and more poorly understood than structure' (Birleson, 1999: 268).

Organizational Focus

Birleson's point about structures links to the need for an organizational focus. The point has been little developed, but it would seem that a focus on either project or programme evaluation, separate from an organization level, will overlook key factors in shaping the project environment.

Patton illustrates this point from a synthesizing evaluation of a large number of Aid to Families in Poverty (FIP) programmes in Minneapolis. 'An important breakthrough in our synthesis came when we understood that project and agency-wide cultures were systematically interrelated … . We found that staff tended to treat participants the way they were treated as professionals within their organisations' (Patton, 1999: 96–7). The systems connections between projects, programmes and organizations operated in both directions, however. 'Programs developed cultures that affected entire agencies and systems of which they were a part' (Patton, 1999: 97). This was particularly the case when projects gained the power and confidence that came from being unusually well resourced. Ordinary projects lacked the power or confidence to challenge system barriers to effectiveness. It was also true where projects and organizations shared a strong sense of mission. However, one important caveat that Patton emphasizes is that a project can be effective in terms of goal attainment measures, and yet make a low contribution to organizational mission (and vice versa). This reinforces our earlier point that accountability evaluation covers different territory from evaluation in a learning organization.

Evaluation Capacity Building

The issue of how organizations, programmes, governments and communities take on and sustain evaluation and its uses as ordinary, everyday practice is a central concern of this chapter. I cited the brief working definition given by Compton and colleagues earlier. More fully, they define evaluation capacity building as: 'A context-dependent, intentional action system of guided processes and practices for bringing about and sustaining a state of affairs in which quality program evaluation and its appropriate uses are ordinary and ongoing practices within and/or between one or more organisations/programs/sites' (Compton, Baizerman and Stockdill, 2002: 8). This definition is limited somewhat because of its restriction of evaluation to programme evaluation. I return to this issue in the following part of the chapter. But, that apart, it is a helpful summary of the process and concepts of capacity building.

I have mentioned already the claim that evaluation capacity building should helpfully be viewed as having different characteristics and requiring skills that are distinct from evaluation. It is a guided process that is ongoing and never complete. It is done collaboratively in teams, and in coalitions and other formal and informal partnerships. It supports the need for evaluation to be useful and conducted in an ethically responsible way. The key concepts include emergence, development, site learning, intention, sustaining and collaboration. A number of these ideas owe a considerable amount to the writing and experience in the field of Third World development policy – an area that social work, to its loss, has generally by-passed. Patton remarks that 'Developmentally-oriented leaders in organisations and programs ... don't aim for a steady state of effectiveness modelling because they're constantly tinkering as participants, conditions, learnings, and context change' (Patton, 1999: 110). The process demands skills of reflection, working in groups, both collaboratively and politically, together with a process orientation and a concern for rigour and relevance.

Learning-Based Practice

Pleas for practice that is evidence-based, and 'best', frequently underplay what is entailed in learning a lesson, and the role of evaluation in this. While it is acknowledged that information is not the same as knowledge, there is nonetheless a simplistic emphasis in social work on the dissemination of research-based knowledge to practitioners. The notion of 'best practice' seems to enshrine the suspect assumption that there must be a single best way of doing something. On the contrary, 'Identifying specific intended uses with specific intended users can only be undertaken in a specific context and situation' (Patton, 2001: 331). This will require close attention to lesson learning, and heeding Patton's sharp interjection that 'all kinds of drivel passes for lessons learned' (Patton, 1999: 106). My own view is that a strong case can be made out for establishing what may be called a 'learning office' in a number of social work agencies, to facilitate appropriate practice in lesson learning.

Preskill and Torres (1999b) have developed a Likert scale to measure organizational readiness for learning and evaluation (ROLE), consisting of 78 items grouped into six dimensions:

- culture;
- leadership;

- systems and structures;
- communication;
- teams;
- evaluation.

The aptness and usefulness of the scale needs field-testing. While it teases out different dimensions, the reliance of the authors on mean scores for interpreting the results risks overlooking the localized, context-specific nature of readiness for lesson-learning.

Organizational critique

I have argued that evaluation in learning organizations requires development of an evaluation culture, an organizational focus for evaluation, a conscious attention to evaluation capacity building, and facilitating learning-based practice. But if it is left without further comment, the suspicion may rightly lurk that there are conservatizing tendencies in the learning organization 'movement'. The suspicions are not without foundation. There are two reservations that I want to reflect on. First, a common-sense inference might suggest that the processes I have described are best reserved for organizational insiders. This is worrisome, particularly if it is also linked to keeping a strong management hold on the process and direction of organizational learning. Second, does embedding evaluation in a learning culture result in a consensual, pluralist and incremental approach to organizational change, and militate against radical critique?

Insiders and Outsiders

An 'insider' stance adopts the view that insiders are best positioned – or even solely positioned – to understand their daily world. Social work has been beset by various strong insider positions, not all of which are conservative in tendency.[7] It has a superficial plausibility. Applied to the previous discussion, it would encourage the view that outsiders – from other agency, government or higher education contexts – are largely or even wholly disqualified from participating in the process. But the insider/outsider split is not that simple. As Sue White concludes in her reflexive account of her own research, 'As anthropologists have debated the in/out, stranger/native, familiar/unfamiliar dichotomies, it has become clear that either/or distinctions of this kind are difficult to measure or sustain in ethnographic fieldwork' (White, 2001: 103).

In the same book, Hall (2001) and White record how they held both insider and outsider roles in relation to their research participants. Hall 'arrived' as an outsider but became in different ways a partial insider. White started as an insider, yet found herself undergoing a fruitful, if potentially hazardous, process of de-familiarization through which she became in some degree a marginal 'inside "out" member'. This suggests that, if only on learning grounds, an assumption that outsiders can and should be neatly identified and excluded is naive and risky.

There are additional considerations. Outside facilitators have value-added benefits. For example, more obviously external facilitators, such as higher education colleagues, can paradoxically provide a key dimension of continuity. Embedding evaluation in the culture of an organization is an extended process that is never complete. If dependent only on insiders it risks being reliant on the enthusiasm of a limited number of good practitioners and managers, who in the nature of things are likely to move on. I have had some involvement with a strong practitioner research interest group in a social services department. The group attracted large numbers of practitioners to its varied meetings, and enjoyed a supportive but helpfully loose link to senior management in the agency. Yet when a key facilitator moved to another post, the group struggled to maintain its energy and activity levels. Furthermore, the experience of insider evaluation in large organizations and smaller agencies suggests that, for internal evaluations to be useful and credible, they must have high status in the organization and real power to make evaluation meaningful (Patton, 1999).

Outsiders-in have an important role to play in fostering the culture and structures of a learning organization. But the justification is not in terms of the supposed objectivity that distant outsiders bring to an organization.

Practitioners and Organizational Critique

The strength of the practitioner research interest group mentioned above stemmed to a significant degree from its relationship to agency management – given space to work, with membership open to managers, but run as a peer learning group. The thrust of this is rather different from the emphases of most literature on evaluation in a learning organization. I entered an earlier caveat about the definition of evaluation capacity building that Compton and colleagues provide, on the grounds that it envisages the evaluation link as being to programme evaluation. Patton, despite his acknowledgement that process evaluation is a key ingredient of organizational learning, tends to locate organizational leaders' relationship to evaluators as the key axis. Owen and Lambert also focus on the evaluator/organizational leader relationship (Owen and Lambert, 1995). Preskill and Torres make clear that their approach to evaluative inquiry for organizational learning is not a form of participatory evaluation.

I associate these emphases in my own mind with the downside to pleas for 'mainstreaming' evaluation such that it becomes a routine part of what happens. What is routine is taken for granted, and what is taken for granted is typically uninspected and part of an organizational equivalent of Thomas Kuhn's notion of 'normal science'. A comparison of American and British texts on evaluation and social work practice helps make the point. The American publishing market has a significant number of synthesizing textbooks on evaluation for social work students. The British market, to my knowledge, has not a single synthesizing social work textbook on this theme. By contrast, the British texts are all aiming, at least in part, to develop a position and make an argument. It would be grossly unfair to imply that British writing is in some way 'better' than American, and the huge difference in market size doubtless contributes to the difference. But the more that any literature becomes dominated by 'mainstream' texts, the less likely it is that practitioner critique will develop and be supported.

This risk of conservatizing tendencies has been noted. 'A concern is that in the ECB literature so far, other stakeholders' voices, in particular the individuals affected by the development programs, are not taken into consideration' (Stockdill, Baizerman and Compton, 2002: 17). They quote Hauge's report on the United Nations Development Programme that 'It is better to have an imperfect answer from someone who has a legitimate claim to concern than a perfect answer from an expert whose mind is elsewhere' (ibid.: 18). Some organizational learning writers are also open to engaging with action research models, and it is noticeable that the action research literature is beginning to offer a possible rapprochement between action research and learning approaches (for example, Reason and Bradbury, 2000).

How can the possibility of organizational critique in the interests of good practice for service users be sustained? Two avenues look promising. First, through a re-visioning of the role of practitioner research and, second, through embedding evaluation processes as part and parcel of practice, rather than as something that is done to practice.

Practitioner Research

Practitioner research – evaluation, research, development, or more general inquiry into services that is small-scale, local, grounded and carried out by professionals who directly deliver those self-same services – is embraced across the professions as good practice. Whether the practice be teaching, nursing, primary health care, pharmacy, counselling, psychotherapy, the various branches of applied psychology, the penal services, medicine or the human services, the desirability of practitioner research is for the most part unquestioned. Much of this activity trundles along with a low profile, rarely unsettling the status quo. It is almost stereotypically Kuhnian – minor puzzle-solving and ordinary. There are the exceptions, such as the classic, even heroic, early developments in self-administered vaccine research and the fashioning of the major depth psychologies in the consulting rooms of Vienna. Practitioner research in social work is no exception. Fellow professionals, agencies and government welcome it as a contribution to the evidence base of social work that is modest in aspiration, small scale and for the most part non-contentious.

Yet there are characteristics of practitioner research that leave it in a weak position – entangled in, yet paradoxically insulated from, larger issues, and unlikely to influence social work services and practice. What are those characteristics? There are six that spring to mind.

Practitioner research often stands in a *client–donor relationship to social work agencies*. It is characteristically performed by direct service people in line posts, or by middle managers. It is often dependent for its completion on the consent of senior managers. In such cases it is employer led and agency owned.

Practitioner research in social work is also typically a *solitary* activity. The paradox of an activity that is both agency owned and solitary is more apparent than real. I estimate that over a half of all practitioner research in social work and social care in the UK is linked to the fulfilment of dissertation requirements for a master's degree.[8] Most practitioner research is solitary because it is non-collaborative and not part of a collective enterprise. Its *non-collaborative* nature springs from economic factors such as the agency costs of simultaneously releasing multiple members of staff to spend time doing research, and from the pressures towards lone research that stem from the assessment criteria that are part of post-qualifying activities and higher degrees in universities. Its *non-collective* character springs from rather different causes, associated with the absence of a critical agenda.

Practitioner research is almost always *insider research*. By 'insider' research, I refer to more than the organizational location and membership of the practitioner. Where I *work* and where I *stand* are two different matters. The point about practitioner research is that it has typically been insider research both in location and standpoint. This becomes transparent when we reflect on the relationship between practitioner research and user-led research. Fisher has argued that

> Genuine involvement of service users (cannot) be taken forward if the focus remains on the researcher-practitioner relationship. In a sense, the idea that problem formulation is/should be resolved through improving the relationship between practitioner and researcher is part of the problem ... . Indeed, there is a clear danger that in focusing on the modes of researcher-practitioner collaboration the voice of the service user is less prominent or simply outnumbered. (Fisher, 2002: 36–7)

Practitioner research stands in a donor–client relationship not only to social work agencies, but also to the methodology of *social science research*. The subordinate stance of practitioner research is also not helped by an occasional insistence from its supporters that practitioner research is a special genre of research (for example, Cochran-Smith and Lytle, 1990). I am not convinced by such territorial claims. Distinctions between 'academic' and practitioner inquiry, based on methodology or epistemology, are 'tenuous if not untenable' (Smith and Kleine, 1986: 55).

Finally, practitioner research tends to be bounded in both *professional and discipline* terms. Despite the well nigh universal professional interest in practitioner research, it is almost never the topic of inter-professional conversation and exchange.

This is a one-sided assessment ignoring the positive gains that come from local relevance, critical assessment of research findings and so on. But the diagnosis suggests directions for a different prognosis. Practitioner research needs to be increasingly collaborative, collective, articulated to user concerns, the subject of active cross-professional conversation and alert to the possibility of critique of both agencies and social science 'donors'. Knud Ramian has directed the development and testing of a collaborative practitioner research network strategy for social workers in the mental health field in Denmark.[9] The central ingredients in the strategy are:

- a procedure for the selection of a small number of research teams;
- no participants are allowed to work alone;
- all teams in a network are committed to the same research question;
- all teams adopt a case study strategy;
- the network is organized around written contracts between the workplace and the network manager;

- the network meets for a seminar every second month.

At the time of writing, the strategy has been tested in seven collaborative research networks, including a total of 45 projects. The existing results show that the network strategy is a method that gives social workers the opportunity to learn, plan, carry out and report case studies. It is conceived in a form that promises well for the delivery of collaborative and collective effort.

While her analysis is not concerned explicitly with organizational learning, White illustrates two ways in which social workers can develop a critical, or analytic, orientation to their practices. It is worth citing at some length.

> First, it was in part a product of particular personal and professional experiences. For example, I remember that, on one or two occasions when my second child was very small, I took him into work with me for a short while. He would sometimes be clingy and sometimes very independent, preoccupied with play, or other people, and hence almost indifferent to my presence. In the company of a group of my social work colleagues, I became acutely conscious that his behaviour could easily be read on any of these occasions as one of the many varieties of 'attachment disorder'. Had this been a clinical assessment, I thought about how vulnerable I would have been to such a diagnosis, and how resistance to it could easily have been written off as defensiveness or denial. Having used the theory routinely in my work for many years, this experience made me much more aware of its incredible malleability and virtual incorrigibility. There are few permutations of infant behaviour which escape its prolific explanatory potential. I came to see attachment theory (indeed all theory) less as a convenient tool, or template, and more as a powerful coloured lens, with the capacity to clarify (by eliminating the 'glare' which we experience when we try to make sense of complex relationships), but which may also cast the world in an over-simplifying monochrome.
>
> The second way in which a more meta-analytic orientation to day to day practices may develop ... is related to 'techniques of organizing knowledge' (Strathern). If practitioners are exposed to different analytic and meta-analytic frameworks from outside their primary discipline, this increases the likelihood of them understanding their practices in new ways. In my own case, this influence came from my academic studies in sociology and social theory. (White, 2001: 105–6)

Evaluating-in-practice

A second route to enabling a reformist organizational critique is through embedding evaluation processes as part and parcel of practice, rather than as something that is done to practice. As with practitioner research, the focus is on the world of direct practice rather than organizational leaders.

Patton hints at aspects of this when he supports helping people in organizations to think evaluatively so as to build evaluation into the organizational culture and engage in evaluation as part of ongoing organizational development. 'Using the processes of evaluation for organisational development and learning can be useful quite apart from the findings that may merge from these processes. Reasoning like an evaluator and operating according to evaluation's values have impacts' (Patton, 1999: 107).

We should not exaggerate the likeness of practice and evaluation, but there is what Riessman has called 'a sympathetic connection' between certain kinds of social work and qualitative kinds of data – 'talk, therapeutic conversation, agency records, narratives about experiences with organisations and macro systems' (Riessman, 1994: ix). The tie is proximate but neither universal, homogenous nor capable of straightforward transfer from one to the other. It requires methodological work, which I have described as involving 'colonizing' and 'translating' (Shaw, 1996; 1997). Colonizing requires practitioners to challenge the conventional donor–client relationship, and act upon research methods rather than simply apply them. Translation raises issues of language and culture, and underscores the interpretative character of the process. Social workers need to develop a dialogic practice, both within social work and with methodologists. For example, Janesick's 'stretching' exercises for qualitative researchers are an example of work based on a learning rationale that provides a fertile basis for professional 'colonizing' and 'translating' (Janesick, 1998). The quality of 'methodological practice' will have an emergent, opportunistic and particularistic character. To maximize the gains from this process social workers need, once again, to avoid remaining too much insiders. 'The familiar not only breeds contempt, it breeds darkness as well' (Eisner, 1988: xii). Above all, 'methodological practice' will have a participatory and collaborative character.

I recently spent six months working on these ideas with senior practitioners and project managers in a large and geographically widely dispersed voluntary children's agency in Britain. Full days spent as a group were interlaced with work-based learning projects. I conveyed to them my belief that evaluating-in-practice requires commitments to evidence, learning and justice, and illustrated the possibilities for methodological practice deriving primarily from qualitative methods.[10] This 'tripod', as the group aptly called it, was critically integrated into their day-to-day practice, and formerly routine events such as annual review days, case closures and so on, became the subject of a new or renewed critical orientation.

Conclusion in a Minor Key

I introduced this chapter with reflection on the tensions between some evaluation models and advocacy of a learning organization. I outlined the core requirements for the evaluative dimension of a learning organization. I then raised two potentially difficult questions, first, about insider/outsider relations in a learning organization and, second, regarding the underlying political thrust of pleas for a learning organization. I partly acknowledged these criticisms, but also responded to them through an outline of evaluating as a direct practice competence, and through a re-visioned practitioner research with a potential for organizational critique. I illustrated these points from recent projects in which I have been involved.

I am not, however, sentimental regarding the feasibility of introducing a critical transformation. Social change tied to barely visible increments remains a serious risk in learning organizations. The arguments remain weak on issues of gender and race (although see Rossiter's chapter in this book). In addition, there is a risk of insularity linked to an undue reliance on intra-organizational learning (there is scope here to draw from work on agency coalitions, for example, Stevenson, Mitchell and Florin, 1996). Rejection of sentimentality, however, does not require abandonment of the project.

Acknowledgement

John Stevenson, University of Rhode Island, for first making me aware of important parts of this literature.

Notes

1   The characteristics of learning organizations are detailed in other chapters of this book. See, for example, Gould's introductory account of the emergence of the concept.
2   The National Science Foundation (NSF) represents the American scientific community. It 'is one of the most prestigious agencies in Washington, and its director reports directly to the President' (House, Haug and Norris, 1996: 137).
3   For a useful and frequently cited discussion of the purposes of evaluation, see Chelimsky (1997). I would add to her list, 'Evaluation for justice' (cf. Shaw, 1999, ch. 1).
4   We have already noted, however, Stockdill et al.'s concern about the discrepancy between what funders say they want and the criteria they subsequently use to assess evaluation reports. I have been on the receiving end, for example, of criticism by the funders of an evaluation project funded to assess agency learning and justice issues, on the grounds of failing to test outcome hypotheses.
5   For a fuller outline of the development and significance of the enlightenment argument about evaluation use see Shaw (1999: 28–30, 73–4, 92–5, 119).
6   Community-based health programmes are one example in the health field (for example, Shediac-Rizkallah and Bone (1998). In Britain, the Economic and Social Research Council has invested heavily in the Research Capacity Building Network for teachers (see http://www.tlrp.org/ and http://www.cf.ac.uk/socsi/capacity/).
7   See Shaw and Gould (2001: 172–3) for an appraisal of strong insider positions in social work.
8   This estimate is taken from a preliminary screening audit of practitioner research in South-East Wales, undertaken in 2002.
9   I am indebted to Knud Ramian's private communication at the 2002 'Evaluation for Practice' conference in Tampere (Finland) and for our workshop collaboration.
10   Kirk and Reid develop a corresponding logic in their critique of science and social work practice in the USA (Kirk and Reid, 2002)

Chapter 9

Reflecting on Practice: Exploring Individual and Organizational Learning through a Reflective Teaching Model[1]

Bairbre Redmond

The degree of effectiveness with which the needs of service users in health and social care are met relies on the ability of individual professionals to recognize, understand and respond to the unique requirements of each service user. Good service delivery also depends on how well employing organizations can encourage and support their practitioners to work in partnership with service users. This chapter examines how, using a reflective training approach, a group of practitioners in the intellectual disability services explored not only their own attitudes to service users, but also how well their different employing agencies functioned as learning organizations, displaying capabilities of changing and responding to service user need. Most importantly, this chapter looks at how individual learning can become a catalyst for wider organizational learning, with practitioners importing new, reflective approaches back into their service agency in a way that can encourage organizational learning.

For the past 20 years the concept of reflective practice (Schön 1983; 1987) has been suggested as a concept that would allow social workers and other practitioners to move beyond inflexible practice guidelines and fixed competencies towards more responsive and thoughtful practice with their service users. Boud, Keogh and Walker (1985: 3) described reflection as 'a generic term for those intellectual and affective activities in which individuals engage to explore their experiences in order to lead to new understanding and appreciation'. Mezirow (1991: 104) considered reflection to be the process by which we 'critically assess the content, process or premise(s) of our efforts to interpret and give meaning to an experience'. Agyris and Schön (1976; 1997), both eminent reflective writers, were also some of the first theoreticians in the area of learning organizations. They proposed that, just as individual reflective practitioners had to learn to question and change their tacit and habitual practice responses, so the learning organization had to be able to review its values, norms and practices in order to restructure its strategies and assumptions in a healthy new way (Coulshed and Mullender, 2001).

Background to the Research

Parents of children with a disability frequently report difficulties in being understood and appreciated by the professionals whom they encounter and of being poorly or insensitively treated by service organizations (Dale, 1996; Read, 2000; Redmond, 1996). As a social worker in the field of intellectual disability and, more recently, as a university-based academic researching in the area, the discontinuity between the needs of family carers and many of the professional and organizational responses offered to them had become depressingly familiar to me (Redmond, 1996; 1997). While much of the literature had previously focused on the pathological problems thought to be inevitably associated with families who had children with a disability, I became more interested in the apparent breakdown in communication between professionals and parents and between parents and service agencies. I also wanted to find ways of encouraging practitioners to re-examine some of their unconscious or tacit beliefs about parents that underpinned their practice. I hoped that, by acknowledging and challenging some of the underlying individual and organizational attitudes towards parents, practitioners might find it easier to appreciate the unique concerns and expectations of individual parents about their children and thus become motivated to alter their practice in order to incorporate such new perspectives.

This led me to examine some general theories of reflection and to consider how the adoption of a reflective stance might assist practitioners in developing more thoughtful and multidimensional perspectives of their clients. In particular I became drawn to the work of Donald Schön (1983; 1987; 1991) and his collaborative work with Chris Argyris (Argyris and Schön, 1974; 1996) which was concerned with developing a concept of reflective practice in order to encourage professionals to adopt a less 'expert' stance with their clients. Schön (1983; 29) claimed that professionals who were capable of adopting such a reflective approach in their work would, among other things, be more responsive to the needs of their clients. He saw the reflective practitioner as being capable of appreciating the uniqueness of the individual client situation and that the working contract forged between client and reflective professional would be marked by accountability, flexibility and accessibility. Importantly, Argyris and Schön also saw reflective change going beyond the scope of the individual practitioner and they considered reflection to be an essential component of a learning organization. Senge (1990a) described such an organization as one where individuals expand their capacity to produce the results they wish to achieve, where new and expansive patterns of thinking are encouraged and where people can learn to learn together.

At the core of my research was the design and implementation of a new reflective model of teaching and learning which I used with a multidisciplinary group of practitioners in a reflective practicum – a university-based learning environment. Over a six-month period, using an action research approach, I applied this reflective model with a group of N = 19 practitioners who were working in the area of intellectual disability and who were also attending a part-time postgraduate course in intellectual disability studies. These practitioners, who were from different professional backgrounds (including social work, nursing, psychology, teaching and medicine), initially examined their existing perceptions of the parents with whom they worked. Through the model's increasingly complex teaching and learning approaches, these practitioners were then encouraged to re-examine some of their perspectives on those with whom they worked and to explore, attempt and critically analyse more reflective and responsive ways of working

Schön (1983; 1987) hypothesized that, if practitioners begin to reflect upon their practice they can then use the knowledge gained from that reflection to develop and improve their practice, making it more responsive to their clients' needs. Simply put, once practitioners begin to think about what they are doing, they are less likely to produce habitual professional responses that may have little to do with their clients' unique and complex needs. Part of such a reflective insight also incorporates how one's professional practice is framed by organization factors that help or hinder positive change and learning in practice. Just as the individual practitioner, through reflection, can learn how to respond more creatively to client need, so too does the organization need to reflect on its tacit routines and procedures that may hinder the development of effective, responsive practice.

Barriers to Change in the Learning Organization

It is important to note that this research was primarily concerned with the analysis of critical change in individual learners in a reflective teaching and training environment, and it was not specifically designed to address organizational problems. If it had been, it could also have been sited within an organization, rather than the more remote university environment. However, the impact of organizational function on individual change became a frequently mentioned issue by the practitioners in the research. This chapter looks specifically at these organizational learning aspects – how individual practitioners saw their work as being constrained or liberated by the organization in which they worked. It also explores how the practitioners used the university-based classroom as a base from which to attempt to effect personal work changes that could also become a catalyst for wider organizational learning.

Argyris and Schön (1996) argued that, in order to understand why unhelpful and unproductive practice exists within an organization, it is necessary to explore the underlying, tacit belief system that controls and shapes the actions that subsequently occur. Central to what Argyris and Schön called 'theory of action' is a recognition of the difference between what individuals say they do in practice (espoused theory) and what they actually end up doing (theory-in-use). The espoused theory represents the public face of an individual or organization's practice, normally articulated in mission statements or best practice guidelines. However, as Flood (1999) points out, the theory of action is primarily concerned with theories-in-use – the kind of professional behaviours that come into play especially when individual practitioners feel embarrassed, stressed or under threat. On such occasions, in a bid to soothe over, cover-up or defend situations, actions of unilateral control, self-protection and defensiveness are more likely to occur. What is important to note about such defensive practice is that practitioners may well be unaware of why they are behaving in this way or what the consequences of such behaviour are likely to be. What is also important is recognizing how organizations, in spite of their public espoused theories of action, may well encourage and foster tacit beliefs that allow unhelpful practice to continue.

Identifying Theories-in-Use

One of the first research tasks I undertook with the professional group was to explore any differences between the way they publicly stated that they worked with families and the underlying, tacit belief systems that might account for their actual practice being different. Within the university classroom the practitioners began to explore the way they felt about the families of children with a disability with whom they worked. A review of the practitioners' references to parents recorded in the early weeks of the research showed them generally not to be related to specific parents, rather to parents as a general group. When analysed, the practitioners' references to parents fell into a number of categories or typologies, the most common of which were:

- parents who were misunderstood and badly treated by the system;
- parents with whom it was difficult to work.

The first category related to parents whom the practitioners felt had been poorly treated by other professionals and by the service organizations.

> Parents are ignored a lot of the time and not listened to, then they get angry with frustration. (Social worker)

> They have to take what's there, rather than what they really need in terms of services, then the service providers are annoyed that they aren't more satisfied with what's being offered. (Doctor)

> Parents often feel they are afraid to complain, that they'll be seen as a 'baddie'. That they will be seen as disruptive, like who would they be to voice criticism? They then give that reinforcement by us [professionals] by saying to them that we're all-knowing, you know, we are the experts, you know best. (Nurse Manager)

> They are required to be grateful a lot of the time, not to make trouble, the services really like thankful parents. (Nurse)

The comments shown above are typical of those recorded in this category. In essence, many of the practitioners argued that the organizations in which they worked often failed to offer adequate services to those with disability and their families. Not only this, but also many of these organizations ignored parents or made it difficult for them to express dissatisfaction at this situation. These views are certainly supported by research findings. Although the past 20 years have seen increasing attempts to include those with disability and their carers more meaningfully in decision-making, evidence exists that parents, in particular continue to remain isolated within organizational structures (see Cunnington and Davies, 1985; McConachie, 1994; Mittler and Mittler, 1983). Pernell (1986) suggests that this type of organizational resistance to change can be traced to growing internal and external pressures on organizations nominally committed to empowerment and openness. Such pressures may then lead to service users becoming frustrated and helpless in their dealings with organizations whose mission is, ostensibly, to serve them. Another pertinent factor is that organizational entropy may also relate to older issues relating to varying professional status. Taylor (2000) notes that the predominantly medical structures in which some social workers and nurses work significantly affect their potential to practice in ways that they might ideally choose.

The comments noted above, however, do not offer much of a clue as to the underlying individual and organizational belief systems that might contribute to this unhelpful practice. However, the comments recorded in the second category showed some practitioners identifying negative parental behaviour as a barrier to good working relationships.

> Sometimes you try very hard to get something for them [parents], it takes a lot of effort, then they say, 'is that all?'. You never seem to get it right sometimes. After a while you sometime don't feel like trying any more. (Social worker)

> We can only offer what we have, but it never seems enough. (Nurse)

> I don't like to say it, but some of them [parents] can be very pushy. No matter what you do, it won't be right. (Nurse)

This final comment demonstrates an important reason why stasis may occur in organizational learning – the identification of a rationale why change in poor practice need not happen. In this case, the practitioners have identified that many parents receive a poor service, but some of them have also made an underlying suggestion that it may not be worth while to change this situation because, no matter what is tried, it will not be enough for the families. Argyris and Schön (1996) called this single-loop learning, a type of instrumental learning that occurs within an organization where underlying assumptions 'excuse' the maintenance of the status quo. Figure 9.1 shows how Argyris and Schön's theory of action can be applied to the practice issues arising for the practitioners in this research. In this incidence, there was clear agreement that the publicly espoused theories of both the individual practitioners and their organizations were that the views of parents should be included and heeded in the process of service provision and delivery. However, the theory-in-use recorded in the research indicated that many of the practitioners felt that parents were difficult to work with. The practitioners also noted that their organizations tended to adopt the same belief system, with the resulting practice strategy of minimizing parental involvement, for example 'parents are ignored a lot of the time and not listened to' thus leading to increased anger and frustration for families.

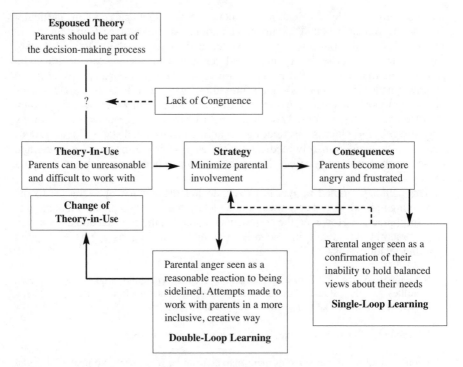

Figure 9.1   Argyris and Schön's theory of action
Source: adapted from Argyris and Schön (1973: 21)

Single-Loop and Double-Loop Learning

The critical issue that now arises is how the individual and the organization choose to learn from this situation. When faced with a poor outcome of an action, Argyris and Schön (1974; 1996) differentiated between two types of learning that can take place for both the individual and the organization, calling them single- and double-loop learning. These terms have similarities with Bateson's (1972) first and second order learning. In general terms single-loop or first order learning describes a conservative response to a situation that seeks to maintain the status quo and to uphold existing values and beliefs. Double-loop or second order learning is characterized by the search for and exploration of alternative routes, rules and goals, rather than attempting to maintain current routines (Lant and Mezias, 1999).

If, in the example below, the parents' anger and frustration is seen as a confirmation of their unreasonable attitudes towards service providers, then no action need be taken and the practice of minimizing parents' contact is justified and can continue. Single-loop learning can then be seen to have occurred with the result that the marginalization of parents may well intensify. However, if the outcome of the action causes a reappraisal of the flawed theory-in-use and parental anger is seen as a justifiable reaction to marginalization that can be ameliorated by more inclusive practice approaches, then double-loop learning has taken place. Unlike single-loop learning where the organizational frames of reference remain static, double-loop learning requires the organization to learn a new frame of references within which to operate (Huber, 1991), thereby making it possible to change the flawed theory-in-use.

As Figure 9.1 demonstrates, as long as the professional belief system remains within the single loop, then little change can occur and flawed reasoning will support this organizational entropy. What is more worrying is that, within the single-loop structure, organizational function will most likely continue to be defective. In this case, it is likely that parents will remain marginalized. Even if, as the comments of the professionals in the research suggested, there is an awareness that the 'system' seems to treat parents badly, unless both individual and organizational learning takes place, then practitioners and service user will remain trapped in a malfunctioning loop.

Systems Thinking

Helping individual practitioners to become capable of double-loop learning involves a number of complex, but interconnected, steps. These involve not only helping practitioners to see how their own tacit belief systems and their theories-in-use effect their practice, but also encouraging them to appreciate the functions of the organization in which they work and recognizing their place and their role within that organizational system. This appreciation of systems thinking is well established within the canon of social work theory. In the 1970s systems theory had a great impact on social work thinking with the work of Pincus and Minihan (1973), Specht and Vickery (1977) and Davies (1977). The belief underpinning much of systems theory was that, in order to bring about change and equilibrium, practitioners had to analyse the social system and find the origin of the current system malfunction (Howe, 1987). This concept has considerable resonance with Peter Senge's (1990a) view of systems thinking as being the cornerstone of the learning organization, as people in organizations begin to appreciate how existing ideas and actions affect practice outcomes, then a newer, more fertile vision of change can emerge. Most importantly Senge argues that systems thinking allows individuals to move from seeing parts to seeing wholes and from seeing people as helpless reactors to seeing them as active participants, capable of creating positive change. Bolam and Deal (1997: 27) state that an inability to understand systems dynamics results in what appears to be a good description of single-loop learning where we are led into 'cycles of blaming and self-defence: the enemy is always out there, and problems are always caused by someone else'.

In order to help the practitioners begin to use systems thinking I became interested in taking some approaches originally designed for use in systemic family therapy and adapting them for use in an organizational sense. I wanted to offer practitioners ways in which they could begin to 'see' the organizational systems within which they were operating and to appreciate the interconnectedness of elements within that system, including their own position and that of their clients. Senge (1990a) also recommends the use of 'system maps' in encouraging systemic thinking. The eco-map was first developed in 1975 by Ann Hartman as a way to help workers in child protection to examine the needs of families (Hartman, 1978). Rooted in systems theory, the eco-map provides a visual representation of the complex connections within elements of a social system. Used in family work it offers opportunities for family members to see the nature of the relationships between different elements of their life system which may be either supportive, stressful, encouraging or openly hostile (Hartman and Laird, 1983). In the context of this research I used organizational eco-maps as a way of getting the practitioners to visualize the complex connections within their employing organization, to map the different subsystems that exist within it and to note the nature of the practitioner's relationship with each element in the system. The organizational subsystems and the nature and quality of the interrelationships between them (such as strong, supportive, hostile and so on) were portrayed in the eco-map by the traditional symbols used in family eco-maps and genograms (see Hartman and Laird, 1983; McGoldrick and Gerson, 1985)

In completing the eco-maps of their employing organizations, many practitioners reinforced the image of themselves as professionals caught in the middle between the 'bad' service and its victim, the complaining parent. Five of the 19 practitioners in the research prepared a graphical representation of their employing organization which placed themselves between the management and the parents. All of these professionals indicated that the relationship in this position was antagonistic or hostile. Four other practitioners represented themselves in the eco-map as being entangled in antagonistic or hostile relationships between doctors and parents. There is a danger that such an image of being an innocent observer caught between two hostile factions within the organization may further remove the practitioner from the need to effect change in his or her own practice. Indeed, in the early stages of the research it was noted that no practitioner talked of testing the validity of this image by engaging with individual parents to see how they perceived the situation, nor did any practitioner suggest that they could advocate with others on behalf of parents.

The Learning Individual and the Learning Organization

Working with individual practitioners in a university environment, away from their organizational settings, offers a challenge to a reflective teacher who is interested in improving not only individual learning, but also seeing how that learning can impact on the employing organization. However, Argyris and Schön (1996) are clear that it is the thinking and acting of individual practitioners that influences the capacity for productive learning at the organizational level. Likewise Senge states that 'organizations learn only through individuals who learn. Individual learning does not guarantee organisational learning, but without it no organisational learning occurs' (Senge, 1990a: 139).

In order to foster such individual reflective learning, the central part of the research consisted of the practitioners being exposed to a number of reflective teaching approaches to encourage them to adopt a double-loop approach to some of the issues arising from their work. These included the drawing up of family-focused plans and using different reflective class exercises aimed at helping the practitioners to explore alternative perceptions of the parents with whom they worked. Parents came into the classroom to discuss pertinent practice issues with the practitioners who were also encouraged to keep learning journals of the changes occurring in their work practices. An important component of this reflective work was the preparation by the practitioners of short written case studies based on a challenging intervention or critical incident that they had encountered with a parent. The practitioners were asked to divide the case studies into an account of the dialogue that occurred, augmented by a record of their own internal thoughts as the interaction progressed. Asking practitioners to recall and record their unspoken opinions behind the interaction was aimed at encouraging them to begin to 're-see' aspects of the action from the parental perspective. This form of case study presentation originally used by Argyris and Schön (1974) in their research into both individual and organizational learning, bears a close resemblance to the process recording used in social work. Papell and Skolnick (1992: 23) see process recording as an important tool for stimulating reflection in social work students and Papell (1976: 1) considers the process recording to be a 'much taken-for-granted instrument for social work learning' which is commonly used without full appreciation of its reflective potential.

The preparation of these case studies and their presentation and analysis in the classroom proved to be an important aspect of helping the practitioners to move beyond single-loop practice. The research revealed that, through the work on their case studies, many of the practitioners began to be able to examine the dichotomies between what they set out to achieve in their work with parents and what ultimately occurred in the practice environment. The practitioners were also challenged to specify their perception of the parents at the start of the interaction and to note how this perception aided or hampered the work they subsequently attempted. Finally, the practitioners were encouraged to reflect upon how successful their espoused theory had been in achieving their perceived goals in the interaction with the parent/s.

Emerging Reflective Change

By the fourth month of the research, a qualitative change was being noted in the content analysis of the practitioners' discussion on their work with parents. Instead of seeing their practice as being constrained by organizational strictures, some of the practitioners began describing changes that they had made in their own practice that challenged poor organizational responses to parents and families. Annette, a nurse in a large residential care setting, had been struggling with the structure of her employing organization, perceiving it as unresponsive to the needs of family carers. Her solution to this difficulty came in the form of a simple but effective change in her own practice.

Annette: I've done something that was a real change in my work that I got
                from this class. In the unit that I work in when inquiries or one of
                the families rang about one of our residents we, the staff, took the
                call and dealt with the enquiry. Now I've begun to say to the family
                member '*would you like to speak to your sister or brother or son*',
                whatever. The first time I did it, the mother said '*why, is there
                something wrong?*', but the families really like to chat with their
                family member now. But there was no reason why we had always
                taken the calls, the person with the disability was just sitting there
                while we took the call on their behalf, but everybody did it. We all
                had the conversation with family, answered questions then said to
                the person '*Your Mum rang*'. It was only when I, like you said,
                reflected on what I was doing, it really was like something out of
                the dark ages, you know."

Social worker: Do a lot of the other staff still do it?

Annette: It's beginning to change since I started doing it, but it just feels so
                strange to me now that I ever did it. It's only a little thing, but, it's
                been really important to me that I made that change. You start to do
                things because everybody else does it that way. Then you see,
                reflect, on the situation from the parents' point of view and try
                something different just to see what will happen, and it's so
                different, like why didn't you see it before.

Annette's description of the small but significant change in her work practice is a
good example of the adoption of newer, double-loop, reflective practice – devising
new action strategies which expose previous inconsistencies and increase effective
practice. In her brief description Annette had identified inconsistent practice
behaviour – taking a telephone call on behalf of a person who is present and able to
use a phone. Annette indicated that her reason for behaving in this way was because
'everybody else did it', revealing how unquestioned organizational practices
contribute to unreflective individual practice behaviour.

In a subsequent discussion, Annette noted that the impetus for her to change her
individual practice and subsequently to create a small learning incident in their
organization came from the completion of her individual case study – 'that exercise
made me think about things I "just do" at work'. 'Just doing' is a good way to
describe tacit practice that is imbedded in single-loop thinking. Such practice occurs
primarily out of habit and professional convenience, is seldom evaluated and may
be replicated, unchallenged, by successive professionals. Annette's story indicates
the effectiveness of creating a reflective training environment that helps
practitioners to begin to examine what they 'just do' with parents and to evaluate its
efficacy both for the parents and for themselves. What also emerged from a content
analysis of the students' discussion was that the time spent on the individual case
studies represented a period of significant critically reflective learning for many of
the practitioners in the class.

An important aspect of reflective teaching and reflective practice also emerges
from Annette's story – the need to help practitioners to incorporate and evaluate the

validity of new perspectives in their ongoing practice. Annette indicated that being in a reflective teaching environment had helped her see her original practice response as being 'like something out of the dark ages', and she wondered why she did not see the inconsistency in her practice before. This highlights a significant part of double-loop, reflective learning – finding previously acceptable practices now inappropriate. Mezirow (1991: 6) called this attitudinal shift 'perspective transformation' and Brookfield (1987: 27–30) named it 'critical learning'. Mezirow saw 'perspective transformation' as an emancipatory process 'of becoming critically aware of how and why the structure of psycho-cultural assumptions has come to constrain the way we see ourselves and our relationships, reconstituting this structure to permit a more inclusive and discriminating integration of experience and acting upon these new understandings' (Mezirow, 1981: 6). Mezirow equated his perspective transformation with Freire's (1972) 'conscientization' and Habermas's (1984) 'emancipatory action' and saw it as a central function of adult learning and education (Mezirow, 1981: 6; 1991: 37–63).

A crucial aspect of perspective transformation or critically reflective learning is that, once achieved, it becomes very difficult for the practitioner to return to earlier unreflective ways of working. Colette, a senior nurse manager commented:

> getting into that way of [reflective] thinking gets to you, once you've looked at the deeper meanings for both yourselves and the parents, how they think, how things really are for them, then you can't go back. It would probably be a whole lot easier if you could but you have to look at things differently now.

Making such a critical transformation is not achieved without difficulty. Colette also highlighted a significant factor in achieving perspective transformation or conscientization – the fact that, by reaching this state of awareness, it is very difficult, if not impossible, to return to one's previous unreflective state. By undertaking critical reflection it becomes difficult or impossible to 'unknow' what has been discovered; as Colette said: 'You can't go back.' What became more evident towards the end of the research was the number of practitioners who were now facing previously routine work situations that had now become less tolerable for them. A number of practitioners used the group for support in such incidences. This is probably best exemplified in Bernie's case. In the last month of the research, Bernie, a psychologist, discussed how a meeting with parents, which would previously have been routine practice, now presented her with considerable difficulties.

Bernie: We had a typical example last week of parents coming in for a case conference, and all the professionals concerned met half an hour before to plan the meeting, to decide what we were going to say to them. I was going to leave and say I'll come back when the parents came in. But I didn't.

Doctor: But do you not have to prepare at some stage? If the professionals hadn't met up before hand, don't they have to get together?

Bernie: Why? Why do the professionals have to get their side of things sorted out before they meet the parents. Why couldn't everybody involved get together at the same time. The parents should have really come in at the beginning and we could brainstorm with them, they could brainstorm with us. It's not like we had answers for them. I just feel such a coward that I didn't make a stand, refused to go in until the parents were invited in. Next time I'm doing it differently, I couldn't be part of that again, it feels wrong now.

There is evidence in the foregoing conversation that some of the practitioners in the research were becoming aware not only that they were capable of seeing new and more complex parental perspectives, but that they were also constrained by organizational perspectives that maintained a more limited, one-dimensional view of parents and their needs. This placed Bernie in a dilemma of whether to work within her new, double-loop model of parents, or to return to the more distant 'expert' stance of her colleagues. Her own response to the dilemma is clear 'next time I'm doing it differently, I couldn't be part of that again, it feels wrong now'.

Reflective Learners, Unreflective Organizations

Ironically, Bernie's case highlights both the success of my reflective model in helping the practitioners to become reflective in their work and the dilemma that this achievement created. Wendy, a family support worker, expressed the predicament well: 'I think that here, with you, on a Friday you can see things clearly, but you get back to work on a Monday, into the system, and the changes you want to make are much harder to implement than you thought.' On a number of occasions practitioners discussed their awareness of the fact that the acquisition of a more reflective, double-loop learning approach in professional practice cannot happen independently of the larger work situation. What also emerged were the difficulties inherent in adopting a more reflective approach within their own work agencies. What began to appear in the later sessions of the research was a growing awareness on the part of the practitioners that, although their practice was becoming more reflective and more double loop in character, many of their employing organizations remained fundamentally single-loop systems.

This awareness that organizational structures limited their ability to become more reflective in their practice confirms Schön's assertion (1983: 328–9) that many organizations tend to resist a professional's attempt to move from single-loop to double-loop, reflective practice. It could be argued that it is unfair to expose individual professionals to a learning environment which causes them to consider fundamental change in their practice when they must return to a work setting that may not support such changes. However, there are a number of separate indications emerging from this research which refute this view. Once reflective, double-loop perspectives have been encouraged then it becomes more difficult for that reflection to be 'undone' and the practitioners are less unlikely to return to a previous unreflective state of awareness. Thus by engaging in active reflection, individuals are fundamentally changed in how they perceive certain situations and in how they behave in such circumstances. This was evidenced in this research by the number of practitioners who talked about 'not going back' to old ways of practice. Not only did these practitioners not want to return to old ways of acting and thinking, they described themselves as being unable to do so. Individuals may also seek to find different ways of incorporating their new perspectives into their work organization at some time in the future. A good example of this is one of the practitioners, a senior doctor, who, seven months after the research ended, contacted me to say that she had drafted a new policy document on parental inclusion that she was preparing to implement in her organization.

Individual change, as discussed above, has the capacity to introduce collective change. Thus, individual practitioners returning to the workplace with new, more reflective perspectives of service users have the potential to become models of change for other practitioners. A danger exists in that a newly reflective practitioner may attempt to 'evangelize' other professionals in a way that elicits defensive responses from colleagues. However, if that practitioner is already thinking reflectively, then it is more likely that he or she will introduce collective change with a sensitivity of how this change may appear to fellow workers. In this way the reflective practitioner can become a reflective teacher in the learning organization. This was evidenced in this research by Bernie's decision to change her method of participation in her agency's case conference practices and by Annette's decision to change her method of dealing with telephone calls from parents. Here a small individual change, initially viewed with suspicion, was gradually accepted as a new practice norm by her co-workers and her agency. More recent research (Redmond and McEvoy, 2002) has looked at longer-term effects of postgraduate education on practitioners in the area of intellectual disability. This research has revealed that 83 per cent of this cohort of practitioners with whom I worked within the reflective teaching model considered that, over two years after the end of the course, they were significantly more confident of being able to introduce change in their organization.

Some Concluding Thoughts

Senge (1990a: 139) talks of the importance of starting, in the learning organization, from the perspective of the individual practitioner and of allowing that personal vision to become the basis of the shared vision of the organization. He warns that when a top-down, organizational vision is imposed 'the result is compliance, never commitment. On the other hand, people with a strong sense of personal direction can join together to create a power synergy towards what [they] truly want' (ibid.). Unfortunately, some practitioners in health and social care areas face the frustration of practice within organizational constraints that fail to encompass their personal vision or view such perspectives as a threat to organizational stability. At worst, barriers to organizational learning and growth can become so insurmountable that practitioners no longer remember that they ever had a vision about their work at all – they have lost what Senge described as their personal mastery, leaving them with little option in how they can practice.

This research suggests that that a reflective training and learning environment offers experienced practitioners a way of reappraising the very value base of their own practice and that of the organization in which they work. Not only that, it allows them to review their approaches to service users and to appreciate the parts of their practice that may be driven or constrained by organizational thinking. Most importantly it can give them both the space and the support to see themselves as innovators of change in the wider organizational sense.

There is a tendency to view the university or college classroom as being only relevant to initial professional training with the added belief that experienced practitioners need only be 'topped up' with newer practice knowledge and advanced competencies at discreet junctures in their careers. Gould (2000) notes that just as the learning organization is not limited to course-based learning, reflective learning goes beyond the inductive application of knowledge or techniques. What this research has demonstrated is that the classroom can also be used as a reflective practicum – somewhere where practitioners can focus on practice issues in a participatory, supportive setting away from the pressures of the workplace. This practicum is also a place where practitioners can review their own position within their organizations and, with help, see how they can operate within that organization in the most effective and professionally satisfying way for themselves and for those with whom they work.

Note

1   The material is this chapter is developed in further detail in the forthcoming publication: Redmond, B. (2004) *Developing Reflective Practice in Health and Social Services: A Model of Teaching and Learning for Students and Professionals*, Aldershot: Ashgate.

Chapter 10

Living out Histories and Identities in Organizations: A Case Study from Three Perspectives

Harjeet Badwall, Patricia O'Connor and Amy Rossiter

This chapter explores the complexity of organizational change as a reflective process by discussing a specific change process in which the authors participated. While there are many different kinds of objectives and change processes in organizations, we are interested in the ways historical identities organized through relations of domination infuse organizations' attempts to manage conflict and difference. Our claim is that such historical relations present deep challenges to identities and that this reality imposes the necessity of connecting reflective processes with larger social struggles.

We will describe a period of conflict during attempted organizational change in a health agency located in the inner city of a large, urban centre. Our reflection is presented from the perspectives of Patricia, a member of management staff at the agency, of Harjeet, a former student in the agency who had been hired on a contract, and of Amy, a visiting professor who was spending part of her sabbatical working at the agency. We are using these accounts in order to explore the complexity and perhaps the limits of critical reflective practice in organizations. We hope to add our experiences to the literature on reflective practice (Fook, 1996; Gould and Taylor, 1996) with particular regard to the organization itself as a site of practice.

The Context

The events at the health agency took place during the zenith of 'reforms' of the neo-liberal government of the province of Ontario, Canada. These 'reforms' involved the cancellation of social housing, welfare cutbacks, agency closings, the decimation of the social safety network and the rise of homelessness as a visible issue, signalling a sea change in Canadian values. Among activists and advocates, hopelessness and despair were mixed with guarded determination to continue to resist government policies and the authoritarian governmental response to protest. While usual practices of holding government accountable did not work, the needs encountered by social service agencies increased exponentially.

As homelessness and substance use became more visible in the agency's neighbourhood, the agency gradually increased the size of its team to work with these populations. In 1997, the organization moved to a new building, and there was great excitement among many staff about the possibilities this new site would offer, especially in responding to the needs of marginalized communities. By 1998, the combination of punitive public policy and visible desperation among marginalized people encouraged some staff towards highly visible public advocacy on behalf of homeless and marginalized people. Hence, staff assumed an important role in advocating for internal resources and values orientated to homeless people and advocating at municipal, provincial and federal levels. This orientation became part of the identity of the agency, and staff activity with homelessness was legitimated and encouraged by the agency, and was seen as an important part of the mandate of the agency. Owing to the politics of the day and heightened client needs visible to the agency, increased advocacy and enhanced service for homeless people became an unspoken high priority. Conflicts arose that contested that priority, but these debates were difficult to conduct openly in the face of the evident valour of the advocacy effort.

At the same time, parts of the organization were making efforts to develop anti-discriminatory and anti-harassment policies and procedures. In informal, private spaces of the organization, discussions about internal racism took place between employees. However, open discussion of race and class were not part of the norms of the agency. At this point, discussions of internal social justice issues concerning race were quite separate from the priority to address external social justice issues such as homelessness. These discussions were carried by separate segments of the organization. Advocacy for homelessness 'belonged' to the homeless and harm reduction team, while people of colour and other staff with mixed agendas took ownership of the internal race issues. This background set the stage for a conflict which centred on race and class: a conflict which positioned social justice issues in competition with each other, thus disabling a view of interlocking social relations. In brief, the conflict centred on whether or not to set limits on clients who, usually while inebriated or delusional, behaved aggressively in the waiting rooms. Support staff, particularly those of colour, argued that working conditions were intolerable because of racist name-calling and threatened physical assault by such clients. They wanted to have clear limits set on clients who were aggressive or disrespectful. Barring some clients temporarily from the agency was a particularly contentious issue. Members of the homeless and harm reduction team (primarily white, middle-class professionals who were heavily committed to advocacy on behalf of homeless people) wanted the agency to be as unconditionally accessible and welcoming to marginalized people as possible. Their position was that support staff, particularly the workers of colour, needed further training to help them deal more successfully with their difficult behaviour.

The Reflective Accounts

The following accounts detail the perspectives of Amy, Harjeet and Patricia from their locations in the organization.

Amy

Two years ago, following eight years of continuous teaching in social work, I decided to return to practice during my sabbatical year. Consequently, I contacted an urban health agency that serves as a field practice site for students in our programme. It was agreed that I would spend some of my sabbatical time at the agency.

I had several motivations for undertaking this project. First, I was interested in exploring how our university-based social work programme could make more substantial links in the community. I wanted to think about how to make multifaceted relations with agencies, which could provide mutual benefits to both agencies and the university. So I began my work with a question about what the role of an academic might be in a community setting. Second, I wanted to reconnect with practice, and I wanted particularly to gain more experience in a community organization.

I began my work at the agency by helping the receptionist at the main reception desk. I had chosen to begin this way because it was an area of the agency that was under pressure and could use some extra staffing, and because I felt it was the best way to get acquainted with staff, clients, procedures and programmes. This work enabled me to begin to develop a picture of how the agency functioned, of its goals and commitments and of its tensions. At the same time, I joined several committees of the agency and began working in particular on projects related to homelessness. It was from the vantage point of an academic whose status and function in the agency was ambiguous that I took part in the issues detailed above. My role became a kind of reflective resource for some staff at the agency. Thus, I talked in depth with Patricia, the agency's health promoter and a Field Supervisor for the School of Social Work, with Harjeet, a former student of mine who had been hired at the agency, and with receptionists and other staff about the issues at the agency. With others, particularly the staff who had primary responsibility for the homeless issues, I had little in-depth interaction.

In this context, I experienced the conflicts about dealing with clients with disruptive or threatening behaviour. During this conflict, issues of social justice within the agency were called into question and contested. The central nub of the argument developed as the homeless and harm reduction team insisted on unconditionally meeting the needs of homeless clients despite the positions of jeopardy these priorities created for the receptionists, particularly those who were women of colour in the agency. At heart was the difficulty within the agency, dominated as it was by white norms, of recognizing that race creates a different social location and causes differential responses to those with racialized identities. Thus, the homeless and harm reduction team's position was that the receptionists, particularly those of colour, required better training to enable them to deal with aggressive and dangerous behaviour. The two receptionists of colour, aided by other support staff, and other people of colour in the agency, attempted to raise consciousness about the issue that their colour and status positioned them to receive very different treatment from inebriated or mentally ill clients. This debate played out as conflict between a demand that the organization take responsibility for maintaining a safe workplace for workers, and the homeless and harm reduction team's demand that marginalized clients be accepted and accommodated as the first priority of the agency.

This debate was complicated by the fact that the team was appreciated and respected for its extraordinary work in the field. Its single-minded dedication to activism clearly produced important political results. Debates were also complicated by the enormous difficulty for people of colour in making race visible within the structure of the invisible domination of white norms. Hence the stage was set for competition between two justice claims: the need for advocacy on behalf of marginalized people, and the need for understanding the dangerous effects of whiteness on people of colour in the agency.

It may be helpful to provide examples of how this conflict played out in the concrete. Receptionists were to some extent, the gatekeepers of the organization. They controlled access to staff, access to resources such as bus tickets, sleeping bags, hygiene supplies, food and clothing. As low-status workers and as people of colour, their decisions were frequently resisted aggressively by clients, who understood quite well that the skin colour of receptionists and their status in the agency 'permitted' a different kind of behaviour than that which would be tolerated by other staff. They also knew that support staff's decisions could be overturned by the homeless and harm reduction team. Thus, if a bus ticket were refused, clients would seek out harm reduction staff and come back to the reception area with ticket in hand. This process had the effect of increasing aggressive behaviour, as it guaranteed access to the team.

Advocacy staff interpreted this process as the failure of the receptionist to deal successfully and empathically with the clients. The message to receptionists was that they should emulate the behaviour of the homeless and harm reduction team – white higher-status workers – and this would end the problems at the front desk. Clients learned that racist, aggressive behaviour was tolerated against receptionists, particularly those who were people of colour. In this process, the differential treatment of receptionists of colour *because of skin colour* was never recognized. Norms based on white privilege were held up as universal: those who failed to meet the standard of those norms were deficient.

My entry into the issue began when I and one of the receptionists experienced a frightening verbal assault and physical threat while working at the front desk. My position there was an anomaly: the professor working as a receptionist. But that position allowed me to experience the same fear that the receptionist experienced. At the level of everyday work, I understood that it was a grossly unfair institutional arrangement, but I also felt rather personally ashamed and inadequate because I was afraid of such incidents, thus exposing me as less able than the staff with sufficient experience and training to 'deal' with such incidents. At the same time, it was clear that the receptionist cared a great deal about these difficult clients. She frequently ignored formal duties in order to serve soup, manage clothing and provide basic care. But as I watched the profusion of racist remarks aimed at the receptionist, I slowly became resentful of the ease with which staff who specialize in work with homeless clients would manage difficult behaviour by taking clients outside for a smoke, distracting them, going for a walk, and so on. I became resentful when any attempts to raise problems that occurred at the front desk seemed to engender calls for 'more training' for the receptionists. Here, my position as a white professor allowed me a unique vantage point: clients, believing I was a receptionist, felt freer to engage in disrespectful behaviour because of their assumptions about my status. It was clear to me that their difficult behaviour was far worse for my co-worker because of her skin colour. This vantage point was quite fundamental to the ensuing development of conflict.

At the same time, my relationships with Patricia and Harjeet were developing. We had connections which predated my sabbatical at the agency: Patricia had been a part-time member of faculty in my programme and was also a field instructor; Harjeet was a former student in our programme. Our programme makes particular claims concerning its emphasis on anti-oppression. It seemed natural that discussions between Harjeet, Patricia and myself began to concentrate on race. Harjeet, who took a major role in the development of an anti-racist policy for the agency, was positioned between Patricia and me, on the one hand, and members of staff who were people of colour, who were growing increasingly angry at the colour-blind performances of the organization, on the other hand.

As tensions arose, the 'safe space committee' on which Patricia, Harjeet and I served, tried to plan some strategies for organizational change concerning the way race was taken up in the organization. This included workshops, a 'retreat' and multiple debriefings. These were attended resentfully by some, homeless advocates, and not attended at all by others. I think it is safe to say that these efforts never produced the 'shock of recognition' or the serious reflection we would have liked concerning the dynamics of race in the agency. My understanding is that little changed, except possibly the kind of changes that may happen when minorities in organizations begin to connect and share their stories with each other.

I want to turn now to dynamics that are at the heart of my interpretation of these events. Barbara Heron (2000) has investigated the relationship of white women to issues of race. Her investigations are on the terrain of international development work in Africa, but her conclusions concerning the conditions of subjectivity for white middle-class women have general applications. Heron traces the formation of subjectivity historically by examining how middle-class white women gained entrance into public space normally controlled by men, through claims to be able to improve the lives of others. They could teach the less fortunate, give charity and alms, and so on. This subject position was at the root of white women's superiority in the British Empire: they knew the 'better' way, they could improve the lives of less fortunate Others. Thus, white middle-class women's identity became elided with morality and goodness. This morality and goodness always required the Other – the degenerate, the poor, the ignorant, the deviant, the foreign – to continuously maintain white women's capacity to recognize themselves as good and moral.

There is, it can be argued, a resulting imperative and sense of entitlement which white, middle-class women care to feel, which has led to intervening in/'improving' the lives of Others. Needing to be morally good colludes with ongoing identity formation – which implies that identities are always in peril of being *un-made* – to produce an urgent need for what Flax refers to as 'innocent knowledge' (cited in Heron, 2000: 30).

Heron goes on to quote Flax's definition of innocent knowledge as 'the discovery of some sort of truth that can tell us how to act in the world in ways that benefit or are for the (at least ultimate) good of all' (Flax cited in Heron, 2000: 30). Says Heron, 'I would suggest, therefore, that the imperative for white women to retain a moral view of self must be understood as heightened by the continuation of the colonial equation of proper womanhood with goodness' (ibid.: 31). I have come to view the events at the agency with a different lens following exposure to Heron's work. Even as I describe this interpretation, I am beset with its partialness as an interpretation as I also claim its accuracy.

At the time of the events, it is interesting to recall my assessment of the homeless and harm reduction team. I saw them as skilled, dedicated people who worked ceaselessly to make a difference in the lives of powerless people. I retain this view to this day. But as well, there seemed to be an implicit claim to moral superiority that protected them from criticism, but which also excluded other white middle-class women from the purest form of bourgeois identity – goodness. There was overt resentment at the way in which homeless advocacy was construed as the dominant and most valued form of goodness.

As the question of race emerged, a kind of two-part space opened up for Patricia and myself. One prong was the provision of support for staff who were people of colour. The other was the desire to have the agency examine the issue of race in the organization in an effort to unsettle the colour-blind orientation of the 'receptionists need training' variety.

In effect, as Patricia and I criticized the moral claims of the homeless team, we cemented our own identity positions within goodness and morality. This could be done by becoming white allies – those white women who act with people of colour around questions of race. But in acting as allies, we at the same time could stake a claim to that purity of intention that is the foundation of white middle-class women's identities. As 'race heroes', we could then challenge the hierarchy of moralities that had been established by the homeless advocates. White women taking up the cause of anti-racism are unassailably innocent.

So a partial interpretation of the events is that they were in effect a contest that grew out of the power relations between white middle-class staff, where each claimed the superior innocence of her particular form of goodness. If this is so, it raises troubling questions about the status of the Others who are required to stabilize the identities of the helpers.

In the case of the homeless Others – and I will unfairly argue the strongest form – being 'helped' requires them to be homogenized as both helpless and harmless. At times, they were infantilized in the agency by the use of methods of dealing with unacceptable behaviour suitable for 2-year olds, such as cajoling, distraction and bribes. These practices helped obscure the forms of very real and very threatening power they exercised over the receptionists. As helpless and harmless, they were also more easily positioned as victims of injustice and oppressive governments. We are familiar, through Foucault's work, with the governmentality that inheres in the process of creating the identities for those who require help (Foucault, 1997: 74–6). The creation of the identity of a homeless person as helpless victim, in dynamic relation with their saviours who fight the system, creates further oppressions (without excluding the possibility of help) through the take-up of these social constructions.

In the case of racialized Others, I think a cleavage developed between Patricia and myself as white allies and people of colour themselves. This cleavage was difficult for me to see because the subjective feeling of being allies obscures the constant operation of white identity formation. Here, Patricia and I took up the cause of ant-racism by talking to other staff, organizing events and, ultimately, by interpreting the concerns of the people of colour to other white staff. These efforts were easily brushed off by homeless advocates as 'complaints' – as rather tiresome distractions from the real work of the agency. But this is where the concept of 'allies' breaks down. During the dismissal of concerns about race, two categories of 'the dismissed' emerged: receptionists of colour, who became complainers trying to cover up their incompetence, and Patricia and myself, who became people who could claim innocence (the foundation of white bourgeois women's identity) because we were pursuing justice and equality.

What about the issue of change? What was responsible for the fact that despite an enormous investment of time and energy, no shared objections and intentions emerged in the organization? I believe in part that what happened was a contest of identity between white women at the agency. The result was the continuation of white middle-class identity as the colonial legacy that continues to circulate and reproduce in modern forms. My guess is that people of colour went underground with their 'complaints' and the diversity and agency of homeless people continues to go untapped as their advocates reinscribe identities of helplessness. Certainly, the examination of how whiteness constructs the conduct of social agencies remains unexamined.

Throughout this account, I have insisted on calling my interpretation partial. That is because I still believe that people of colour and white people need to be allies. I also believe that we cannot abandon people made helpless by conditions of extreme poverty, illness and hopelessness. These beliefs in some way have to be part of the interpretation. But is unclear to me how to move 'help' beyond my historical identity which demands that I am only real when I am moral and helpful and good. I am deeply troubled by the knowledge that my search for innocence was complicit with the inability of the organization to make change. Yet I cannot find forms which are good without reinscribing my identity as 'good'.

Harjeet

My entry into this discussion is as a woman of colour, a former student/staff member at the agency, and someone who took up race issues during this organizational crisis. The discussion will purposely focus on my reflections and learning about race issues during my time at this organization. I first arrived at the health centre on a social work student placement. Patricia was my field instructor and supervisor at the site. It was during my student placement that Patricia and I revived the Anti-Discrimination Committee. Once the Anti-Discrimination Committee was reinstated and staff was approached to join the committee, we began our work. Much of our focus was around developing an anti-harassment policy for the centre. A few short months after completing my student placement, I was approached by the agency and offered a staff position. I was hired for an eight-month contract position. It was at this time that Amy joined the centre on a sabbatical from teaching. Amy and I had previously known each other from the social work programme.

There were select staff members who illustrated a commitment to anti-discrimination issues but, like many organizations, people were at various points in their understanding of the issues. The staff was made up of mainly white workers and management, with a small number of people of colour workers mainly in administrative positions. The client population consisted of members from homeless communities, immigrant populations, low-income populations and members of aboriginal communities. My job description covered a variety of areas, from individual support to clients, to running groups and supervising social work students. Because of my previous work on the Anti-Discrimination Committee during my student placement, co-ordinating the efforts of the committee was included within my job description.

Tensions were rising in the agency over the mistreatment of receptionists (mainly women of colour) who were being racially harassed and threatened by clients from homeless populations. The receptionists' attempt to gain support around protecting themselves from racial harassment was interpreted by management and programme staff (who were dominantly white) as evidence for their need for further training in dealing with 'disruptive' clients and in de-escalating difficult client situations. Instead of seeing the tension as acts of racial oppression, management and programme staff misplaced their struggle as a *job performance* issue. At the same time, members of homeless populations were being positioned as 'difficult, disruptive' as a whole group of people.

Very quickly, the agency had a situation in which race was being pitted against class, and vice versa. Organizationally, the agency had little in place in terms of policies to respond to the complexities that this tension was presenting. The anti-harassment and safe space policies were still in progress and did not offer the receptionists the support needed from programme staff and management to address the discrimination they were facing. Amy, Patricia and I began addressing and responding to the struggle using the Anti-Discrimination Committee. Upon being hired as an official staff member, my responsibilities increased around the facilitating of the agency's anti-discrimination efforts. Other areas of my job description became marginal over time. Useful skills that I possessed or wanted to develop further were minimized. From my location as a worker who went from being a student to a member of staff, I was being positioned to analyse, provide support and, in some relationships, to 'resolve' the brewing tensions around race and class. The transition from student to employee was not smooth. Many staff still viewed me as a student and therefore, hierarchically, I was located on the margins of the organization. At the same time, I was being positioned to 'fix' the current problems around discrimination.

I was reminded by my white colleagues about how valuable I was to the agency, and how my analysis was useful and greatly appreciated, but the systemic supports that were needed to respond to the tensions were not in place. These supports included a demonstrated commitment to organizational change, management being fully involved in the change process, and everyone taking responsibility. In my role as a community health worker, I was also facilitating and organizing the Anti-Discrimination Committee. Management had set up a situation in which, in my role, I was taking a leadership position around the anti-oppression efforts. By positioning me to take a leadership role around facilitating this change, management was able to transfer responsibility for the issues onto my role. In addition, lines of accountability were not clear because responsibility was not shared by the whole organization. Staff members at the agency possessed various understandings of social justice. In my role, I was positioned as the 'expert' on the issues. Co-ordinating the Anti-Discrimination Committee was a part of my job description. Therefore, it was challenging to negotiate the degree to which I was going to engage or not engage in the work. My role was set up to be both critical and vulnerable at the same time. Just as the receptionists' issues around racism were being dismissed under the guise of job performance, the struggles in my role on the Anti-Discrimination Committee had the potential to be taken up as job competency as well. I was torn between wanting to do a great job, be the 'fix-it' person, maintain good relations with staff, and critically challenging racist dynamics and practices of the agency.

Informally, women of colour in the organization confided in me about the racism they encountered on the job. The discussions were filled with pain, anger, hopelessness and desperation, in addition to a sense of connection, safety and relief. All of these impacts were the result of how racism was operating and being revealed in the organization. I went from hearing their stories of struggle and anger, to promoting organizational change with white management. Not only was I set up by management to take leadership in this area, my colleagues, who were women of colour informed me that the struggles 'needed' the role I was in to take leadership 'on behalf' of race issues. I was positioned around white staff, white management and women of colour in the organization. I was put in the position of making the situation 'better' for both the staff being affected by the tensions, and for management who were not fully involved in the change process.

In my relationships with my colleagues of colour, I was set up to be the 'race hero': someone who was going to remove the incredibly taxing struggles faced by the group. I was struggling with my own privilege in relationship to the receptionists, both in terms of my status at the agency and my educational privilege. I was set up to be the 'expert'. Uncomfortably, I used the status of 'expert' to make gains with the management team. It was a privileged position, and I benefited from this privilege when I went into meetings with management, but it was also a disadvantaged position. I occupied my role, holding many of the stories my colleagues shared, in addition to the effects I was experiencing around racism. The complexities around the advantages and drawbacks were becoming more apparent over time. It was very difficult for me to exercise my own agency and intentionality, because many aspects of the organization were dependent on my role. In addition, I could not speak from my own location, without my opinions being seen as representative of all people of colour. With the benefit of hindsight, it was a lesson I learned around exercising boundaries and using my own agency, wherever I realistically could, recognizing that survival and agency takes place *within* systems of power and domination.

I worked very closely with the receptionist team to *collaborate* around exploring various strategies that might support anti-racist change. I attempted to highlight how difficult this role was in my location as a woman of colour working in an agency that is affected by racism. What people of colour were experiencing was the direct result of white supremacy and white norms of intervention. As a result, I did not have a place within the organization to explore the challenges I was facing in this role, and therefore could not obtain much needed supports. In limited ways, I would turn to Amy and Patricia, who were allies, for support around the struggles. We could find points of connection in those discussions some of the time. At other times, I was guarded for reasons that supported my survival and maintained my relations with them as allies. I believed during many moments of extreme stress, that management was relieved that someone, other than themselves, was addressing the issues around race and class. The organization was in crisis.

Once discussions about race moved from informal spaces within the agency to the Anti-Discrimination Committee, staff members who worked closely with homeless populations began associating the anti-discrimination work exclusively with anti-racism efforts and did not feel issues around class were being adequately addressed. It became clear that the Anti-Discrimination Committee's efforts and tensions were challenging some staff at the agency. Amy and I began meeting with the teams separately to explore people's concerns and understanding of social justice. The teams were becoming divisive around what anti-oppression and social justice meant for the agency. Each group felt that their concerns were not being addressed. Programme team members continued to advocate for homeless populations and issues around class. Highlighting the critical issues around homelessness and poverty was needed and necessary as part of a social justice agenda. Unfortunately, the process around challenging class issues took place without exploring the role staff was playing in perpetuating racism in the organization. Amy, Patricia and I engaged in critical discussions about these dynamics. At the same time, there were members of the organization with mixed agendas who were aligning themselves with the struggles experienced by the receptionists due to their own challenges about homeless populations.

Each of the groups spoke passionately about their 'truth' and these 'truths' were imposed on the organization. In my co-ordinating role on the Anti-Discrimination Committee, I was in a vulnerable position with my colleagues, and feared the great possibility of a backlash. The struggle was complex, challenging and needed an organizational response, one that incorporated everyone's ideas and concerns about the issues. When addressing issues of racism, simply acknowledging a difference of opinions among staff about what social justice means is not enough, particularly when the majority of the organization comprises white workers. Social justice that strives to address and critically respond to racism is vulnerable within a complex yet dominantly white space. McLaren (1993) in his article titled, 'Multiculturalism and the postmodern critique: towards a pedagogy of resistance and transformation', highlights the importance of locating difference in socio-political contexts: 'difference is politicised by being situated *in* real social and historical conflicts and

not simply *over* abstract differences or between semiotic contradictions ...
Difference needs to be understood as social contradictions, as difference in relation,
rather than dislocated, free-floating difference' (McLaren, 1993: 124–32). All facets
of an organization need to be involved in change, which occurs at both local and
systemic levels, with recognition that we do not enter the arena of organizational
change *equally*.

This crisis raises many challenging issues. Within the context of this
organization, women of colour who were the recipients of racial abuse were told
they were not performing their job duties adequately. Management therefore
dismissed the operation of racism in these incidents. Homeless clients were being
homogenized as a population that is 'difficult'. There was an assumption being
made by management and programme staff that one generic training manual about
'safe space' can assist all workers around de-escalating 'difficult clients'. There was
little recognition of multiple identities that exist in the social locations of clients and
staff. The 'safe space' policy located tensions and struggles *within* clients and
receptionist staff, promoting an individualized, competency-based analysis which is
largely removed and decontexualized from social locations. White workers who
worked closely with homeless clients often undermined any agency and authority
receptionists of colour exercised in the face of racist attacks, by excusing the racist
behaviour of homeless clients. Client-centredness was framed simplistically and
this philosophy allowed for unclear boundaries and accountability, among both
workers and clients. Being client-centred is necessary, but it cannot be practised
without limits and boundaries.

The change process had neglected to acknowledge how race, class and gender
were pitted against one another. White women workers in the organization received
quick responses to discrimination based on gender, again centralizing gender, but
the racism being experienced by women of colour was not acknowledged. When we
(the women of colour in the agency) attempted to exercise our boundaries as a
means of protecting ourselves from discrimination, our efforts were turned around
into job performance issues or were viewed upon as 'complaints'. Our resistance to
these acts of oppression were individualized and located within the sphere of
competence and not seen as outside of us, in the racist systems of the health agency.

During one of our interactions, Patricia and I were discussing issues of
oppression and I was attempting to draw out the issues specifically related to race.
In an effort to recognize the interconnectedness of oppressions, the discussion
centred on how race was not the only form of oppression. This understanding of
oppression is valuable when we need to explore the complexities surrounding social
locations. However, this analysis minimizes the unique impacts of racism, and it is
done by *equalizing* the effects of multiple forms of oppression. Patricia was a friend,
a colleague, my manager and someone I deeply respect. I automatically heard
myself sounding apologetic for focusing on race, even though the incident in
question dealt with racism, and the majority of the workers in the organization were
white women. The ways in which people negotiate systems of oppression is not
equal, there is a hierarchy involved when the majority of workers in the agency are
white.

Within this setting, focusing on race politics alone is discouraged. Even more difficult to illustrate is the complexity of racial identities. All the people of colour in the organization came from many diverse communities. People of colour may hesitate to speak openly about the diversity of racial identities for fear that their experience of racial oppression will be denied (Razack, 1998). These dynamics are the result of white supremacy, and examples of how racism within organizations operates in multiple ways in daily relations. White people in positions of power, determine the issues and how the issues are addressed. Sherene Razack's *Looking White People in the Eye* (1998) is an analysis of oppression that reveals the silencing dynamics of the politics of inclusion which were operating at the agency during its crisis. Razack stresses the importance of recognizing specific oppressive hierarchies, and that it is not enough to simply state that all people are oppressed:

> While I have relied on postmodernism theories for understanding the construction of subjectivity, I tried to keep a modernist eye on domination. Who is dominating whom is not a question I reply to with the answer that we are all constituted as simultaneously dominant and subordinate. While we are all simultaneously dominant and subordinate, and have varying degrees of privilege and penalty, this insight is not the most relevant when we are seeking to end specific hierarchies at specific sites. (Razack, 1998: 161)

Racially, there were clear hierarchies at the agency. The organization was dominantly made up of white workers, mainly white women. Razack is naming what some would identify as controversial and divisive to the work around anti-oppression theory and practice, because she is naming the existence of *hierarchies* based on oppression, and more specifically white supremacy. Razack explains this point by describing race relations in academic settings:

> For example, when we confront the whiteness of the academy and note that an overwhelming majority of professors are white, we cannot change this situation by responding that white professors also belong to subordinate groups – some are women, some are disabled, some are lesbians. Such a response amounts to a statement that race does not matter, an outright denial of the impact of white supremacy on the lives of people of colour. (Ibid.: 161)

Instead of a politics of inclusion, Razack (1998) stresses a *politics of accountability*. Accountability requires us to examine relations of privilege and penalty, and guides us to explain the social hierarchies around us and our participation in them (ibid.: 170).

Razack's analysis of a politics of accountability, which responds to power based on privilege, is useful in deconstructing discourse about inclusiveness. Taking discourse around privilege further, critical social work practice can assist social justice work in drawing out the complex expression of privilege, therefore we can avoid homogenizing the operations of power and privilege. Razack has also pointed out that we cannot, in the spirit of recognizing diversity, dismiss white supremacy and the impacts it has on workers and clients of colour, especially because social services are run mainly by the white dominant class. The importance of diversifying how we address oppression creates unfair critiques from white people, that people of colour are now essentializing race (Razack, 1998). White people or conservative postmodernists assume that this totality is based on cultural essence, where in reality it is based on the need to organize against and resist white supremacy.

The danger in making the argument that differences are now essentialized is to miscalculate how far we have actually come on the road of racial equality. We risk ignoring the relentless whiteness of the academy and thus the social context in which our descriptions of inequality are *heard*. It has been far too easy to confuse an argument about the constructedness of all identities with the view that the oppression of specific groups of peoples does not exist. Racism is, of course, anything but ambiguous to its victims, but a social construction approach can easily be harnessed by those who do not experience racism to deny its existence. (Ibid.: 164)

Social work situates itself with social justice. Within the context of this organization, social justice was a practice workers engaged in with their clients. Social justice was seen as something outside of ourselves, something we fought for, for our clients and out in the community. However, social justice was not taking place internally among staff relations. This is a critical reflection, because it speaks to the power imbalances between staff and the denial of those power imbalances within social service organizations. What is critical is to examine the complexity of power relations, and the multiple ways in which oppression is expressed. For example, race, class, gender, sexual orientation are words that have a great deal more to do with creating the illusion of *inclusion* around being oppressed, whereas, racism, sexism, classism acknowledge the operations of power and privilege.

The role of allies is critical during such a process. An important question for the discussion is, 'How can we be responsible allies?' Having allied colleagues, as Amy and Patricia were to this process, is critical. In our relationships, we demonstrated an openness to the struggle and to taking responsibility. In their roles, I experienced them as supports and as open to critically analysing the crisis and their involvement in it. They engaged in and promoted anti-racist organizational development during this crisis. I have often found myself in many work and academic settings, automatically looking for potential allies, people who share a similar commitment to social justice, across a diversity of issues. Even within these relationships, issues of race may not always be taken up by addressing white supremacy. White supremacy may be seen as something outside our organizations and our allied relations. If race issues are addressed, even in a remote manner, people of colour are set up to feel relief and/or a sense of gratitude. I have experienced and witnessed this dynamic in many settings. These dynamics and feelings are problematic because anti-racism must be owned and invested into by everyone. As a woman of colour, I am set up by white supremacy to find and connect with white allies upon my entry into any organization. This is done for survival and, hopefully, some sense of protection.

The importance of having allies makes attempts to discuss some of the struggles within allied relations difficult. In efforts to maintain allied relationships, I could not always critically challenge Amy and Patricia in their roles, and this dynamic supported them in their position to benefit from their privilege as white women who were 'race heroes'. Being white 'race heroes' meant they did not at all times have to critically examine their position as 'innocent'. In my role at the agency, I could highlight some of the dynamics around race relations, but not entirely, for fear of damaging the strong relations I had developed with them. They were a part of a very small group in the agency that was committed to anti-racism, and this made it challenging to name the ways in which they were also participating in their privilege as white women. I could not afford to lose them or anyone else committed to anti-racism as allies. There was little room to discuss the impacts this situation had produced for people of colour at the agency. Because of their privilege as white women, it was 'safer' for them to take up issues around race. This is not necessarily a problematic initiative. I do believe white people need to take up issues of race, to critically examine their participation in privilege and penalty. Where this may break down is when members of the organization can connect with messages about anti-racism more easily from them as white women, as opposed to women of colour in the agency. Not necessarily specific in this context, there is also a tendency in some settings for white allies to speak *for* people of colour, as opposed to *with* people of colour. Women of colour are positioned in a vulnerable location due to the multiple ways in which racism operates. The education and insight that we provide about issues of race has the potential to be appropriated by white allies. These dynamics beg the question: 'How do white people and people of colour work collaboratively?' I do believe white people have a responsibility to take up race issues, as Amy and Patricia did at the agency. It needs to be facilitated in a manner, which openly and critically examines how 'allied' relations can potentially reproduce systems of privilege and penalty.

Why was race pitted against class? Why was the discussion taken up in this manner? The needs of one group were silenced by the needs of another group. Responding to these challenging questions would require the organization to critically examine their identity as a social justice agency. The organization would have to admit its shortcomings. It would mean holding each other responsible and accountable, and hopefully from there finding points of connection where change can be implemented. There were a number of sources that were imposing their understanding of social justice and resistance onto the receptionist staff, people of colour and homeless populations. In my role, I became the representative of people of colour – an extremely uncomfortable position. In some organizations, anti-discrimination committees are established to keep a watchful eye on oppressive systems. If an organization has an anti-discrimination/harassment policy in place, they believe they have fulfilled their responsibility. Unfortunately, it has been my experience that anti-discrimination initiatives continue to exist on the *margins* of social service practices. Rhetoric about anti-discrimination is prevalent, and the rhetoric is not translated into practice.

Upon leaving the agency, I asked for an exit interview. I articulated many of the issues outlined in this discussion at this meeting. The fear exists that such issues can be pathologized or located within the person addressing them. I wanted the organization to understand that what I experienced was connected to larger expressions of white privilege. I recall a discussion Amy and I had had after I left the agency. We were reflecting on the struggles and I was attempting to discuss the continued impacts of the experience. Amy felt that personal agency or boundaries in my role had not been fully expressed and that many impacts around racism were allowed to take place. The discussion called into question the ways in which we *resist* oppressive systems. How Amy, as a white woman who is an ally, resists systems of discrimination is going to be very different from how I as a woman of colour will exercise and *demonstrate* resistance. Demonstrating resistance is not always safe for people of colour, and often at times it is a risk in terms of job security, continued harassment and so on. Therefore, how people of colour resist discrimination and exercise agency is multiple, complex and located within the contexts of systems of power. Amy was measuring agency and resistance based on what resistance and boundaries *meant to her as a white woman*. There is the danger of allies critiquing methods of survival and resistance. McLaren (1994: 322) emphasizes that 'agency is never complete, as subjects are continually being produced within and by relations of power and systemic structures of exclusion, disempowerment, abjection, deauthorization and erasure'. In other words, how people of colour may navigate and negotiate resistance is deeply complex and located *within* power relations. Even though white people cannot understand the 'lived' experiences of racism, there must be in place a commitment from all involved, to finding points of connection. It is in this most challenging arena, we can attempt to create change.

Patricia

At the time of this example, I had been working at the health agency for almost four years. I knew Amy from my previous work as a part-time social work instructor, and I had supervised Harjeet's undergraduate social work field placement at the health agency. Since coming to the agency, and as one part of my job duties as Health Promoter, I had initiated and played a lead staff role in anti-discrimination policy development and implementation. I led the committee's work reviewing employment practices and creating an employment equity plan, and organized staff training sessions on anti-discrimination issues. Harjeet had worked closely with me on this work during her earlier placement at the agency; together we drafted an anti-harassment policy and supported committee work.

During the time covered by this chapter, I had agreed to assume a management position on a temporary basis for a 10-month period. This position involved supervising the front desk receptionist, the harm reduction team and some programme staff. Harjeet was hired to work part-time to cover some of my previous job responsibilities during this time. Also that year, as mentioned above, several new staff were hired as the organization expanded better to serve the needs of homeless and substance using community members.

Barbara Heron's work (Heron, 2000), as well as the challenging and candid discussions I have had recently with Harjeet and Amy, has helped me to begin to unravel the complexities of that period of time in the organization in which I still work. It is clear to me now that the intense feelings of inadequacy, frustration and hopelessness that I often experienced that year had their roots not just in the worsening circumstances of our clients, the demanding workload I was carrying and organizational shortcomings, but also, and probably primarily, in the threats I experienced to key aspects of my identity.

There were many conflicting claims to my need to demonstrate my position of 'moral goodness'. I had worked hard to raise awareness of discrimination, particularly racial discrimination – in my earlier teaching and in the organization. At some level, I was seeking confirmation that these 'noble' efforts were recognized and appreciated (by people of colour, including Harjeet) and were incrementally contributing to lasting organizational change in the health agency, even though there was little evidence that this was happening.

At the same time, I was also worried that there were some staff who were not eager to further extend services to homeless people, or people with substance use problems. They were, I felt, sometimes looking for ways to have them barred or otherwise excluded. In response to clients' occasional racist outbursts and other disruptive behaviours, these staff demanded quick action to protect both workers and other clients from abuse. I did, at times, see this as a blatant backlash against homeless people, as resistance to changes in the health agency and, even, in some cases, as a convenient and opportunistic time to embrace anti-racism when previous efforts to raise consciousness had been dismissed. It also contained overtones of paternalistic protection of some staff by those with more power, thus replicating the traditional doctor/receptionist dynamic (which, because of the power imbalance, could be turned around at any time from protection to criticism). I saw myself, and wanted staff from the homeless team to see me, as someone who cared about homeless people, who understood the systemic issues they faced, who was committed to improving access to services and who shared the staff's commitment to social justice, even if I was not as heavily involved in it. The 'race hero' within me was now competing with the 'class hero' as the conflicts intensified.

I had also just become a manager, supervising some people who had previously been my peers, but mostly new staff – committed, skilled workers who came into the organization expecting systems that worked, policies and protocols in place, and staff and management who shared their passion for the work they were doing in harm reduction and homelessness. Instead, they found an organization struggling with too much change too fast, new teams that had not yet gelled, a lack of clear direction and chaotic administrative procedures. As their manager, I often bore the brunt of their frustration, and as I lacked the time and skill and organizational support to make the necessary changes fast enough, I was often left feeling hurt, overwhelmed and inadequate. So now the 'race hero', the 'class hero' and the 'good manager' were all under attack, and all were exposed not only to staff, but to the critical eye of two people I very much respected and whose approval I sought – Harjeet, skilled in anti-racism work, and Amy the visiting social work professor.

My efforts, my 'pure intentions', were not able to resolve much, as I struggled to prove my credentials as someone who thought she understood racism in the dynamics at play, as someone who was defending the right of marginalized and homeless people to be in the health agency in the midst of some degree of backlash, and as a new manager who could be supportive and helpful to staff and who could play a role in remedying long-standing organizational flaws. I spun between the three, at times feeling 'disloyal' to the workers of colour by focusing on the backlash against homeless people, at other times feeling frustrated by the refusal of some workers to examine their role in perpetuating racism and my inability adequately to bring to the surface and confront these dynamics. As a new manager in a temporary position, in an organization with poorly developed systems for supervision and accountability, I was unable to wield much influence with my management colleagues or contribute significantly to positive changes.

But there were also many aspects of my identity and position that served to protect me and to enable me to remain in a position where I could still choose whether or not to respond. As a white woman, I was not experiencing the racism directly, nor was the expectation by the staff who were women of colour to 'fix it' placed on me to the extent that it was placed on Harjeet. My relief that she was there, that she could share (if not fully assume) this work, and likely do it more successfully than I had been able to, blinded me to the fact that I and the organization were unfairly placing her in an untenable position. Also, although I faced some criticism as a manager, I still had seniority and security in the organization, and my newness in the position and my temporary status absolved me somewhat from too high expectations. My reputation in the community as a committed worker and as a teacher who brought a social analysis to the classroom also insulated me somewhat from some sense that I was a disappointment to the advocates for the marginalized. And the fact that I was working hard, putting in many hours of overtime, helped preserve the position of 'innocence' and 'goodness' of which Heron speaks.

This example, and the organizational dynamics and activities that both pre-dated and followed it, illustrate how 'dabbling' in anti-oppression work by mainstream organizations does little good and can, in fact, reinforce inequity and oppression. As long as we were doing some anti-discrimination or advocacy work, even though we could suspend it whenever other 'important' work needed attention, we as white, middle-class managers and workers could locate ourselves morally and ethically on the 'right side', handing out samples of anti-oppression like we did samples of shampoo and socks, when we wanted to or had some in stock. It was the charity model wearing a disguise of social justice. Few were holding us accountable, and those who tried had less power and thus could be ignored, pathologized, told to wait or to fix it themselves. I was a white woman allegedly wanting to be an ally to women of colour, yet I was unable or perhaps unwilling to acknowledge the complexity of Harjeet's position or to ensure that the management team took seriously these issues and used its privileged position to act responsibly. Only by embracing this complexity, by demonstrating together and across differences and over time our commitment to being reflective, open, honest, vulnerable and strong can we avoid the repetition of these dynamics or a retreat to cynicism.

Conclusion

Clearly, our analysis of the complexities confronting the process we have described does not lend itself to easy prescriptions regarding the role of reflection in organizational change. In this regard, we are interested in the kind of challenges our case study puts to models of reflection and action within democratic norms. While recognizing that change projects and processes vary considerably with different intentions, needs and circumstances in organizations, we would like to suggest that reflection in organizations is produced out of histories of relations of domination that take the form of personal identities which are part and parcel of organizational conflicts and which may be outside experienced intentionality. We therefore want to consider the idea that organizational reflection never exists outside the histories of identities that partially create the organization itself, although these impacts are variable in terms of intensity and effect.

For example, what has remained consistent throughout the process described in this chapter is that white supremacy/privilege dictates what the issues of importance are and to what degree organizational change will occur. People of colour continue to have the responsibility of eradicating discrimination imposed on them by white organizations. The minority worker who is responsible for anti-discriminatory change, in this case, Harjeet, became the 'representative' for all of the issues that fall under the umbrella of anti-oppression. The choices for people of colour are limited. They do not carry the same privilege white people possess, the privilege that allows them not to be involved in change processes, or to step in and out of it as needed. Moreover, there continues to be a lack of awareness around *how* privilege operates in practice, policy and staff relations. Power relations are multiple and are expressed in many complex systems. Anti-racism efforts continue to be explored at the expense of people of colour. However, white people and people of colour need to work together around the issues in organizations. We need each other to stay connected to the ways we *all* participate in privilege and penalty, as Razack (1998) has pointed out in her expression of a politics of accountability, rather than a politics of inclusion. But in normative organizations, can white management be relied upon for accountability? What motivates an organization to become accountable?

Our case study fuels in-depth questioning about the possibilities and limits to reflection and organizational change. When historical identities are constantly reproduced in the day-to-day functioning of the organization, how can reflective processes work with the tensions and conflicts when such reproduction is challenged? What role does authority play in hierarchical organizations which are confronting such issues? What do we expect from participants in change? We have described how the conflicts in this study arose from historically racialized identities. Is it our intention to change identities themselves through reflective processes? What are the limits to our expectations of just norms in the workplace? Finally, what is the nature of conflict in reflective processes? There may be an ideal norm concerning reflection that organizations should engage in open and democratic participation aimed at exposing multiple points of view to the participants. In this case, where the pain of inequity, the invisibility of privilege and the normalcy of historical legacies prevail, what are the limits that can be expected from reflective dialogue? Are there ways to maximize benefits? Despite our lack of clear answers to these questions, it is probable that raising them at the beginning of the process might have facilitated a more proactive approach. Nevertheless, we learned to respect the complexity of competing agendas, power and historical subjectivities in reflective processes.

Chapter 11

Conclusions: Optimism and the Art of the Possible

Mark Baldwin

Introduction

We have not set out just to theorize the learning organization for the personal social services in this book. We do not want to limit our exploration of the concept of the learning organization to investigating what it can tell us about how personal social services organizations *ought* to be structured and managed, or how far from this normative ideal so many managerialist organizations in which social workers practice have slipped. We have argued that the learning organization as a concept is ideally suited to providing a normative structure for complex and fluid personal social services organizations, but we also want to explore how we can get there from here. To what extent can the ideas and the examples of organization and practice revealed in this book give us hope of a move towards that democratic, dynamic and developmental ideal that is the learning organization?

That is what I am going to explore in this final chapter. Nick Gould has provided a range of definitions of the learning organization in the introductory chapter, noting the way in which it has been used in the literature as both normative and critical device. Each chapter has then woven its story around the concept or aspects of it such as critical reflection and organizational learning. Sadly, but unsurprisingly, the book is no revelation of the dawn of the learning organization within the personal social services, although there are examples of elements of the concept in some quarters of some organizations. For this final chapter I want to pull together some of the lessons from the theoretical and empirical work reflected in the chapters to provide hope for the future as well as practical ideas for the introduction of key aspects of the learning organization. This will be of help to social workers and managers within organizations as well as to academics and social work students who are interested in the development of the concept within the personal social services.

Before embarking on this optimistic look at the art of the possible, however, I want to dwell upon some fundamental difficulties with the concept of the learning organization and attempts to introduce aspects of it into current personal social services organizations. First and foremost, there is a problem in the way that the philosophical basis to the learning organization is different to that of most current personal social services organizations. There is a clash of paradigms for both understanding how organizations work and how they ought, normatively, to be structured. Secondly, and this is still within the realms of paradigm, even if we were to agree that the learning organization is what we want for the personal social services, there is then the fraught question of how you get there from here. Implementation theory for social policy suggests differing models, and it would help to be clear about how effective top-down, bottom-up, incremental or mixed approaches to implementing change are in achieving the change required.

These philosophical questions are important because we all have differing ways of making sense of the world and the parts of it which are important to us. Unless those that have control over organizations and organizational change actually believe that change is possible outside of a top-down rational approach, or those that believe that change in organizations is only possible with a fundamental change in the structure of society, then the inclusive, democratic and participative approach to change posited within the learning organization concept will not happen. We have here the radical social worker's dilemma. The analysis is that social work will not become a liberating activity without structural change and yet there is no appetite for that change. The radical social worker is then stuck within a profession which, by his or her own analysis, is a part of the very machinery of state oppression that they want to see an end to. How, similarly, does the social worker, manager, researcher or consultant who is interested in the development of the learning organization for the personal social services, work for change within the managerialist organization which fundamentally undermines the concept of participation for learning and change?

We need to explore these problems and dilemmas before going on to recapitulate the lessons from this book about the art of the possible.

Understanding Organizations – A Clash of Perspectives?

Chapters within this book have added to other writing which has started to look at (Baldwin, 2000a) or has built a focus upon the learning organization within the personal social services (Gould, 2000; Pottage and Evans, 1994). People writing about the personal social services are seeing the learning organization as a useful analytical and critical concept for investigating the future of the personal social services. These are writers who, like Donald Schön (1983), see the terrain in which social workers practice as the 'swampy lowlands' of messy personal and organizational relationships, rather than the 'sunny uplands' where clear technocratic solutions can be found to deal with the problem of uncertainty.

Nick Gould has already reminded us of the writers who, like himself and Richard Pugh (Pugh and Gould, 2000), have offered an analysis of the increasingly fragmented nature of the welfare world. In social policy analysis there is talk of the 'wicked issues' that social welfare has to deal with and others (for example, Taylor, Chapter 5 in this volume) have noted the degree of change that is necessary to respond to the increasing demands to involve service users in the development and delivery of services. It is no longer good enough (when was it ever?) to rest solely upon professional assessments of what is appropriate for service users. This is true for the assessment of individual service user assessments as it is for more strategic development of services or methods of practice that 'work'. In this context of uncertainty and constant change, an organizational framework that can respond to such fluidity is indispensable.

And yet the cry seems to be '*plus ça change, plusieurs la même chose*', as the personal social services constantly reorganize while remaining fundamentally the same. Organizations re-create themselves within very similar frameworks – the bureaucratic or, more recently, managerial hierarchy (Challis, 1990; James, 1994; Clarke, Gewirtz and McLaughlin, 2000). I want here to note the way in which the dominant paradigm for understanding and constructing organizations has remained largely similar, and how the concept of the learning organization stands in opposition to this paradigm. Morgan and Burrell (1979) established a helpful framework for understanding the ways in which organizations are conceptualized. Social workers may be familiar with the model as it was adapted by Whittington and Holland (1985) to help us understand the differing paradigms that construct social work theory (Payne, 1997). Without needing to go into detail here, Morgan and Burrell position organizational theory along two axes. The horizontal axis defines theories that are more or less built upon objective or subjective views of reality. The vertical axis defines theories as more or less wedded to the maintenance of the status quo or to change. In this model bureaucratic or managerialist organizations are typecast as objective and status quo – determined by their structure, with the structure determining the roles and relationships of those who work within them. The learning organization, on the other hand, is a concept founded more within a social constructivist paradigm in which the organization is conceptualized as constructed through relationships which hold the opportunity for change and development on a day-to-day basis.

Clearly this is only a model for understanding theories of organization and not the organizations themselves, and we have to be careful of vulgarizing certain types of organization such as the managerialist. There is a wealth of literature dedicated to the analysis of managerialism within the public sector (James, 1994; Clarke, Gewirtz and McLaughlin, 2000). This literature explains the complexity of these organizations, and the degree to which the most objective and rationalist versions of managerialism have been introduced into the personal social services, under considerable pressure from the Department of Health, through the introduction of measurable targets and a range of other devices for ensuring certainty of outcome and enabling comparison between personal social services organizations. This tendency within public service started under the Thatcher government of the 1980s but has continued under New Labour (Baldwin, 2002). This general tendency should not, however, lead us to believing that complex organizations such as the personal social services are only the managerialist equivalents of machine bureaucracies. So managerialism as a concept is a useful device for recognizing certain types of organization. As concepts, however, managerialism along with the learning organization, reveal very different ways of understanding organizations. Holding to one or the other of these perspectives will provide beliefs about what organizations are like or could be like, and how people who work within them should be treated.

We have here a clash of paradigms, although the contemporary story is more complex. While I argue that managerialism and the learning organization are interpreted by different epistemological phrase books, there is evidence of the language of the learning organization starting to creep into some government commitments to organizational development. Any UK government website that addresses the organization of public services will speak the language of the learning organization. (See Taylor, Chapter 5 in this volume for an example.) All organizations in the UK are encouraged to be 'Investors in People', and many public sector organizations have put their eggs into that basket. A glance at the criteria for an organization that is an 'investor in people' (http://www.iipuk.co.uk/) tells us that we are looking at the normative learning organization. The reality, however, is of these often remaining identifiably managerialist organizations. Tony Blair almost apologized recently for his public sector reforms sounding too technocratic and managerialist when what he wanted to convey was a concern for people who work within and receive services from these organizations.

Advocates of the learning organization, therefore, have to take note of this anomaly in public sector discourse. There is a fair amount of policy and organizational philosophy within government discourse that supports notions such as stakeholder involvement in the development of services, and other aspects of the learning organization. Several of these features are investigated in this book. Examples would be supervision, double-loop learning, co-operative teamwork, evaluation, training, education and continuing professional development. It is almost as if this discourse has taken the words of learning organization development and subverted them in a tokenistic fashion that enables the speaker to sound as if that is the goal while never having to walk down the road towards that destination. This is a problem for the implementation of the learning organization that any model for change will have to take into consideration.

Implementation Theory and Practice

If the learning organization is where we want to be within the personal social services then how do we get there? Social policy implementation theory (see Hill, 1993, for a synopsis of the arguments) provides a helpful set of perspectives for understanding how change might work within organizations and the type of blocks that arise to thwart developments.

Having said that, debate about implementation theory has got rather stuck between top-down rationalist approaches (Hogwood and Gunn, 1984) and others such as Lipsky (1980) who argues that policy is better seen as what is actually acted out in organisations, mainly by practitioners whom he refers to as street level bureaucrats who determine policy from the bottom up. Majone (1989) is not happy with a scientific model of policy analysis and introduces other factors that are neglected in rationalist theory, such as 'inference' and 'articulation of values'. He argues that these different approaches are equally valid, especially when recognizing the 'legitimacy of different perspectives' (Majone, 1989: 9). Policy analysis that claims to be value-free is described as 'decisionism', a scientific approach which fails to address differences of perspective and the way they are dealt with in policy processes. For Majone policy implementation is better seen as a political and participative process, and the ways in which some voices are allowed to be articulated and not others reminds us that policy implementation is a locus for the wielding of power in political processes. Majone argues that the process of decision-making is better described as 'mutual learning' (Majone, 1989: 41). This connection between policy-making and learning takes us to the heart of the literature on organizational learning (Argyris and Schön, 1996), in which we have seen that an organization's identity is largely accounted for by the construction of 'theory-in-use' by members of the organization working in relationship together. Failure to appreciate that perspective and value are articulated in a process of 'persuasion' (Majone, 1989) in policy implementation means that scientific rationalist theory is unable to reveal the complete picture when it makes the positivist claim that human action can be understood objectively, without taking into account actors' interests, their perspective or their values.

Top-down implementation theory, typified by Hogwood and Gunn (1984), has provided some useful theoretical and empirical evidence of the blocks to 'perfect implementation', and is thus somewhat prescriptive in tone. Most notably they point to the actions of professionals as they use their discretion in professional practice. While other writers such as Lipsky focus on such use of professional discretion as a key aspect that defines what policy is, the rationalists are looking for ways of organizing such discretion out of the equation in the search for perfect implementation. It is this search for certainty that is closely associated with managerialism.

Bottom-up analyses tend to be more descriptive of how things are, although such analysis still provides guidance to understanding and action, in two main forms. First, we need to think of implementation as decision-making within 'successive limited comparisons' (Lindblom, 1988: 188) and therefore incremental in nature. Secondly, as mentioned above, we are urged to study the behaviour of key implementers such as street level bureaucrats (Lipsky, 1980). Lipsky explores discretion and accountability in policy implementation so is investigating the part played by key people in organizations, as the concept of the learning organization requires us to do. Lipsky helps us to understand the way in which policy is constructed by implementers, particularly at the street level in organizations, although, of course, within the organizational learning literature there is an argument that this occurs throughout organizations that are successful at generating an environment of organizational learning (Argyris and Schön, 1996).

One further tension, which has developed in more recent years with the burgeoning service user movement, exists between the arguments for 'democratic' accountability (that is, the actions of elected politicians) and the weight given to the 'voice' of service users. Politicians may feel they have some justification in arguing that it is they who have a responsibility to determine policy derived from their electoral mandate. This notion is increasingly challenged by the concept of participatory democracy in which other stakeholders – users, carers and professional service providers – have been encouraged to demand a say. Indeed, this concept is written into the community care legislation through the requirement on local authorities to consult with their communities and voluntary organizations when they put together their Community Care Plans. This is another example of the ways in which the top-down and bottom-up arguments are played out.

Lindblom's incrementalism also provides a critique of rationalist theory, noting that there is seldom such a thing as new policy. Any new policy will be built upon a history of policy initiatives that have been tried and tested, and to which different stakeholders will attach varying value. We only need to think, within social work, of the community care arena as a good example of this (Baldwin, 2000a). Because rationalist perspectives do not address the concept of value, they are unable to provide anything more than an 'ideal-type' for policy implementation theory. This partial explanation for important areas such as organizational behaviour and the actions of 'street level' (Lipsky, 1980) implementers means that we need to look elsewhere for help in imagining the implementation of the learning organization.

Lindblom argues incrementalism as a process of 'partisan mutual adjustment' (Lindblom, 1988: 252) in which differing perspectives are introduced to the policy process. This is very similar to Majone's argument about 'different perspectives' (see above). What we do not have here is an analysis of power relationships in policy implementation and organizational process. We need to acknowledge and explain the process by which some perspectives are permitted in the decision-making process and others are not (Bachrach and Baratz, 1962; Lukes, 1974).

So although there are problems with Lindblom's 'muddling through', and Lipsky's bottom-up approach, they are useful ways of understanding what happens in organizational development. If we have a mind to the criticisms implicit within Majone's perspective and those who analyse power within organizational processes, then bottom-up and incremental approaches can help us to understand the implementation of the learning organization. The evidence is that top-down rationality does not work so we have to take into account the part played by street level bureaucrats (particularly if we extend this to a whole range of 'stakeholders' within personal social services organizations) as well as incrementalism which fits with the concept of the learning organization in which all stakeholders throughout organizations should be involved to ensure organizational learning. If we also add the concept of iterative learning described by Argyris and Schön (1996) in double-loop learning (see Baldwin, Chapter 3 in this volume), then we can start to see the way in which the learning organization might become reality within personal social services organizations. Accepting muddling through rather than seeing it as an unfortunate inevitability might actually validate this as an approach within organizations. The search for structure and certainty might then be seen to be the waste of time that it is. Muddling through is perhaps the way of approaching organizational learning and development in the swampy lowlands of Schön's world of organization, which included the personal social services. 'Muddling through the swampy lowlands' may not be the prettiest of mixed metaphors but probably rings true to the experience of many people working at all levels in personal social services organizations!

So what can we do? If we are persuaded by Lindblom's analysis, then how can we maximize the chances of collective involvement and critical analysis within double-loop learning in this process of development? I am reminded of some of the arguments around the elimination of institutional racism – Gillborn (1995: 176) argues for 'struggling where we are' rather than trying to root out racism root and branch. There is a lot of rhetorical noise in anti-racism and this has transferred into policy as a managerialist search for targets met that will indicate progress. Increasing the numbers of black police officers is an example of one such target, but it will not eradicate racism either at individual or institutional levels. This will require individual and organizational *learning*. By learning here I mean in the sense of knowledge gained, understood and *owned* by everyone within the organization, with this understanding fed into the structures and processes of the organization. Learning is that which leads to the changes necessary to deal with the novelty that is diversity in personal social services organizations.

The Evidence from this Book

In order to check the existence of, even, aspects of the learning organization, let alone a mature learning organization as we have presented it in its normative form, there is a need for more empirical research. The same goes for testing development or implementation of the same ideal type of organization. Well-considered evaluation or action research projects need to be initiated. At this stage, however, what can we present as evidence of nascent learning organizations from the chapters in this book?

In re-reviewing the chapters written for this book, I looked for evidence of the aspects of the learning organization that Gould has outlined in his introductory chapter, although, given the contested nature of the concept, I did not exclude other characteristics that might match our overarching definition of the learning organization. A learning organization is one that, through its constituent parts, and notably through the learning of the individuals who work within it, can learn, developing new ways of understanding and dealing with unfolding problems and issues. There is a fundamental value base to this notion of the learning organization. The learning organization is participative and democratic, facilitating the learning of all its members in order to ensure learning and development within the whole organization.

In order to structure this analysis of the chapters I have looked at two aspects of the learning organization. The first explores whether the chapters provide evidence of the learning organization in social care organizations, or whether it remains, from this book, little more than a theoretical idea with no current practical consequences. The second aspect of the analysis involves looking for ways in which the learning organization is being implemented in social care organizations. I will be looking particularly at the opportunities and threats to such implementation, as I feel this should provide a helpful guide to organizations and the managers and practitioners who work within them to the art of the possible. I also feel such an analysis will assist researchers and students who are interested in the concept of the learning organization as an analytical tool for the organization and management of the personal social services.

Evidence for the Learning Organization, or Aspects of it, within the Organizations Investigated in the Chapters

As I said at the outset of this chapter, there is no evidence that social care organizations have become fully functioning learning organizations. There are, however, encouraging indications that aspects of the learning organization are appearing in some organizations. I will state the reasons why I feel these developments are encouraging as I progress, but all of them point to individuals and collections of individuals recognizing the need for their organization or the part of it in which they work to operate a flexible and responsive approach to the demands that are made on contemporary social care organizations. These are people, managers and practitioners who understand that they operate in Schön's swampy lowlands and that they need to adopt a collective and dynamic approach to service developments at either individual or strategic levels in order to work their way through that terrain.

One aspect of the learning organization that Gould notes in the initial chapter is the need to locate learning in the work base – within practitioners' practice. Allan and Sage in Chapter 6 describe such a process. The Housing Association investigated in their chapter created reflective groups across a wide part of the organization, to facilitate the development of a reflective approach to practice and practice development. This development was partly a response to the difficulties with managerialist supervision which gave lesser priority to practice development. This is an aspect of supervision in modern social care organizations also noted in Karvinen-Niinikoski and Jones's chapters. While supervision might be a site for both professional development and managerial concerns, the setting up of alternatives to replace the loss is perhaps a more helpful response than other organizations that seem happy to lose that aspect of professional supervision. In this organization, senior management recognized the importance of reflective discussion of practice. Such a commitment would seem central to the success of such initiatives.

In Badwall, O'Connor and Rossiter's chapter there was also evidence of structures being set up to deal with a lack of progress in dealing with racism in the organization. While there were clearly problems with this highlighted in the chapter, it is another example in which opportunities for critical reflection are seen as having a developmental purpose in organizational processes.

More than one of the chapters provides evidence of structures for critical reflection which are actually situated outside of the organization, set up for post-qualifying or other training purposes, or as research or evaluation projects. There is a question here as to whether such external structures can facilitate organizational learning, which would largely hinge on the legitimacy of those structures within managerial power structures. Certainly the work I write about in Chapter 3 with colleagues from a children's charity fell into this category, with the outcomes not, ultimately, being accepted by senior management as they moved on to other concerns.

One of the chapters that charts the development of externally situated reflective learning opportunities for social work staff is that by Bairbre Redmond. The reflective groups that she facilitated were designed to explore a move beyond habitual professional practices which were, upon reflection seen to be counter-productive to effective service delivery. Redmond describes the way in which the groups addressed the gap between espoused theory and theory-in-use, by developing understanding and seeking to change behaviour. Practitioners were able to take this learning back into their own practice and, through modelling, into the organizational setting. Redmond also notes how group learning led, through changed practice, to perspective transformation, critical learning and emancipatory action. There could, then, have been some degree of the double-loop learning that Argyris and Schön (1996) argue is essential to organizational learning. In the final analysis, however, Redmond observed reflective practitioners but unreflective organizations. We need to flag up why it is that there is so much resistance to practice learning from senior management in organizations. We must remind ourselves that managers are generally on the side of the angels in this matter and often feel buffeted by policy initiative and organizational processes in the same way as people lower down organizations (Baldwin, 2000a). While this might seem a substantial block to the realization of the learning organization in social care organizations, Redmond reminds us of the importance of becoming a change agent in your own organization. Social workers will be familiar with the notion of modelling good practice, and it reflects the systems model of change agent and Senge's argument of change coming from the bottom up.

Judith Thomas also investigates the usefulness of groups meeting externally to organizations. The use of critical incident analysis in supportive reflective groups, working within Habermas's framework of emancipatory knowledge was helpful in moving people from understating to action. We have already seen the importance of locating learning in practice. Again, however, the problem for these groups was embedding their individual learning into the organization. Even more than that, some of the participants were finding it hard to persuade their organizations to grant them workload relief to create reflective space. Very much the same problem arose with the co-operative inquiry groups I describe in Chapter 3 where the groups spent some of their reflective time trying to establish strategies for persuading first and middle managers to allow them this time for collective critical reflection. We have already heard how, in the managerial world of social care organizations, supervision is not likely to include this space for professional development. If practitioners are also denied other opportunities in these organizations, then there is little likelihood of the conditions being created for an organization to learn and develop strategies for effective practice.

Jan Fook, in Chapter 4, describes an attempt by a human services agency to introduce aspects of the learning organization. Setting up a training programme to teach practitioners critical reflection came as part of a broader move to introduce quality improvements, so the organization's management saw critical reflection as a part of that process of improvement. The concept was that individuals would, through this programme, maximize changes in learning culture, in much the way described by Senge (1990) and Argyris and Schön (1996).

Yet again, critical incident analysis was the tool used to facilitate critical reflection suggesting this is an effective tool for practice development. The problem was one of time and a failure adequately to cover service delivery to allow participants to attend. Sporadic attendance then undermined the effectiveness of the groups. So, again, the message is that such programmes can facilitate individual learning from critical reflection, and that this aids practice development. Practice became more reflective and less reactive and 'robotic', avoiding the technical solutions that Schön (1983) argues are so unhelpful in the swampy lowlands of organizational practice. There was a better understanding of organizational dilemmas, even while organizational processes were preventing their learning from becoming embedded within the organization. As Fook helpfully points out, lack of time was blamed for failures to maintain critical reflection when actually what had failed was adequate priority for critical reflection as an integral organizational activity.

Another interesting block to moving learning from these sort of groups into organizational learning was that participants tended to see themselves as individual learners. If practitioners do not see themselves as potentially contributing to organizational learning and development, then it is unlikely to have that double-loop learning effect.

Evidence of the Opportunities and Threats to Implementation of the Learning Organization or Aspects of it in the Organizations Detailed in the Chapters

There is one threat above all others that recurs throughout the chapters in this book. That is, the introduction of managerialism into social care organizations. The focus on management issues at the expense of other organizational processes such as professional development is one of the things that characterizes managerialism (Baldwin, 2000a; Clarke, Gerwitz and McLoughlin, 2000) and there is plenty of evidence that it is alive and well in a variety of organizations and internationally. In relation to supervision, for instance, both Jones and Karvinen-Niinikoski tell of the overbearing emphasis on management concerns within supervision. The co-operative inquiries I detail in Chapter 3 also provide such evidence. I need to say again here that this is not, in my view, a sinister conspiracy by managers to take over the world of personal social services organizations. They have their own pressures that they have to respond to.

Jones argues persuasively that the introduction of managerial instruments into supervision while intended to introduce a degree of certainty into practice such as child protection can, by reducing the opportunity for moderating value conflicts that arise, actually result in dangerously unreflective practices. Efficient managerialism can, therefore, result in ineffective services. At the same time Jones introduces an interesting threat to the effective introduction of the learning organization. His contention, backed by some empirical evidence suggests that the learning organization could become a cover for top-down implementation of ideas that would undermine the basic principles of the concept as we have argued them in this book. Imogen Taylor gives a similar warning in the final section of Chapter 5.

While contemporary managerialism is seen as a threat, so is traditional professionalism. Karvinen-Niinikoski and myself in Chapters 2 and 3 highlight concern with belief in the certainty of professional knowledge. This belief is reflected most notably in positivist adherence to evidence of what works as the basis to good practice. Such a professionalism, Karvinen-Niinikoski argues, is a threat because it will fail to be responsive to the changed and changing world of service user involvement where the formal knowledge and understanding of professionals is not adequate of itself in making sense of a contemporary climate of uncertainty and ambiguity in social care organizations.

A similar failure is seen to occur even when professionals have a well-developed sense of responsiveness to service users, as occurs in a story of clashing perspectives in the chapter by Badwall, O'Connor and Rossiter. On this occasion the block to the sort of professional development that is required to introduce anti-racism into organizations came from a failure to listen to the voice of all stakeholders in organizational improvement. In this case predominantly black administrative staff's concerns were not listened to by white professionals. There is a cautionary tale here about addressing problems by building structures outside of mainstream activity in the organization. The appointment of a 'race' expert to deflect such problems allows the rest of the organization to avoid owning learning about anti-racism. If learning is not owned by all within the organization then it cannot become organizational learning. Institutional racism, so slippery as a concept, does help us understand that sometimes an organization can experience a problem such as endemic racism despite the best intentions of workers within it. There is a requirement for continuous collective learning within the concept of the learning organization which is an essential characteristic of organizational change and development.

Badwall, O'Connor and Rossiter also pose an interesting and pertinent question about the limits to reflection. Where there is disagreement reflective approaches may help, but conflict may require something different the chapter argues. Where there are relationships of power then who decides what will be dealt with in organizational processes is an important point. Nick Gould argues strongly in the introductory chapter for all that we have learnt about power in social work to be influential in the developing concept of the learning organization. If the normative learning organization is a democratic and inclusive structure then it will need to take seriously the relationships of power constructed by 'race', class, gender, disability, sexuality and age.

Ian Shaw, in his chapter on evaluation, presents another potential block to organizational learning where there is a belief in an organization that information counts as learning and knowledge created. He speaks of organizations in which information is disseminated in this way. Knowledge becomes learning and learning becomes knowledge in a dynamic process which is well documented elsewhere. When information is disseminated it is not necessarily learnt by its recipients because it may well not be understood, believed and owned by them. Only then might that information become knowledge in the sense of making a difference to people's practice. There is a strong parallel then with the notion of 'best practice' in which it becomes the norm that there is one way of doing things that is best. Neither approach is helpful in dealing with the diversity of problems and situations which we argue defines contemporary social care organizations.

I want now to move on to look at the opportunities for implementation of aspects of the learning organization in social care organizations. The chapter is entitled the art of the possible and that is what I want to end up by focusing upon. It is to be hoped that this book makes the case for the learning organization as a concept with some relevance for the future of social care organizations if they are to maintain their effectiveness in dealing with the kind of needs and wishes which service users present to them. So what do the chapters in this book tell us about what is possible, and what can we conclude would be appropriate action for individuals and organizations to foster in their future practice?

If managerialism is seen in the previous section as a major threat to the learning organization, then that does not mean that management cannot be a catalyst to the positive aspects of the concept. In his investigation of the part supervision plays in organizations, Jones suggests a management approach that facilitates the participation of the whole workforce. His persuasive argument suggests that the collation of reflections that occur within supervision could provide organizations with a wealth of knowledge to influence strategic decisions that managers have to make.

In another argument Jones explores the possibilities for what he refers to as 'network learning' in which the professional development and critical reflective aspects of supervision are sought elsewhere than from line managers. Practitioners would then, as Redmond, Fook, Allan and Sage, Thomas and I suggest in our respective chapters, become receivers and generators of knowledge. The sort of collective learning that these chapters all describe provides ample empirical evidence of what is possible when groups of practitioners involve themselves in critical reflection upon their practice. If nothing else, we have seen how such reflections can lead to the avoidance of rule-governed practice in favour of a practice that responds to uniqueness, diversity and change in the way social care organizations' mission statements claim they do.

I have argued above that power relationships in organizations are a major threat to the democratic and participative approach required for the learning organization. As is often the case, the threat is but one side of a coin. The other side is an opportunity in which recognizing power relationships, ensuring legitimation, building trust and shared communication between all stakeholders in an organization (service users, managers, support staff and practitioners) could build individual and organizational learning into complex social care settings such as multi-professional teams. Taylor makes this argument strongly in Chapter 5.

Taylor expands this thread by looking in some detail at the participation of service users in the development of services. She argues that such involvement can only increase learning for professionals, even if the current empirical evidence is of a painfully slow implementation of any real degree of such involvement. So, service user involvement is a major key to the development of useful learning by all stakeholders within social care organizations.

Bairbre Redmond's chapter provides a great sense of optimism for future development. Her reflective teaching model, in working with professional groups, enabled them to move beyond expert models which, in their analysis, were stifling effective practice. Greater responsiveness to service user need could only then be enhanced by greater involvement by service users in all aspects of organizational process. Again, however, we confront the problem for practitioners of taking this learning back into their organizations. Redmond argues strongly the case that practitioners can become change agents in their own organizations. However, while such critical reflection might reduce the degree of tacit or unreflective practice (Baldwin, 2000a) by individual social workers, there is a further jump to be made before this learning becomes embedded within organizational learning through Argyris and Schön's (1996) double-loop concept.

Another key area for future development is argued in both Shaw's chapter on evaluation and my own on co-operative inquiry. Shaw argues that it is the participatory nature of research and evaluation that is a key aspect of effective evaluation, especially if it is to have an effect on practice development. This has been a key aspect of my work too. I have argued here as well as elsewhere (Baldwin, 1998; 2000) that participation is important because, unless all stakeholders in an organization feel that knowledge being used has some meaning for them, they are unlikely to own it. This level of acceptance of knowledge is essential to learning becoming embedded in practice or service development.

Understanding and Taking Action

To suggest a blueprint for action at this point would be to undermine the principle we have argued in this book that there is no such thing. Organizational learning will occur, within broad principles, according to the circumstances of each separate organization. So what can people who work in organizations, or students of organizations look for as examples of effective implementation for organizational learning? I will end then, by listing the policy and organizational imperatives that will support any such attempts.

Critical Reflection

Evidence from the chapters in this book suggest strongly that critical reflection enables practitioners to analyse and adapt their practice in more effective directions. We would want to emphasize the necessity for such reflection to be critical in nature (Fook, 2002). In order to question accepted and powerful forms of practice and hold them up to scrutiny in the contemporary world of social care requires a challenging approach in a supportive environment. Some social workers are adept and good at this. Less effective social workers, especially those who are more susceptible to traditional professional or managerialist certainties, will require a great deal of assistance with this.

Embedding Critical Reflection within Organizations

We have observed how such critical reflection that changes individual practice can get lost as it is transferred back into organizational settings. Practitioners are struggling hard to fulfil a 'change agent' role in their organizations. They will continue to struggle unless senior managers recognize the worth of critical reflection as a tool for practice and service development, and provide space and time for it as a priority activity alongside other organizational concerns such as service delivery. As long as it is seen as less important, it will always be squeezed out by service delivery priorities in pressurized social care organizations. The notion of reflective practitioners being let down by unreflective organizations is an indictment of management failure to envision the bigger picture.

Encouraging Participation by All Stakeholders

This notion of democratic organizations that encourage participation and involvement can be seen as de rigueur in mission statements and the introduction of organizational good practice such as Investors in People in the UK. Such participation is a central aspect of the concept of the learning organization, if organizations are to connect individual and organizational learning. This means that there must be encouragement of developments from the bottom up as well as information and guidance in the other direction. Unless people at all levels in an organization understand what the organization is about, and have at least a degree of ownership of this, then knowledge for action in social care organizations will continue to be something which is imposed from above and undermined from below.

It also needs to be said, here, that encouragement of stakeholder involvement requires an analysis of power relationships to ensure that voices are not marginalized. Denial of any valid voice in an organization will again undermine organizational learning and development.

Service User Involvement

A special footnote to the previous point is that service user involvement is a key to organizational learning and development in the personal social services. Not only is this law, policy and good practice in social care in many countries around the world, it is becoming an increasingly effective catalyst for individual and organizational change. This is a major conclusion for this book.

Addressing Managerial Practice and Analysing its Effectiveness in Advancing General and Organizational Policy

Much of the evidence for blocks to organizational learning and the embedding of individual learning in organizations is placed at the door of managerial processes within this book. Although managers are in position to make decisions about organizational development, it would assist the making of effective decisions if organizations paid regard to the connections between managerial practice and organizational mission statement. In relation to supervision and the facilitation of critical reflection, this book provides ample evidence that management undermines these aspects of organizational behaviour. We do not believe this to be the fault of individual managers within social care organizations. The circumstances are much more complex than that, and we have to look more deeply at the ethos that underpins organizational culture to see where managerial practice is located. This is, as I have argued above, an instance of paradigm clash.

This is something which, outside any consideration of the effectiveness of organizational learning, will have to change if the lessons of the Climbié Report in the UK are to be taken seriously. Lord Laming's report is hardly the first to list professional supervision (not just the management of tasks and targets) as a key to preventing the lapses in practice that lead to child deaths. There is much in the learning that comes from this book which could assist organizations introduce the sort of changes that might reduce the likelihood of yet another such inquiry in years to come.

Conclusions

We have laid out what is, we feel, evidence that the learning organization is a useful concept for analysing social care organizations around the world. The concept gives pointers to what an effective social care organization might look like as well as a tool for critically evaluating how they currently are. The book also provides empirical and theoretical evidence about the learning organization which indicates just how effective it might be if implemented.

While there are probably more threats than opportunities at the current time, there are also an increasing array of legal and policy imperatives for organizations to take the implementation of aspects of the learning organization much more seriously. In the specific context of institutional racism, the guidance emanating from the Commission for Racial Equality in the UK, which is intended to enable local authorities to implement their duty to promote racial equality is clearly informed by concepts of involvement and continuing development and learning. Initiatives such as Investors in People, post-qualifying training, the new UK degree in social work and other initiatives on continuous professional development all point to the importance of organizations taking individual learning seriously as a catalyst to organizational learning and development. Many social care organizations profess to do as much in their mission statements.

The concept of service user involvement is also argued here as of fundamental importance in ensuring services continue to develop in effective ways. While service user views are not the only perspectives that are important, including them as of equal importance in consideration of strategic decision-making will make a substantial difference to the whole flavour of service development. A participative approach to organizational learning and development is, along with service user involvement, a key lesson from this book.

Finally, as social work moves towards greater professionalization in many quarters, so pointers to good organizational and individual learning such as that provided by the UK's General Social Care Council will emerge. The GSCC Codes of Practice provide the imperative for both employers and employees such as social workers to work together in alliance with the people who use their services, to ensure that those services provided through individual practice actually results in disadvantaged and marginalized people being able to take more positive control of their lives. The wit that stems from the knowledge and experience of social work practitioners, along with the optimism essential for a profession that is motivated by a sense of social justice, are our greatest assets. Working with others (managers and service users) in a participative fashion is the way forward.

Bibliography

Abbott, A. (1988), *The System of Professions: An Essay on the Division of the Expert Labour*, Chicago: University of Chicago Press.

Abbott, A. (1995), 'Boundaries of social work or social work of boundaries', *Social Service Review*, **4**, December, 545–62.

Adams, R. (2002), 'Developing critical practice in social work', in Adams, R., Dominelli, L. and Payne, M. (eds), *Critical Practice in Social Work*, Basingstoke: Palgrave.

Adams, R., Dominelli, L. and Payne, M. (eds) (2002), *Critical Practice in Social Work*, Basingstoke: Palgrave.

Agger, B. (1998), *Critical Social Theories*, Boulder, CO: Westview.

Aleszowski, A., Harrison, L. and Manthorpe, J. (1998), *Risk, Health and Welfare*, Buckingham: Open University Press.

Alvesson, M. (1998), 'Knowledge work: ambiguity, image and identity', in Cayley, L., 'Fostering effectiveness of work related training', unpublished PhD dissertation, University of Sussex.

Argyris, C. (1999), *On Organisational Learning*, 2nd edn, Oxford: Blackwell.

Argyris, C. and Schön, D. (1974) *Theory in Practice: Increasing Personal Effectiveness*, San Francisco, CA: Jossey Bass.

Argyris, C. and Schön, D. (1976), *Theory in Practice: Increasing Professional Effectiveness*, San Francisco, CA: Jossey-Bass.

Argyris, C. and Schön, D. (1978), *Organisational Learning: A Theory of Action Perspective*, Reading, MA: Addison-Wesley.

Askeland, G.A. (forthcoming) 'Focus on the facilitator'.

Argyris, C. and Schön, D. (1996), *Organisational Learning II: Theory, Method and Practice*, Reading, MA: Addison-Wesley.

Austin, M. (1988), '"Managing up" – relationship building between middle management and top management', *Administration in Social Work*, **12** (4), 29–46.

Auvinen, A. and Karvinen, S. (1993), *Työnohjaus, reflektiivisyys, kehitys. Sosiaalityön työnohjaajakoulutuksen perusteita (Supervision, Reflection, Development. Educating Social Work Supervisors)*, Center for Training and Development. Research Reports 1/1993, University of Kuopio.

Bachrach, P. and Baratz, M. (1962), 'The two faces of power', *American Political Science Review*, **56**, 947–52.

Baldwin, M. (1996), 'White anti-racism: is it really "no go" in rural areas?', *Social Work Education*, **15** (1), 18–33.

Baldwin, M. (1998), 'The positive use of discretion in social work practice: developing practice through co-operative inquiry', *Issues in Social Work Education*, **18** (2), 42–8.

177

Baldwin, M. (2000a), *Care Management and Community Care: Social Work Discretion and the Construction of Policy*, Aldershot: Ashgate.

Baldwin, M. (2000b), 'Learning to practice with the tensions between professional discretion and agency procedure', in Napier, L. and Fook, J. (eds), *Breakthroughs in Practice: Theorising Critical Moments in Social Work*, London: Whiting & Birch.

Baldwin, M. (2001), 'Working together, learning together: co-operative inquiry in the development of complex practice by teams of social workers', in Reason, P. and Bradbury, H. (eds), *Handbook of Action Research: Participatory Inquiry & Practice*, London: Sage.

Baldwin, M. (2002) 'New Labour and social care: continuity or change?', in Powell, M. (ed.), *Evaluating New Labour's Welfare Reforms*, Bristol: Policy Press.

Balloch, S. and Taylor, M. (eds) (2001), *Partnership Working Policy and Practice*, Bristol: Policy Press.

Banks, S. (1999), 'The social work professions and social policy: proactive or reactive?', *European Journal of Social Work*, **2** (3), 327–39.

Banks, S. (2001), *Ethics and Values in Social Work*, 2nd edn, Basingstoke: Palgrave.

Barlow, C., Coleman, H. and Rogers, G. (2000), 'Beyond orientation: a model for field instructor development and support', paper presented to the First European Conference on Practice Teaching and Field Education in Health and Social Work, York, UK, September.

Barnes, G.G., Down, G. and McCann, D. (2000), *Systemic Supervision. A Portable Guide to Supervision Training*, London: Jessica Kingsley.

Bateson, G. (1972), *Steps to an Ecology of Mind*, New York: Ballantine Books.

Bauman, Z. (1992), *The Intimations of Postmodernity*, London and New York: Routledge.

Beddoe, L. (1997), 'Best practice in social work supervision: education and accreditation issues', *Social Work Review*, **9** (4), 37–42.

Bell, D. (1973), *The Coming of Post-Industrial Society: A Venture in Social Forecasting*, New York: Basic Books.

Bell, L. and Webb, S. (1992), 'The invisible art of teaching for practice: social workers perceptions of taking students on placements', *Social Work Education*, **11** (1), 28–46.

Benner, P. (1984), *From Novice to Expert: Excellence and Power in Clinical Nursing Excellence*, Menlo Park, CA: Addison-Wesley.

Bereiter, C. (2002), *Education and the Mind in the Knowledge Age*. Mahwah, NJ: Erlbaum.

Besthorn, F. (2003), 'Radical ecologisms: insights for educating social workers in ecological activism and social justice', *Critical Social Work*, **3** (1), 66–107.

Beynon, H. (1973), *Working for Ford*, London: Penguin.

Birleson, P. (1999), 'Turning child and adolescent mental-health services into learning organisations', *Clinical Child Psychology and Psychiatry*, **4** (2), 265–74.

Bolam, L.G. and Deal, T.E. (1997), *Reframing Organizations: Artistry, Choice and Leadership*, 2nd edn, San Francisco, CA: Jossey-Bass.

Boud, D. (1995), *Enhancing Learning through Self Assessment*, London: Kogan Page.

Boud, D. (1999), 'Avoiding the traps: seeking good practice in the use of self-assessment and reflection in professional courses', *Social Work Education*, **16** (2), 121–32.

Boud, D. and Knights, S. (1996), 'Course design for reflective practice', in Gould, N. and Taylor, I. (eds), *Reflective Learning for Social Work*, Aldershot: Ashgate.

Boud, D. and Walker, D. (1998), 'Promoting reflection in professional courses: the challenge of context', *Studies in Higher Education*, **23** (2), 191–206.

Boud, D., Cohen, R. and Walker, D. (1993), *Using Experience for Learning*, Buckingham: Open University Press.

Boud, D., Keogh, R. and Walker, D. (eds) (1985), *Reflection: Turning Experience into Learning*, London: Kogan Page.

Braye, S. (2000), 'Participation and involvement in social care: an overview', in Kemshall, H. and Littlechild, R. (eds), *User Involvement and Participation: Research Informing Practice*, London: Jessica Kingsley.

Brew, A. (1999), 'Towards autonomous assessment: using self-assessment and peer assessment', in Brown, S. and Glasner, A. (eds), *Assessment Matters in Higher Education*, Buckingham: Open University Press.

Brockbank, A. and McGill, I. (1998), *Facilitating Reflective Learning in Higher Education*, Buckingham: SHRE and Open University Press.

Brookfield, S. (1987), *Developing Critical Thinkers*, San Francisco, CA: Jossey-Bass.

Brookfield, S. (1995), *Becoming a Critically Reflective Teacher*, San Francisco, CA: Jossey-Bass.

Brown, A. and Bourne, I. (1996), *Social Work Supervision*, Buckingham: Open University Press.

Bruce, E. and Austin, M. (2000), 'Social work supervision: assessing the past and mapping the future', *Clinical Supervisor*, **19** (2), 85–107.

Bunker, D.B. and Wijnberg, M.H. (1988), *Supervision and Performance: Managing Professional Work in Human Service Organizations*, San Francisco, CA: Jossey-Bass.

Butler, B. and Elliot, D. (1985), *Teaching and Learning for Practice*, Aldershot: Gower.

Capra, F. (2002), *The Hidden Connections: A Science for Sustainable Living*, London: HarperCollins.

Cayley, L. (2000), 'Fostering the effectiveness of work-related training', unpublished PhD dissertation, University of Sussex.

CCETSW (1995), 'Rules and Requirements for the Diploma in Social Work', Paper 30, London: The Stationery Office.

Challis, L. (1990), *Organising Public Social Services*, Harlow: Longman.

Chelimsky, E. (1997), 'Thoughts for a new evaluation society', *Evaluation*, **3** (1), 97–118.

Chief Secretary to the Treasury (2003), *Every Child Matters*, London: The Stationery Office.

Clare, M. (1988), 'Supervision, role strain and the Social Services Department', *British Journal of Social Work*, **18** (6), 489–507.

Clare, M. (2001), 'Operationalising professional supervision in this age of accountabilities', *Australian Social Work*, **54** (2), 69–79.

Clarke, J. and Newman, J. (1997), *The Managerial State*, London: Sage.

Clarke, J., Gerwitz, S and McLaughlin, E. (eds) (2000), *New Managerialism, New Welfare?* London; Sage.

Cochran-Smith, M. and Lytle, S. (1990), 'Research on teaching and teacher research: the issues that divide', *Educational Researcher*, **19** (2), 2–22.

Compton, D.W., Baizerman, M. and Stockdill, S.H. (eds) (2002), *The Art, Craft and Science of Evaluation Capacity Building New Directions for Evaluation*, no. 93, San Francisco, CA: Jossey-Bass.

Cooper, B. and Rixon, A. (2001), 'Integrating post-qualification study into the workplace: the candidate's experience, *Social Work Education*, **20** (6), 701–16.

Coulshed, V. and Mullender, A. (2001), *Management in Social Work*, 2nd edn,. Basingstoke: Palgrave.

Cowan, J. (1981), 'Struggling with self-assessment', in Boud, D (ed.), *Developing Student Autonomy in Learning*, New York: Kogan Page.

Crisp, B.R. and Green Lister, P. (2002), 'Assessment methods in social work education: a review of the literature', *Social Work Education*, **21** (2), 259–67.

Crozier, M. (1964), *The Bureaucratic Phenomenon*, Chicago, IL: University of Chicago Press.

Cunningham, C.C. and Davis, H. (1985), *Working with Parents: Frameworks for Collaboration*, Milton Keynes: Open University Press.

Dale, N. (1996) *Working with Families of Children with Special Needs – Partnership and Practice*, London: Routledge.

Dalrymple, J. and Burke, B. (1995), *Anti-Oppressive Practice: Social Care and the Law*, Buckingham: Open University Press.

Davies, H. and Kinloch, H. (2000), 'Critical incident analysis: facilitating reflection and transfer of learning', in Cree, V.E. and Macauley, C. (eds), *Transfer of Learning in Professional and Vocational Education*, London: Routledge.

Davies, M. (1977), *Support Systems in Social Work*, London: Routledge and Kegan Paul.

Davies, P. and Bynner, J. (1999), 'The impact of credit based systems on learning cultures', ESRC, Report of the Learning Society Programme, www.regard.ac.uk.

DeGale, H. (1991), 'Black Students' Views of Existing CQSW Courses and CSS Schemes: 2', in *Setting the Context for Change*, edited by Northern Curriculum Development Project, London: CCETSW.

Department for Education and Employment (DfEE) (1998), *The Learning Age: A Renaissance for a New Britain*, London: HMSO.

Department of Health (DoH) (1989), *Community Care in the Next Decade and Beyond*, London: HMSO.

Department of Health (DoH) (1998), *Modernising Social Services*, London: The Stationery Office.

Department of Health (DoH) (1999), *Quality Protects*, London: The Stationery Office.

Department of Health (DoH) (2001a), *Working Together Learning Together: A Framework for Lifelong Learning for the NHS*, London: HMSO.

Department of Health (DoH) (2001b), *Mental Health National Service Framework, Summary Report by Workforce Action Team on Workforce Planning, Education and Training*, London: HMSO.

Department of Health (DoH) (2001c), *Mental Health National Service Framework, Full Report by Workforce Action Team on Workforce Planning, Education and Training*, London: HMSO.

Department of Health (DoH) (2001d), *The Expert Patient: A New Approach to Chronic Disease Management for the 21st Century*, London: HMSO.

Department of Health (DoH) (2002a), *Modernising Services to Transform Care: Inspection of How Councils Are Managing the Modernisation Agenda in Social Care*, London: HMSO.

Department of Health/Social Services Inspectorate (2002b), *Modernising Mental Health Services, Inspection of Mental Health Services*, London: HMSO.

Department of the Environment, Transport and the Regions (DETR) (1999), *Supporting People*, London: The Stationery Office.

DeSouza, P. (1991), 'A review of experiences of black students in social work training', in *One Small Step Towards Racial Justice*, The National Steering Group on the Teaching of Race and Antiracism in the Personal Social Services, London: CCETSW.

Dick, E., Headrick, D. and Scott, M. (2002), *Practice Learning for Professional Skills: A Review of the Literature*, report commissioned by the Scottish Executive.

Doel, M. and Marsh, P. (1992), *Task-Centred Social Work*, Aldershot: Ashgate.

Doel, M., Shardlow, S., Sawdon, C. and Sawdon, D. (1996), *Teaching Social Work Practice*, Aldershot: Arena.

Dominelli, L. (1997), *Sociology for Social Work*, London: Macmillan.

Dominelli, L. and Hoogvelt, A. (1996), 'Globalisation and the technocratisation of social work', *Critical Social Policy*, **16** (2), 45–62.

Dovey, K. (1997), 'The learning organisation and the organisation of learning', *Management Learning*, **28** (3), 331–49.

Dreyfus, H. and Dreyfus, S. (1986), *Mind Over Machine: The Power of Human Intuition and Expertise in the Era of the Computer*, Oxford: Basil Blackwell.

Driver, M. (2002), 'The learning organization: Foucauldian gloom or utopian sunshine?', *Human Relations*, **55** (1), 33–53.

Easterby-Smith, M., Araujo, L. and Burgoyne, J. (eds) (1999), *Organisational Learning and the Learning Organisation*, London: Sage.

Eby, M. (2000), 'Understanding professional development', in Brechin, A., Brown, H. and Eby, M. (eds), *Critical Practice in Health and Social Care*, London: Sage.

Egelund, T. (1999), 'Om nordisk supervisionsteori – teoretisk orientering og organisatorisk forankring', *Nordisk Sosialt Arbeid*, (3), 138–48.

Egelund, T. and Kvilhaug, A. (2001), 'Supervisonens organisering', *Socialvetenskaplig tidskrift*, (3), 180–200.

Eisner, E. (1988), 'Educational connoisseurship and criticism: their form and functions in educational evaluation', in Fetterman, D.M. (ed.), *Qualitative Approaches to Evaluation in Education*, New York: Praeger.

Elliot, J. (1991), *Action Research for Educational Change*, Milton Keynes: Open University Press.

Engeström, Y. (1987), *Learning by Expanding: An Activity-Theoretical Approach to Developmental Research*, Helsinki: Orienta-Konsultit.

Engeström, Y. (1992), 'Interactive expertise: studies in distributed working intelligence', *Research Bulletin*, 83, Department of Education, University of Helsinki, Yliopistopaino.

Engeström, Y., Engeström, R. and Vähätalo, T. (1999), 'When the center does not hold: the importance of knotworking', in Chaickling, S., Hedegaard, M. and Juul Jensen, U. (eds), *Activity Theory and Social Practice*, Aarhus: Aarhus University Press.

Engeström, Y., Miettinen, R. and Ounamäki R. (eds) (1999), *Perspectives on Activity Theory*, Cambridge, MA: Cambridge University Press.

England, H. (1986), *Social Work as Art*, London: Allen & Unwin.

Epstein, L. (1980), *Helping People: The Task-Centred Approach*, St Louis, MO: CV Mosby.

Eräsaari, R. (2002), 'Avoimen asiantuntijuuden analytiikka', in Pirttilä, I. and Eriksson, S. (eds), *Asiantuntijoiden areenat*, Jyväskylä: SoPhi.

Eräsaari, R. (2003), 'Open-Context Expertise', in Bamme, A., Gertzinger, G. and Wieser, B. (eds), *Yearbook 2003 of the Institute for Advanced Studies on Science, Technology and Society*, Tecknik- und Wissenschaftsforschug (Science and Technology Studies) Vol. 41, München-Wien: Profil, 31–65.

Eraut, M. (1992), 'Developing the knowledge base: a process perspective on professional education', in Barnett, R. (ed.), *Learning to Effect*, Buckingham: Open University Press.

Eraut, M. (1994), *Developing Professional Knowledge and Competence*, London: Falmer Press.

Eraut, M. (2001), 'Learning Challenges for Knowledge-based Organisations', in Stevens, J. (ed.), *Workplace Learning in Europe*, London: Chartered Institute of Personnel and Development (CIPD).

Eraut, M. (2002), 'Conceptual analysis and research questions: do the concepts of "learning community" and "community of practice" provide added value?', paper presented at the Annual Conference of the American Educational Research Association, New Orleans, April.

Eraut, M., Alderton, J., Cole, G. and Senker, P. (1998), 'Learning from other people at work', in Coffield, F. (ed.), *Skill Formation*, Bristol: Policy Press.

Eraut, M., Alderton, J., Cole, G. and Senker, P. (1999), 'The impact of the manager on learning in the workplace', in Coffield, F. (ed.), *Research and Policy*, Bristol: Policy Press.

European Commission (1995), *Towards the Learning Society*, Brussels: European Union.

Evans, D. (1999), *Practice Learning in the Caring Profession*, Aldershot: Ashgate.

Fielding, M. (2001), 'Learning organisation or learning community? A critique of Senge', *Reason in Practice*, 1 (2), 17–29.

Fisher, M. (2002), 'The role of service users in problem formulation and technical aspects of social research', *Social Work Education*, 21 (3), 305–12.

Fisher, T. (1990), 'Competence in social work practice teaching', *Social Work Education*, 9 (2), 9–24.

Flood, R.L. (1999), *Rethinking the Fifth Discipline: Learning within the Unknowable*, London: Routledge.

Fook, J. (ed.) (1996), *The Reflective Researcher: Social Theories of Practice Research*, Sydney: Allen & Unwin.

Fook, J. (1999), 'Critical reflectivity in education and practice', in Pease, B. and Fook, J. (eds), *Transforming Social Work Practice: Postmodern Critical Perspectives*, London: Routledge.

Fook, J. (2000), 'Deconstructing and reconstructing professional expertise', in Fawcett, B. (ed.), *Practice and Research in Social Work: Postmodern Feminist Perspective*, London: Routledge.

Fook, J. (2002), *Social Work: Critical Theory and Practice*, London: Sage.

Fook, J., Ryan, M. and Hawkins, L. (1997), 'Towards a theory of social work expertise', *British Journal of Social Work*, **27**, 399–417.

Fook, J., Ryan, M. and Hawkins, L. (2000), *Professional Expertise: Practice, Theory and Education for Working in Uncertainty*, London: Whiting & Birch.

Foucault, M. (1997), *Ethics: Subjectivity and Truth*, New York: New Press.

Freire, P. (1972), *Pedagogy of the Oppressed*, London: Penguin.

Frydman, B., Wilson, I. and Wyer, J. (2000), *The Power of Collaborative Leadership: Lessons for the Learning Organisation*, Boston, MA: BH.

Gardiner, D. (1989), *The Anatomy of Supervision: Developing Learning and Professional Competence for Social Work Students*, Stratford: Open University Press.

General Social Care Council (2002), *Requirements for Social Work Training*, London: General Social Care Council.

George, M. (2002), 'Trust in social care', *Care and Health*, 16–29 October, 28–9.

Ghaye, T. and Lillyman, S. (1997), *Learning Journals and Critical Incidents: Reflective Practice for Health Care Professionals*, Wiltshire: Mark Allen Publishing.

Gherardi, S. (1999) 'Learning as problem-driven or learning in the face of mystery', *Organization Studies*, **20** (1), 101–24.

Gibbs, J.A. (2001), 'Maintaining front-line workers in child protection: a case for refocusing supervision', *Child Abuse Review*, **10** (5), 323–35.

Giddens, A. (1984), *Yhteiskuntateorian keskeisiä ongelmia (Central Problems in Social Theory: Action, Structure and Construction in Social Analyses)*, Keuruu: Otava.

Gillborn, D. (1995), *Racism and Anti-Racism in Real Schools*, Buckingham: Open University Press.

Gonczi, A. and Hager, P. (1998), 'Development of professional competencies – a case study in the complexities of corporatist policy implementation', in Yeatman, A. (ed.), *Activism and the Policy Process*, Sydney: Allen & Unwin.

Gould, N. (1996), 'Introduction: social work education and the "Crisis of the Professions"', in Gould, N. and Taylor, I. (eds), *Reflective Learning for Social Work*, Aldershot: Arena.

Gould, N. (1999), 'Qualitative practice evaluation', in Shaw, I. and Lishman, J. (eds), *Evaluation and Social Work Practice*, London: Sage.

Gould, N. (2000), 'Becoming a learning organisation: a social work example', *Social Work Education*, **19** (6), 585–96.

Gould, N. (2003), 'The caring professions and information technology: in search of a theory', in Harlow, E. and Webb, S.A. (eds), *Information and Communication Technologies in the Welfare State*, London: Jessica Kingsley.

Gould, N. and Taylor I. (eds) (1996), *Reflective Learning for Social Work*, Aldershot: Arena.

Greene, J. (2001), 'Evaluation extrapolations', *American Journal of Evaluation*, **22** (3), 397–402.

Gregory, R. (1997), 'The peculiar tasks of public management', in Considine, M. and Painter, M. (eds), *Managerialism: The Great Debate*, Melbourne: Melbourne University Press.

Guttman, E., Eisikowits, Z. and Malucchio, A. (1988), 'Enriching social work supervision from the competence perspective', *Journal of Social Work Education*, Fall (3), 27–88.

Habermas, J. (1972), *Knowledge and Human Interests*, London: Heinemann.

Habermas, J. (1984), *Theory of Communicative Action*, Boston, MA: Beacon Press. (First published as *Theorie des kommunikativen Handelns*, 2 vols, Frankfurt: Suhrkamp in 1981.)

Habermas, J. (1987), *The Theory of Communicative Action, Vol 2: Lifeworld and the Rationalization of Society*, Boston, MA: Beacon Press.

Hakkarainen, K., Paavola, S. and Lipponen, L. (2002), 'Käytäntöyhteisöistä innovatiivisiin tietoyhteisöihin' ('From the communities of practice towards innovative knowledge communities'), forthcoming (article submitted for publication), www.helsinki.fi/science/networkedlearning.

Hakkarainen, K., Palonen, T., Murtonen, M., Paavola, S. and Lehtinen, E. (2003), 'Assessing networked expertise: a multi-level inventory', University of Helsinki and University of Turku, forthcoming (article submitted for publication). www.helsinki.fi/science/networkedlearning.

Hall, T. (2001), 'Caught not taught: ethnographic research at a young peoples' accommodation project', in Shaw, I. and Gould, N. (eds), *Qualitative Research in Social Work*, London: Sage.

Handy, C. (1989), *The Age of Unreason*, London: Arrow Business Books.

Harlow, E. (2000), 'New managerialism and women: changing women's lives', in Harlow, E. and Lawlor, I. (eds), *Management, Social Work and Change*, Aldershot: Ashgate.

Harris, J. (1998), 'Scientific management, bureau-professionalism and new managerialism: the labour process of state social work', *British Journal of Social Work*, **28** (6), 839–62.

Hartman, A. (1978), 'Diagrammatic assessment of family relationships', *Social Casework*, **55**, October, 465–76.

Hartman, A. and Laird, J. (1983), *Family Centred Social Work Practice*, New York: Free Press.

Hawkins, P. and Shohet, R. (1989), *Supervision in the Helping Professions*, Milton Keynes: Open University Press.

Hawkins, P. and Shohet, R. (2000), *Supervision in the Helping Professions*, 2nd edn, Buckingham: Open University Press.

Hay, J. (1992), *TA for Trainers*, London: McGraw-Hill.

Healy, K. (2000), *Social Work Practices: Contemporary Perspectives on Change*, London: Sage.

Hearn, J. (1992), *Men in the Public Eye: The Construction and Deconstruction of Public Men and Public Patriarchies*, London: Routledge.

Heikkilä, M., Kaakinen, J. and Korpelainen, N. (2003), Kansallinen sosiaalialan kehittämisprojekti (The National Programme for Social Welfare). Helsinki: STM.

Heron, B. (2000), 'Taking it to heart: whiteness and claims to a non-racist self', paper presented at the era21 (End Racism! Activism for the 21st Century) conference in Vancouver, Canada, November.

Heron, J. (1981), 'Assessment revisited', in Boud, D. (ed.), *Developing Student Autonomy in Learning*, New York: Kogan Page.

Heron, J. (1996), *Co-operative Inquiry: Research into the Human Condition*, London; Sage.

Heron, J. and Reason, P. (2001) 'The practice of co-operative inquiry: research "with" rather than "on" people', in Reason, P. and Bradbury, H. (eds), *Handbook of Action Research*, London; Sage.

Hess, P. (1995), 'Reflecting in and on practice', in Hess, P. and Mullen, E.J. (eds), *Practitioner–Researcher Partnerships*, Washington, DC: NASW.

Hess, P. and Mullen, E.J. (eds) (1995), *Practitioner–Researcher Partnerships*, Washington, DC: NASW.

Heywood, F. (2001), *Money Well Spent: The Effectiveness and Value of Housing Adaptations*, Bristol: Policy Press.

Hill, M. (ed.) (1993), *The Policy Process: A Reader*, Hemel Hempstead: Prentice-Hall.

Hinett, K. and Thomas, J. (1999), *Staff Guide to Self and Peer Assessment*, Oxford: Centre for Staff Development.

Hinks, N. (2000), 'Introducing a culture of reflective learning in a non-statutory social work agency: an action inquiry', in Napuer, L. and Fook, J. (eds), *Breakthroughs in Practice: Theorising Critical Moments in Social Work*, London: Whiting & Birch.

Hogwood, B. and Gunn, L. (1984), *Policy Analysis for the Real World*, Oxford: Oxford University Press.

Hough, G. (1996), 'Using ethnographic methods to research the work world of social workers in child protection', in Fook, J. (ed.), *The Reflective Researcher: Social Workers' Theories of Practice Research*, Sydney: Allen & Unwin.

Hough, G. (2003), 'Enacting critical social work in public welfare contexts', in Allan, J., Pease, B. and Briskman, L. (eds), *Critical Social Work: An Introduction to Theories and Practices*, Crows Nest, NSW: Allen & Unwin.

House, E. (1980), *Evaluating with Validity*, Beverly Hills, CA: Sage.

House, E. and Howe, K. (1999), *Values and Evaluation*, Thousand Oaks, CA: Sage.

House, E., Haug, C. and Norris, N. (1996), 'Producing evaluations in a large bureaucracy', *Evaluation*, **2** (2), 135–50.

Howe, D. (1987), *An Introduction to Social Work Theory*, Aldershot: Ashgate.

Howe, D. (1996), *Surface and Depth in Social Work Practice*, London: Routledge.

Huber, G. (1991), 'Organizational learning: the contributing processes and the literatures', *Organization Science*, **2** (1), 88–115.

Hudson, B. (ed.) (2000), *The Changing Role of Social Care*, London: Jessica Kingsley.

Hughes, L. and Pengelly, P. (1997), *Staff Supervision in a Turbulent Environment: Managing Process and Task in Front-Line Services*, London: Jessica Kingsley.

Hugman, R. (1991), *Power in Caring Professions*, Basingstoke: Macmillan.

Humphrey, J. (2002), 'Joint reviews: retracing the trajectory, decoding the terms', *British Journal of Social Work*, **32** (4), 463–76.

Humphries, B. (1988), 'Adult learning in social work education: towards liberation or domestication?', *Critical Social Policy*, **23**, Autumn, 4–21.

Hyrkäs, K. (2002), 'Clinical supervision and quality care: examining the effects of team supervision in multi-professional teams', PhD dissertation, Acta Universitatis Tamperensis 869, University of Tampere.

Ife, J. (1997), *Rethinking Social Work: Towards Critical Practice*, Melbourne: Longman.

Ife, J. (2001), *Human Rights and Social Work: Towards Rights Based Practice*, Cambridge: Cambridge University Press.

Isaac-Henry, K., Painter, C. and Barnes, C. (1997), *Management in the Public Sector*, 2nd edn, London: International Thompson Business Press.

Issit, M. (1999), 'Towards the development of anti-oppressive reflective practice: the challenge for multi-disciplinary working', *Journal of Practice Teaching in Health and Social Work*, **2** (2), 21–36.

Ixer, G. (1999), 'There's no such thing as reflection', *British Journal of Social Work*, **29** (4), 513–27.

James, A. (1994), *Managing to Care: Public Services and the Market*, Harlow: Longman.

Janesick, V.J. (1998), *'Stretching' Exercises for Qualitative Researchers*, Thousand Oaks, CA: Sage.

Jarvinen, A., and Kohonen, V. (1995), 'Promoting Professional Development in Higher Education through Portfolio Assessment', *Assessment and Evaluation in Higher Education*, **20** (1) 25–36.

Jones, A. and May, J. (1992), *Working in Human Service Organisations: A Critical Introduction*, Melbourne: Longman.

Jones, M. (1999), 'Supervisor or superhero: new role strains for frontline supervisors in human services', *Asia Pacific Journal of Social Work*, **9** (1), 79–97.

Jones, M. (2000), 'Hope and despair at the front-line: integrity and change in the human services', *International Social Work*, **43** (3), 365–80.

Jones, M. and Jordan, B. (1996), 'Knowledge and practice in social work', in Preston-Shoot, M. and Jackson, S. (eds), *Educating Social Workers in a Changing Policy Context*, London: Whiting & Birch.

Jordan, B. (1998), *The New Politics of Welfare: Social Justice in a Global Context*, London: Sage.

Jordan, B., with Jordan, C. (2000), *Social Work and the Third Way: Tough Love as Social Policy*, London: Sage.

Juuti, P. (1999), 'Ohjauksellinen näkökulma organisaatioiden johtamisessa' ('The mentoring and supervisory view in organizational leadership'), in Onnismaa, J.,

Pasanen, H. and Spangar, T. (eds), *Ohjaus ammattina ja oppialana: Ohjauksen toimintakentät*, Jyvaskyla: PS-Kustannus.

Kadushin, A. (1968), 'Games people play in supervision', *Social Work*, **13** (3), 23–32.

Kadushin, A. (1992), *Supervision in Social Work*, 3rd edn, New York: Columbia University Press.

Kadushin, A. and Harkness, D. (2002), *Supervision in Social Work*, 4th edn, New York: Columbia University Press.

Karvinen, S. (1987), *Sosiaalityön ajolähtö. Sosiaalityön ohjausprojekti. Sosiaalihallituksen julkaisuja (The Crisis of Social Work. Developing Management and Supervision in Social Work)*, Helsinki: Department of Social Welfare.

Karvinen, S. (1993), 'Kehittävä työnohjaus sosiaalityön reflektiivisen ammatillisuuden edistäjänä – työnohjausteorian hahmotusta' ('Outlines for a theory of supervision'), in Auvinen, A. and Karvinen, S., *Työnohjaus, reflektiivisyys, kehitys. Sosiaalityön työnohjaajakoulutuksen perusteita. (Supervision, reflection, development. Educating Social Work Supervisors)*, Kuopio: University of Kuopio, Koulutus- ja kehittämiskeskus. Tutkimuksia ja selvityksiä 1/1993.

Karvinen, S. (1996), 'Sosiaalityön ammatillisuus modernista professionaalisuudesta refleksiiviseen asiantuntijuuteen' ('Social work professional competence from modernity towards reflective expertise'), in Karvinen, S., *Sosiaalityön ammatillisuus modernista professionaalisuudesta reflektiiviseen asiantuntijuuteen (The Ideas of Professional Method and Reflective Practice in Social Work from Modern Professionalism to New Expertise)*, Kuopio: Kuopio University Publications E, Social Sciences.

Karvinen, S. (1999), 'The methodological tensions in Finnish social work research', in Karvinen, S., Pösö, T. and Satka, M. (eds), *Reconstructing Social Work Research: Finnish Methodological Adaptations*, Jyväskylä: SoPhi, pp. 277–303.

Kearney, P. (1996), *The Management of Practice Expertise: Project Report*, London: National Institute for Social Work.

Kemmis, S. (1985), 'The politics of reflection', in Boud, D., Keogh, R. and Walker, D. (eds), *Reflection: Turning Experience into Learning*, London: Kogan Page.

Kemp, E. (2001), 'Observing practice as participant observation: linking theory to practice', *Social Work Education*, **20** (5) 527–37.

Kincheloe, J.L. (1991), *Teachers as Researchers: Qualitative Enquiry as a Path to Empowerment*, London: Falmer Press.

Kirk, S. and Reid, W. (2002), *Science and Social Work: A Critical Appraisal*, New York: Columbia University Press.

Kolb, D. (1984), *Experiential Learning: Experience as the Source of Learning and Development*, Englewood Cliffs, NJ: Prentice-Hall.

Kramer, R.M. (1999), 'Social uncertainty and collective paranoia in knowledge communities: thinking and acting in the shadow of doubt', in Thompson, L.L., Levine, J.M. and Messic, D.M. (eds), *Shared Cognition in Organizations: The Management of Knowledge*, Mahwah, NJ: Erlbaum.

Laming, Lord (2003), *The Victoria Climbié Inquiry: Report of an Inquiry by Lord Laming Presented to Parliament by the Secretary of State for Health and the Secretary of State for the Home Department*, London: The Stationery Office.

Lant, T.K. and Mezias, S.J. (1996) 'An organizational learning model of convergence and reoreintation', in Cohen, M.D. and Sproull, L.S. (eds), *Organisational Learning*, London: Sage.

Laragy, C. (1997), 'Social workers in the year 2000', *Asia Pacific Journal of Social Work*, **7** (1), 47–58.

Latour, B. and Woolgar, S. (1979), *Laboratory Life: The Social Construction of Scientific Facts*, Sage: London.

Lave, J. and Wenger, E. (1991), *Situated Learning: Experience as a Source of Learning and Development*, Englewood Cliffs, NJ: Prentice-Hall.

Le Grand, J. and Bartlett, W. (eds) (1993), *Quasi-Markets and Social Policy*, Basingstoke: Macmillan.

Leathard, A. (ed.) (1994), *Going Inter-Professional: Working Together for Health and Welfare*, London: Routledge.

Lewis, J. and Glennester, H. (1996), *Implementing the New Community Care*, Buckingham: Open University Press.

Lewis, J.A., Lewis, M.D., Packard, T. and Souflee, F. (2001), *Management of Human Service Programs*, 3rd edn, Stamford, CA: Wadsworth.

Lewis, S. (1998), 'Educational and organisational contexts of professional supervision in the 1990s', *Australian Social Work*, **51** (3), 31–9.

Lindblom, C. (1988), *Democracy and Market Systems*, Oslo: Norwegian University Press.

Lindsey, J. (1988), *Research into the Careers of Practice Teachers*, London: Kingston University.

Lipsky, M. (1980), *Street Level Bureaucrats: Dilemmas of the Individual in Public Services*, New York: Russell Sage Foundation.

Lister, R. (1998), 'Citizenship on the margins: citizenship, social work and social action', *European Journal of Social Work*, **1**, 5–18.

Longworth, N. and Davies, W. (1996), *Lifelong Learning: New Visions, New Implications, New Roles for People, Organisations, Nations and Communities in the 21st Century*, London: Kogan Page.

Lorenz, W. (2003), 'Understanding the "Other": European perspectives on the ethics of social work research and practice', forthcoming.

Lukes, S. (1974), *Power: A Radical View*, Basingstoke: Macmillan.

Macdonald, G. (2000), 'Social care: rhetoric and reality', in Davies, H., Nutley, S. and Smith, P. (eds), *What Works? Evidence-Based Policy and Practice in Public Services*, Bristol: Policy Press.

Macdonald, G. (2002), 'Transformative unlearning: safety, discernment and communities of learning', *Nursing Inquiry*, **9** (3), 170–78.

Majone, G. (1989), *Evidence, Argument and Persuasion in the Policy Process*, New Haven, CT: Yale University Press.

Malpass, P. and Murie, A. (eds) (1999), *Housing Policy and Practice*, London: Macmillan.

Mandy, P. (1996), 'Interdisciplinary rather than multidisciplinary or generic practice', *British Journal of Therapy and Rehabilitation*, **3**, 110–12.

Manthorpe, J. (2002), 'Settlements and social work education: absorption and accommodation', *Social Work Education*, **21** (4), 409–18.

Margerison, C. (1994), 'Action learning and excellence in management development', in Mabey, C. and Iles, P. (eds), *Managing Learning*, London: International Thomson.

Marshall, J. and McLean, A. (1988), 'Reflection in action: exploring organisational culture', in Reason, P. (ed.), *Human Inquiry in Action*, London: Sage.

Marsick, V. (ed.) (1987), *Learning in the Workplace*, London: Croom Helm.

Maslow, A. (1968), *Towards a Psychology of Being*, New York: Van Nostrand.

Masschelein, J. (1991), 'The relevance of Habermas's communicative turn', *Studies in Education*, **11**, 95–111.

Mattaini, M.A. and Meyer, C. (1995), *The Foundations of Social Work Practice*, Washington, DC: NASW.

McConachie, H. (1994) 'Changes in family roles', in Mittler, P. and Mittler, H. (eds), *Innovations in Family Support for People with Learning Disabilities*, Chorley: Lisieux Hall.

McGoldrick, M. and Gerson, R. (1985), *Genograms in Family Situations*, New York: W.W. Norton.

McLaren, P. (1993), 'Multiculturalism and the postmodern critique: towards a pedagogy of resistance and transformation', *Cultural Studies*, **7** (1), 118–46.

McLaren, P. (1994), 'Critical pedagogy, political agency, and the pragmatics of justice: the case of Lyotard', *Educational Theory*, **44** (3), 319–40.

Means, R. and Smith, R. (1994), *Community Care, Policy and Practice*, Basingstoke: Macmillan.

Means, R., Brenton, M. and Harrison, L. (1997), *Making Partnerships Work in Community Care: A Guide for Practitioners in Housing, Health and Social Services*, Bristol: Policy Press.

Mezirow, J. (1981), 'A critical theory of adult learning and education', *Adult Education*, **32** (1), 3–24.

Mezirow, J. (1991), *Transformative Dimensions of Adult Learning*, San Francisco, CA: Jossey-Bass.

Middleman, R. and Rhodes, G. (1985), *Competent Supervision*, Englewood Cliffs, NJ: Prentice-Hall.

Miettinen, R. (1998), 'Materiaalinen ja sosiaalinen: Toimijaverkkoteoria ja toiminnan teoria innovaatioiden tutkimuksessa' ('Material and social: actor network theory and action theory in the research on innovations'), *Sosiologia*, 1/1998, 28–42.

Milburn, A. (2002), 'Reforming social services', paper presented to National Social Services Conference, Cardiff, 17 October.

Miller, C. (2002), 'Individual beliefs about clinical teamworking and their impact on interprofessional work and learning', paper presented at the Annual Conference of the American Educational Research Association, New Orleans, April.

Miller, C., Ross, N. and Freeman, M. (2001), *Interprofessional Practice in Health and Social Care: Challenging the Shared Learning Agenda*, London: Arnold.

Mitchell, C. (2001), 'Partnership for continuing professional development: the impact of the Post Qualifying Award for Social Workers (PQSW) on social work practice', *Social Work Education*, **20** (4), 433–45.

Mittler, P. and Mittler, H. (1983) 'Partnership with parents, an overview', in Mittler, P. and McConachie, H. (eds), *Parents, Professionals and Mentally Handicapped People*, London: Croom Helm.

Moffat, K. (1996), 'Teaching social work as a reflective process', in Gould, N. and Taylor, I. (eds), *Reflective Learning for Social Work*, Aldershot: Arena.

Morgan, G. and Burrell, G. (1979), *Sociological Paradigms and Organisational Analysis: Elements of the Sociology of Corporate Life*, Aldershot: Ashgate.

Morrison, K. (1996), 'Developing reflective practice in higher degree students through a learning journal', *Studies in Higher Education*, **21** (3), 317–32.

Morrison, T. (1993), *Staff Supervision in Social Care: An Action Learning Approach*, Harlow: Longman.

Morrison, T. (1997), 'Learning, training and change in child protection work: towards reflective organisations', *Social Work Education*, **16** (2), 20-43.

Morrison, T. (2001), *Staff Supervision in Social Care: Making a Real Difference for Staff and Service Users*, 2nd edn, Brighton: Pavilion.

Muetzelfeldt, M. (2001), 'Managing professionalism and organisational learning between state agencies and non-profit human service providers: Australian experience and possibilities', paper presented at the Fifth International Research Symposium on Public Management, Barcelona, 9–11 April.

Muetzelfeldt, M. and Briskman, L. (2000), 'Market rationality, organisational rationality and professional rationality: experiences from the "Contract State"', paper presented at the conference Playing the Market Game? Governance Models in Child and Youth Welfare, University of Bielefeld, 9–11 March.

Muetzelfeldt, M., Briskman, L. and Jones, M. (2002), 'Brokering knowledge: managing knowledge in a network of government and non-government human service delivery agencies', in Considine, M. (ed.), *Knowledge, Networks and Joined-Up Government: Conference Proceedings*, Melbourne: University of Melbourne.

Napier, L. and Fook, J. (eds) (2000), *Breakthroughs in Practice: Social Workers Theorise Critical Moments in Practice*, London: Whiting & Birch.

Närhi, K., Matthies, A. and Ward, D. (eds) (2002), *Eco-Social Approach in Social Work*, Jyväskylä: SoPhi.

Newman, J. (2000), 'Beyond the new public management? Modernizing public services', in Clarke, J., Gewirtz, S. and McLaughlin, E. (eds), *New Managerialism, New Welfare?* London: Sage.

Nonaka, I., Toyama, R. and Konno, N. (2000), 'SECI, Ba and leadership: a unified model of dynamic knowledge creation', *Long Range Planning*, **33**, 5–34.

Nordlander, L. and, Norlander, B. (2002), 'How social workers reason about the work with clients and its conditions – an explorative case study', paper presented at the Fourth International Conference on Evaluation for Practice, Tampere, Finland, 4–6 July.

Nowotny, H. (2000), 'Transgressive competence. the narrative of expertise', *European Journal of Social Theory*, **3** (1), 5–21.

Nyhan, B., Cressey, P., Tomassini, M., Kelleher, M. and Poell, R. (2003), *Facing up to the Learning Organisation Challenge: Key Issues from a European Perspective*, vol. 1, Thessaloniki: CEDEFOP.

O'Neill, O. (2002), *A Question of Trust: BBC Reith Lectures 2002*, Cambridge: Cambridge University Press.

Ovretveit, J. (1993), *Co-ordinating Community Care: Multidisciplinary Teams and Care Management*, Buckingham: Open University Press.

Owen, J.M. and Lambert, F.C. (1995), 'Roles for evaluation in learning organisations', *Evaluation*, **1** (2), 237–50.

Papell, C. (1976), *Process Recording Revisited: A Contemporary Look at the Unique and Much Taken for Granted Instrument for Social Work Learning*, paper presented at the Annual Spring Meeting of Field Instructors, May.

Papell, C. and Skolnik, L. (1992), 'The reflective practitioner: a contemporary paradigm's relevance for social work education', *Journal of Social Work Education*, **28** (1), 18–25.

Parton, N. (1994), 'The nature of social work under conditions of (post)modernity', *Social Work & Social Sciences Review*, **5** (2), 93–112.

Parton, N. (1998), 'Risk, advanced liberalism and child welfare: the need to rediscover uncertainty and ambiguity', *British Journal of Social Work*, **28** (1), 5–27.

Parton, N. and O'Byrne, P. (2000), *Constructive Social Work*, London: Macmillan.

Patton, M.Q. (1999), 'Organisational development and evaluation', *Canadian Journal of Program Evaluation*, special issue, 93–113.

Patton, M.Q. (2001), 'Evaluation, knowledge management, best practices, and high quality lessons learned', *American Journal of Evaluation*, **22** (3), 329–36.

Payne, M. (1991), *Modern Social Work Theory: A Critical Introduction*, Basingstoke: Macmillan.

Payne, M. (1997), *Modern Social Work Theory*, 2nd edn, Basingstoke: Macmillan.

Payne, M. (1999), 'Social construction in social work and social action', in Jokinen, A., Juhila, K. and Pösö, T. (eds), *Constructing Social Work Practices*, Aldershot: Ashgate.

Payne, M. (2000), *Teamwork in Multiprofessional Care*, Basingstoke: Macmillan.

Peck, E. and Barker, P. (1997), 'Users as partners in mental health – ten years of experience', *Journal of Interprofessional Care*, **11** (3), 269–77.

Peck, E., Gulliver, P. and Towell, D. (2002), *Modernising Partnerships: An Evaluation of Somerset's Innovations in the Commissioning and Organisation of Mental Health Services; Final Report*, London: Kings College.

Peltola, T. and Åkerman, M. (1999), *Toimijuus, verkostot ja valta toimijaverkkoteoriassa (Agency, Networks and Power in the Actor Network Theory)*, Finland: University of Tampere, World Wide Web publication.

Pernell, R.B. (1986) 'Empowerment and social group work', in Parnes, M. (ed.), *Innovations in Social Group Work: Feedback for Practice to Theory*, New York: Hayworth.

Phillipson, J. (1992), *Practising Equality: Women, Men and Social Work*, London: CCETSW.

Phillipson, J. (2002), 'Supervision and being supervised', in Adams, R., Dominelli, L. and Payne, M., *Critical Practice in Social Work*, Basingstoke: Palgrave.

Pincus, A. and Minihan, A. (1973), *Social Work Practice Model and Method*, Ithaca, IL: Peacock.

Platt, D. (2001), *Modern Social Services 10th Annual Report of the Chief Inspector of Social Services*, London: Department of Health.

Pottage, D. and Evans, M. (1994), *The Competent Workplace: The View from Within*, London: NISW.

Preskill, H. and Torres, R.T. (1999a), 'Building capacity for organisational learning through evaluative inquiry', *Evaluation*, **5** (1), 42–60.

Preskill, H. and Torres, R.T. (1999b), *Evaluative Inquiry for Learning in Organizations*, Thousand Oaks, CA: Sage.

Preston-Shoot, M. (1996), 'On retaining a reflective space: making sense of interactions in work and work groups', *Journal of Social Work*, **10** (1), 11–21.

Preston-Shoot, M. and Jackson, S. (1996), 'Social work education in a changing policy context: an introduction', in Preston-Shoot, M. and Jackson, S. (eds), *Educating Social Workers in a Changing Policy Context*, London: Whiting & Birch.

Pritchard, P. and Pritchard, J. (1994), *Teamwork for Primary and Shared Care: A Practical Workbook*, 2nd edn, Oxford: Oxford University Press.

Pugh, R. and Gould, N. (2000), 'Globalization, social work and social welfare', *European Journal of Social Welfare*, **3** (2), 123–38.

Raitakari, S. (2002), 'Sosiaalityön marginaalistatus. Asiakkuus ja asiantuntijuus modernin ja postmodernin tulkintakehyksessä' ('Marginalisation and social work. Clients and experts in Frame of Postmodernity'), in Juhila, K., Forsberg, H. and Roivainen, I. (eds), *Marginals and Social Work: Social Work Research Yearbook 2001*, The Finnish Society of Social Work Research and the Finnish Professional Union of Social Workers, Jyväkylä: SoPhi.

Ranson, S. and Stewart, J. (1994) *Management for the Public Domain: Enabling the Learning Society*, Basingstoke: Macmillan.

Raunio, K. (2002), 'Managerismi – haaste sosiaalityön autonomiselle asiantuntijuudelle' ('Managerialism as a challenge to the autonomy of social work expertise'), *Yhteiskuntapolitiikka*, **67** (6), 600–603.

Razack, S. (1998). 'To essentialize or not to essentialize', in S. Razack, *Looking White People in the Eye*, Toronto: University of Toronto Press.

Read, J. (2000), *Disability, the Family and Society: Listening to Mothers*, Buckingham: Open University Press.

Reamer, F. (ed.) (1994), *The Foundations of Social Work Knowledge*, New York: Columbia University Press.

Reason, P. (ed.) (1994), *Participation in Human Inquiry*, London: Sage.

Reason, P. and Bradbury, H. (2000), *Handbook of Action Research*, London: Sage.

Redmond, B. (1996), *Listening to Parents – the Aspirations, Expectations and Anxieties of Parents about their Teenagers with Learning Disability*, Dublin: Family Studies Centre, University College Dublin.

Redmond, B. (1997) 'Family services – power or patronage?', *Irish Social Worker*, **15** (4), Winter.

Redmond, B. and McEvoy, J. (2002), 'Learning to change: a study of perceived changes in attitudes and practice of staff following their completion of a postgraduate diploma in intellectual disability studies', paper given at IASSID Europe Conference, Dublin, June.

Reed, M. (1995), 'Managing quality and organisational politics: TQM as a governmental technology', in Kirkpatrick, I. and Lucio Martinez, M. (eds), *The Politics of Quality in the Public Sector*, London: Routledge.

Reid, B. (2001), 'Partnership and change in social housing', in Balloch, S. and Taylor, M. (eds), *Partnership Working*, Bristol: Policy Press.

Revans, R. (1980), *Action Learning: New Techniques for Management*, London: Blond & Biggs.

Riessman, C.K. (1994), 'Preface: making room for diversity in social work research' in Riessman, C.K. (ed.), *Qualitative Studies in Social Work Research*, Thousand Oaks, CA: Sage.

Rosenman, L. (2000), 'Turning threats into challenges: a positive perspective on the future', in O'Connor, I., Smyth, P. and Warburton, J. (eds), *Contemporary Perspectives on Social Work and the Human Services: Challenges and Change*, Malaysia: Longman.

Ruch, G. (2002), 'From triangle to spiral: reflective practice in social work education, practice and research', *Social Work Education*, **21** (2), 199–216.

Saaristo, K. (2000), *Avoin asiantuntijuus. Ymparistokysymys ja monimuotoinen ekspertiisi (Open Expertise. The Environmental Question and Multiple Expertise)*, Research Center for Contemporary Culture, University of Jyväskylä.

Sackett, D.L, Roseburg, W.M., Gray, J.A.M., Haynes, R.B. and Richardson, W.S. (1996), 'Evidence based practice: what it is and what it isn't', *British Medical Journal*, **312** (7023), 71–2.

Salonen, J. (2003), 'Miten sosiaalityön työnohjausta tutkitaan. Katsaus empiiriseen tutkimukseen' ('How to research social work supervision. A review on empirical research'), unpublished paper given at the conference on supervision, Hämeenlinna, Finland, August.

Sanders, C. (2002), 'Harassed, pulled every which way, but committed to her workers', *Times Higher Education Supplement*, 7 June.

Satka, M. and Karvinen, S. (1999), 'The contemporary reconstruction of Finnish social work expertise', *European Journal of Social Work*, **2** (2), 119–29.

Satyamurti, C. (1981), *Occupational Survival: The Case of the Local Authority Social Worker*, Oxford: Blackwell.

Scarborough, H. (ed.) (1996), *The Management of Expertise*, London: Macmillan.

Schein, E. (1992), *Organisational Culture and Leadership*, 2nd edn, San Francisco, CA: Jossey-Bass.

Schein, E. (1994), *Organisational Psychology*, 3rd edn, Englewood Cliffs, NJ: Prentice-Hall.

Schein, E.H. (1989), *Organisational Psychology*, Englewood Cliffs, NJ: Prentice-Hall.

Schön, D.A. (1983), *The Reflective Practitioner: How Professionals Think in Action*, New York: Basic Books.

Schön, D.A. (1987), *Educating the Reflective Practitioner: Towards a New Design for Teaching and Learning in the Professions*, San Francisco, CA: Jossey-Bass.

Schön, D.A. (1991), *The Reflective Turn: Case Studies in and on Educational Practice*, New York: Teachers College Columbia University.

Scott, D. and Farrow, J. (1993), 'Evaluating standards of social work supervision in child welfare and hospital social work', *Australian Social Work*, **46** (2), 33–41.

Sealey, C. and Cowl, J. (2002), 'Developing mental health guidelines', presentation at the Social Care Institute for Excellence's Knowledge into Practice conference, London, December.

Senge, P. (1990), *Fifth Discipline: The Art and Practice of the Learning Organisation*, New York: Doubleday.

Senge, P. (1991), 'The learning organisation made plain', *Training and Development*, October, 37–44.

Senge, P. et al. (1999), *The Dance of Change: The Challenges of Sustaining Momentum in Learning Organizations*, New York: Doubleday.

Shapiro, M. (2000), 'Professions in the post-industrial labour market', in O'Connor, I., Smyth, P. and Warburton, J. (eds), *Contemporary Perspectives on Social Work and the Human Services: Challenges and Change*, Malaysia: Longman.

Shaw, I. (1996), *Evaluating in Practice*, Aldershot: Ashgate.

Shaw, I. (1997), *Be Your Own Evaluator: A Guide to Reflective and Enabling Evaluating*, Wrexham: Prospects Publishing.

Shaw, I. (1999), *Qualitative Evaluation*, London: Sage.

Shaw, I. and Gould, N. (2001), *Qualitative Research in Social Work*, London: Sage.

Shediac-Rizkallah, M.C. and Bone, L.R. (1998), 'Planning for the sustainability of community based health programs: conceptual frameworks and future directions for research, practice and policy', *Health Education and Research Theory and Practice*, **13** (1), 87–108.

Sheldon, B. and Chilvers, T. (2000), *Evidence-Based Social Care: A Study of Prospects and Problems*, Lyme Regis: Russell House.

Simons, P.R.J. and Ruijters, M.C.P. (2001), 'Work related learning: elaborate, extend and externalise', in Nijgjof, W.J. and Nieuwenhuis, L.F.M. (eds), *The Dynamics of VET and HRD Systems*, Enschede: Twente University Press.

Sing, G. (1994), 'Anti-racist social work: political correctness or political action', *Social Work Education*, **13** (1), 26–31.

Smale, G., Tuson, G. and Statham, D. (2000), *Social Work and Social Problems: Working towards Social Inclusion and Change*, Basingstoke: Palgrave.

Smith, C. (2001), 'Trust and confidence: Possibilities for social work in "High Modernity"', *British Journal of Social Work*, **31** (2), 287–305.

Smith, L. and Kleine, P. (1986), 'Qualitative research and evaluation: triangulation and multi-methods reconsidered', in Williams, D.D. (ed.), *Naturalistic Evaluation, New Directions in Program Evaluation*, no. 30, San Francisco, CA: Jossey-Bass.

Smyth, J. (1991), *Teachers as Collaborative Learners*, Buckingham: Open University Press.

Smyth, J. (1996), 'Developing socially critical educators', in Boud, D. and Miller, N. (eds), *Working with Experience: Animating Learning*, London: Routledge.

Socialstyrelsen (2000), Nationellt stöd för kunskapsutveckling inom socialtjänsten, SoS -rapport 2000: 12. Stockholm: Socialstyrelsen.

Specht, H. and Vickery, A. (eds) (1977), *Integrating Social Work Methods*, London: Allen & Unwin.

Stanley, J. and Goddard, C.R. (1993), 'The effect of child abuse and other family violence on the child protection worker and case management', *Australian Social Work*, **46** (2), 3–10.

Stanley, L. (ed.) (1990), *Feminist Praxis*, London: Routledge.

Stefani, L (1998), 'Assessment in partnership with learners', *Assessment and Evaluation in Higher Education*, **23** (4), 339–50.

Stevenson, J.F., Mitchell R.E. and Florin, P. (1996), 'Evaluation and self-direction in community prevention coalitions', in Fetterman, D.M., Kaftarian, S.J. and Wandersman, A. (eds), *Empowerment Evaluation: Knowledge and Tools for Self-Assessment and Accountability*, Newbury Park, CA: Sage.

Stockdill, S.H., Baizerman, M. and Compton, D.W. (2002), 'Towards a definition of the ECB process: a conversation with the ECB literature', in Compton, D.W., Baizerman, M. and Stockdill, S.H. (eds), *The Art, Craft and Science of Evaluation Capacity Building*, *New Directions For Evaluation*, no. 93, San Francisco, CA: Jossey-Bass.

Stonham Housing Association Ltd. (1999), Care Practice Manual for Supported Housing, London: SHA.

Stromfors, G. (2002), 'Hva er faglig veiledning i socialt arbeid?' ('What is professional supervision in social work?'), in Stromfors, G. and Vindlegg, J. (eds), *Faglig veiledning i sosialt arbeid (Supervision in Social Work)*, Oslo: Kommuneforlaget.

Syrett, V., Jones, M. and Sercombe, N. (1996), 'Practice supervision: the challenge of definition', *Practice*, **8** (3), 53–62.

Taylor, B.J. (2000), *Reflective Practice: A Guide for Nurses and Midwives*, Buckingham, Open University Press.

Taylor, C. and White, S. (2000), *Practising Reflexivity in Health and Welfare: Making Knowledge*, Buckingham: Open University Press.

Taylor, I., Thomas, J. and Sage, H. (1999), 'Portfolios for learning and assessment: laying the foundations for continuing professional development', *Social Work Education*, **18** (2), 147–60.

Thomas, J. (1997), 'Yesterday's practice, today's learning, tomorrow's teaching resource', *Learning for Competence*, London: CCETSW.

Tidd, J., Bessant, J. and Pavitt, K. (1997), *Managing Innovation: Integrating Technological, Market and Organizational Change*, Chichester: Wiley.

Titterton M. (1999), 'Training professionals in risk assessment and risk management', in Parsloe, P. (ed.), *Risk Assessment in Social Care and Social Work*, London: Jessica Kingsley.

Toffler, A. (1971), *Future Shock*, London: Pan.

Torres, R.T. and Preskill, H. (2001), 'Evaluation and organisational learning: past, present and future', *American Journal of Evaluation*, **22** (3), 387–95.

Tsang, E. (1997), 'Organizational learning and the learning organization: a dichotomy between descriptive and prescriptive research', *Human Relations*, **50** (1), 73–89.

Tsui, M. (1997a), 'The roots of social work supervision: an historical review', *Clinical Supervisor*, **15** (2), 191–8.

Tsui, M. (1997b), 'Empirical research on social work supervision: the state of the art (1970–1995)', *Journal of Social Service Research*, **23** (2), 39–51.

Tuomi, I. (1999), *Corporate Knowledge: Theory and Practice of Intelligent Organisations*, Helsinki: Metaxis.

Turner, M. and Balloch, S. (2001), 'Partnership between service users and statutory social services', in Balloch, S. and Taylor, M. (eds), *Partnership Working: Policy and Practice*, Bristol: Policy Press.

Tynjälä, P. (2003), 'Ammatillinen asiantuntijuus ja sen kehittäminen tietoyhteiskunnassa' ('Developing professional expertise in a knowledge society'), in Kirjonen, J. (ed.), *Tietotyö ja ammattitaito (Knowledge Work and Occupational Competence)*, Jyyaskla: University of Jyväskylä.

Tynjälä, P., Nuutinen, A., Eteläpelto, A, Kirjonen, J. and Remes, P. (1997), 'The acquisition of professional expertise – a challenge for educational research', *Scandinavian Journal of Educational Research*, **41** (3–4), 475–94.

Urry, J. (2003), *Global Complexity*, Cambridge: Polity Press.

Usher, R., Bryant, I. and Johnston, R. (1997), *Adult Education and the Postmodern Challenge: Learning beyond the Limits*, London: Routledge.

Uttley, S. (1994), 'Professional "moving down": rationalisation, routinisation and displacement', in Ife, J., Leitmann, S. and Murphy, P. (eds), *Advances in Social Work and Welfare Education: Education for Post-Industrial Practice*, Perth: University of Western Australia Press.

van der Knaap, P. (1995) 'Policy evaluation and learning: feedback, enlightenment or argumentation?', *Evaluation*, **1** (2), 189–216.

Virkkunen, J. (2001), 'Konseptien kehittäminen osaamisen johtamisen haasteena'. ('Business concepts as challenges to the knowledge management'), in Virkkunen, J. (ed.), *Osaamisen johtaminen muutoksessa. Ideoita ja kokemuksia toisen sukupolven knowledge managementin kehittelyyn (Changing Knowledge Management. Ideas and Experiences on the Development of the Second Generation Knowledge Management)*, Helsinki: Työministeriö.

Walker, S. (2001), 'Tracing the contours of postmodern social work', *British Journal of Social Work*, **31** (1), 29–39.

Ward, A. (1995), 'Opportunity led work: 1. The concept', *Social Work Education*, **14** (4), 89–105.

Watson, M. (2003), Using the Internet for evidence based practice', in Harlow, E. and Webb, S.A. (eds), *Information and Communication Technologies in the Welfare State*, London: Jessica Kingsley.

Webb, S. (2001), 'Some considerations on the validity of evidence-based practice in social work', *British Journal of Social Work*, **31** (1), 57–9.

Wenger, E. (1998), *Communities of Practice: Learning, Meaning and Identity*, Cambridge: Cambridge University Press.

White, P. (2003), 'The joy of sadness', *Guardian Review*, 30 August, pp. 14–15.

White, S. (2001), 'Auto-ethnography as reflexive inquiry: the research act as self-surveillance', in Shaw, I. and Gould, N. (eds), *Qualitative Research in Social Work*, London: Sage.

Whittington, C. and Holland, R. (1985), 'A framework for theory in social work', *Issues in Social Work Education*, **5** (1), 25–50.

Winter, R. (1990), *Methods of Analysing Social Work Practice*, Essex: ASSET.

Wistow, G. (1999), 'Community care in the twenty-first century: choice, independence and community integration', in Spiers. F. (ed.), *Housing and Social Exclusion*, London: Jessica Kingsley.

Wright, N. (1993), 'Partnership for Initial Teacher Training: retrospect and prospect', *Aspects of Education* (48), 69–85.

Yelloly, M. (1995), 'Professional competence and higher education', in Yelloly, M. and Henkel, M. (eds), *Learning and Teaching in Social Work: Towards Reflective Practice*, London: Jessica Kingsley.

Yelloly, M. and Henkel, M. (eds) (1995), *Learning and Teaching in Social Work: Towards Reflective Practice*, London: Jessica Kingsley.

Yliruka, L. (2000), *Sosiaalityön itsearviointi ja hiljainen tieto (Self-Evaluation and Tacit Knowledge in Social Work)*, Helsinki: Stakes.

Index

accountability
  concept of 118
  consequences of 84
  and evaluation 117, 118
  and learning 20
  politics of 154, 160
  and supervision 6, 20–1
accreditation, and learning 80
action learning 17
  and Revans 3
action research
  and evaluation 124
  and supervision 31
action, theory of 131, 133–4
activity system
  mediated 34–5, 36, 37, 38
  as multi-voiced system 35
activity theory 32
  see also activity system
actor network theory 29
Adams, R, and the reflexive cycle 33
Aid to Families in Poverty programmes
  120
Argyris, C
  and client relationship 130
  and double-loop learning 49, 134–5
  and individual learning 136
  and learning 18, 26, 28, 29
  and the learning organization 129
  and organizational learning 38, 43–4, 47,
    72–3
  and productive learning 72
  and single-loop learning 133, 134–5
  and theory of action 131, 133–4
audit culture 7, 20
Australia, supervision study 15–16
autonomy
  and management 28
  and supervision 31

Badwall, H, reflective account of
  organizational change 149–57

Baizerman, M, and evaluation 118, 120–1,
  124
Bateson, G, and learning 134
Bell, D 3
best practice 118–19, 121
Birleson, P, and learning organization 120
Blair, T 164
Boud, D
  and critical incident analysis 109
  and feelings 51, 111
  and learning 43
  and reflection 129
Braye, S, and service user involvement 78
Brew, A, and self-assessment 114
Bristol, University of 87
  and portfolio assessment 92
brokers, and multi-professional teamwork
  81
Brookfield, S
  and critical incidents 104
  and critical learning 139
bureaucracy
  and learning 18
  Weber's theory of 2
Burke, B, and anti-oppressive social work
  106
Burrell, G, and organizational theory 163
Bynner, J, and credit-based systems 80

Calgary University, and peer collaboration
  91
Canada
  homelessness 143–4
  neo-liberal reforms 143
  organizational change case study
    Badwall's account 149–57
    O'Connor's account 157–9
    Rossiter's account 145–9
Care Practice Standards Manual 87
  development of 89
  feedback 97
  implementation of 87, 88, 90, 95–6, 97, 99

perceptions of 97
and portfolios 93
and professional competence 93
provisions of 94, 95
Cayley, L, organizations and learning 80
Centre for Evidence Based Social Services
48, 104
certainty, and the learning organization 171
change
adapting to 21
barriers to 9, 131–2, 164
and co-operative inquiry 52–3
complexity of 117
consequences of 32
continuous nature of 3, 163
and globalization 6, 27
individual and organizational 66–7, 68
and the learning organization 6, 79
organizational 9, 159–60
Badwall's reflective account 149–57
O'Connor's reflective account 157–9
Rossiter's reflective account 145–9
resistance to 49, 169
and systems thinking 135
child deaths, inquiries into 1–2, 12, 175
Clarke, J, and the managerial state 84
class
and organizational conflict 144, 148–9,
150, 152
and race 147, 148, 150, 156
Climbié, V, Laming report on death of 1–2,
175
co-operative inquiry
advantages of 50–1, 52–3
and participation 173
Colwell, M 1
Commission for Racial Equality 175
communication, and multi-professional
teamwork 84–5
Community Care Plans 166
competence, assessment of professional
92–3, 112–13
Compton, D W, and evaluation 118, 120–1,
123, 124
consumerism
and service user involvement 78
and social welfare 46
Cook, P 1
Coopey, J, and the learning organization 5
Cowl, J, and service user involvement 85–6
critical incident analysis 169

and critical reflection training 63, 70,
169
definition 104
and effective practice 8
and practice teachers 101–2
and practice teaching courses
choosing an incident 110–11
and competency frameworks 112–13
feedback on 111
guided structure 108–9
and learning transfer 111
and oppression 109–10
and power differentials 113–14
process of 107–8
value of 109
reflective perspectives on 105–6
and reflective teaching 137
use of 104–5
critical practice 33
critical reflection
and co-operative inquiry
development of innovation 52
and managing discretion 51–2
methods 50–1
and cultural identification 43, 45
definition problems 104
and discretion 45, 46
external structures for 168–9
implementation problems 140–1
importance of 41
and individual learning 46
and learning 42–3
and the learning organization 47
and managerialism 53
opportunities for 49–54
and organizational learning 72–3, 173–4
and perspective transformation 139, 169
polarizing effect 71
and power relationships 58–9
process of 58, 104
and professional practice development
46, 51, 54
and reflection 58
and social work 57–9
and supervision 38
theoretical concepts 102–4
threats to
and evidence of what works 48
failure of critical analysis 49
managerialism 48
rational policy implementation 49

training programme 7, 169
  attendance 70–1
  content and format 61–3
  context of 59–60
  contractual problems 70–1
  critical incident technique 63, 70
  and diversity 69–70, 72
  evaluation 63, 66–9
  and individual learning 66, 67
  and organizational learning 64, 66–9
  and perceived dilemmas 67–8
  planning of 60–1
  and power 68–9
  practical problems 71
  results 63–6
  and time 71
  and uncertainty 114
cultural difference
  and reflexivity 24
  and social work 26
culture, broad concepts of 43

Dalrymple, J, and anti-oppressive social
  work 106
Davies, P, and credit-based systems 80
decision-making
  and discretion 51–2
  and implementation 165
  and judgement 7
  as mutual learning 165
deconstruction, and critical reflection 58
democracy, participatory 165–6, 174
disability, and practitioner attitudes towards
  parents 130, 132–5, 137–40
discretion
  and changes in service provision 19–20
  and critical reflection 45, 46
  and decision-making 51–2
  and effective practice 7, 46, 50
  and learning 19
  managing professional 51–2
  necessity for 45–6
  negative impact of 44
  and policy 165
  unreflective 44–5
diversity
  and corporatist policy 69
  and critical reflection training 69–70, 72
double-loop learning 47, 49, 51, 71, 72,
  134–5, 139, 140–1, 166
Dovey, K

and the learning organization 79
and power 84
Driver, M, and the learning organization 6

Eby, M, and reflective practice 102
eco-maps, and systems thinking 136
Elliot, J, and reflective practice 103
empowerment, and the learning
  organization 80
Engeström, Y 37
  and expansive learning 35
  and human activity system 31
  and mediated activity system 34–5
Environment, Transport and the Regions,
  Department of, and care practice
  standards 87
Eräsaari, R
  and closed expertise 25, 26–7
  and expert knowledge 24
Eraut, M
  and co-operation 82
  and formal learning 79
  and qualifications 80
  skill development 94
  and trust 84
ethnicity, and power 84
evaluation
  and accountability 117, 118
  and action research 124
  and insider/outsider split 122–3
  and the learning organization 8, 117,
    118, 171
    capacity building 119, 120–1
    culture 119–20
    learning-based practice 121–2
    organizational focus 120
    mainstreaming 119
  and participation 173
  and practice 126–7
  and practitioner critique 123–4
  purpose of 118
  and trust 120
  value of 8
evidence, and critical reflection 48
evidence-based practice 7, 28, 90, 104, 119
  and expertise 27
expansive learning 7, 21, 26
  Engeström's model of 35
  and expertise 37
  and supervision 31, 33
experience, and problem-solving 4

experiential learning 3, 4, 17, 35, 38
expert patient 78
expertise
    closed 25, 26–7
    crisis of 25
    and evidence-based practice 27
    generation of 30
    nature of 23
    open 25, 37
    paradox of 23
    reflexive 27, 37
    and social work 26, 46
    supervision and promotion of 25–7, 32

feelings, and learning 43, 51, 111
Fielding, M, and power 83–4
Finland, and knowledge-based practice 28
Fisher, M 125
Flood, R L, and theory of action 131
Fook, J 43
Fordism 2
Freeman, M, and multi-professional
    teamwork 82–3

gender
    and discrimination 153
    and management 84
    and power 84
    and reflexivity 24
    and supervisory arrangements 14
General Social Care Council 102, 175
    and social work education 94
    and work-based learning 90
Gherardi, S, and the learning organization 5
globalization
    and change 6
    and organizational change 27
Gonczi, A, diversity and corporatist policy
    69
goodness, and bourgeois identity 148
Gould, N 1
    and critical reflection 41
    and welfare fragmentation 162
governance
    emergence of different forms of 17
    and organizational change 27
    and supervision 13, 14
Greene, J, and evaluation 118
Gregory, R, and organizational learning 19
Griffiths Report 88
Gunn, L, and implementation theory 165

Habermas, J 103, 105
Hager, P, diversity and corporatist policy 69
Hall, T 122
Handy, C 3
    and the learning organization 79
Harlow, E, and managerialism 84
Hartman, A, and eco-maps 136
Hawkins, P, and supervision 110
Health Act (1999) 77
Health and Social Care Act (2001) 77
Health and Social Care trusts 77
Health, Department of, 'A Quality Strategy
    for Social Care' 87
Heron, Barbara 157
    race and white women 147–8
Hill, O 89
Hogwood, B, and implementation theory
    165
homelessness, Canada 143–4
House, E, and evaluation 118, 119
Housing Act (1996) 87
    provisions 88
housing associations, and partnership
    working 88
Housing Corporation 88
    and *Care Practice Standards Manual* 89
housing, supported
    and qualification problems 97
    and staff qualifications 96
    see also Stonham Housing Association
Hughes, L, and child death inquiries 12
human relations movement 3
Humphries, B, and structured learning 109

identity
    bourgeois 148
    historical 143, 160
    multiple 153
    and organizations 165
    professional 13, 26, 86
    and race 149, 154
    and reflection 159–60
    threats to 157–8
    and white middle class women 147, 149
Ife, J, ethical mission of social work 27
implementation theory 164
    bottom-up 165, 166
    and incrementalism 166
    top-down 165, 166
Improving Working Lives standard 77
inclusive learning 21

incrementalism 166
indeterminacy
    and judgement criteria 16
    and practice 19
    and supervision 6
individual learning
    and critical reflection 46
    and critical reflection training 66, 67
    and organization 4
    and organizational change 68
    and organizational learning 3, 43–4, 46,
        72, 129, 136–7, 141, 170
information
    management of 85
    supervision and processing of 15
innovation
    and critical reflection 52
    and knowledge production 24, 36, 36–9
    and learning 18
    and organizational learning 26
    and supervision 7, 37
    and working practices 8
interpersonal relationships, and discretion
    45
Ixer, G
    and critical reflection 41, 59
    and reflection 92, 102

Janesick, V J 127
judgement, *see* discretion

Kadushin, A, and supervision 12, 17
Kemp, E, and participant observation 90
Keogh, R, and reflection 129
Kirk, S, and accountability 117–18
Knights, S, and critical incident analysis
    109
knotworks, hybrid 27
knowledge
    approaches to creation of 26
    construction and development of 23
    and context of 25
    and expertise 25
    generation of 30
    orientation 26, 37
    and practice 4
    production of innovative 24, 36, 36–9
    supervision and brokering of 21, 22
knowledge-based practice 119
knowledge communities 26
Kolb, D

and experiential learning 26, 38
    and learning cycle 42, 102
Konno, N, and innovative learning
    community 36
Kuhn, T, and normal science 123

Lambert, F C, and evaluation 118, 123
Laming, Lord, and Victoria Climbié report
    1–2, 175
Latour, B 29
leadership
    and organizational change 27
    and organizational learning 29
learning
    and accountability 20
    and accreditation 80
    as behavioural process 42
    context of 21, 43
    and critical reflection 42–3
    as cumulative process 42
    cycles of 33, 42, 102
    embeddedness of 3, 4
    and human service organizations 17–19
    inclusive 21
    and innovation 18
    inter-professional 5
    iterative 166
    and management 3, 18–19
    and multi-professional setting 8
    and organizational structures 80–1
    paradox of 29
    and participation 80
    personal nature of 43
    and power 17, 19
    and practice 4, 79
    problematic concept of 3
    productive 72
    and professionalization 2
    prospects for 19–21
    and qualifications 80
    and reflection 42
    and reflection-in-action 42
    and transferability of 4
    as way of life 79–80
    see also action learning; double-loop
        learning; expansive learning;
        experiential learning; individual
        learning; learning organization;
        lifelong adult learning; network
        learning; organizational learning;
        reflective learning; single-loop

learning; transformative learning;
    work-based learning
learning-based practice, and evaluation
    121–2
learning community 80
    innovative 36
learning organization 18
    and action-learning 3
    and certainty 171
    characteristics of 46–7, 76–7, 167
    as contested theory 5–6
    and context-based learning 4
    core aspects of 9
    and critical reflection 47
    critiques of 11
    diffïculties with concept 2, 161–2
    and evaluation 8, 117, 118
        capacity building 120–1
        culture 119–20
        insider/outsider split 122–3
        learning-based practice 121–2
        organizational focus 120
    evidence of 168–70
    implementation of 161, 162, 164–7,
        172–3
    and knowledge production 23
    and lifelong learning 76
    and multi-professional teamwork 75, 81,
        82–3
    need for 37
    and New Labour 76, 164
    obstacles to 54
    and organizational theory 163
    and participation 53
    and power 171, 172
    and public policy discourse 76
    and reflective practice 4, 59
    and responsiveness to change 6, 79
    and service user involvement 85
    and social work 2
    and structures 80–1
    and systems thinking 119, 135–6
    and teamwork 2, 53, 82
    theory of 2–3
    threats to 170–1
    and uncertainty 163
    usefulness of concept 162, 175
    and work-life balance issues 80
lifelong adult learning 26
    and the learning organization 76
    and portfolios 87, 92–4

Lindblom, C, and incrementalism 166
Lipsky, M 7, 44, 51, 164
    and discretion 165
Lorenz, W, ethical mission of social work
    27

Macdonald, G, and unlearning 86
McGregor, D 3
McLaren, P 152–3, 157
McLean, A 102
Majone, G
    and mutual learning 165
    and policy analysis 164
management
    and action-learning 3
    and organizational learning 174–5
    and promotion of learning 81
managerialism
    and autonomy 28
    and certainty 165
    and change 3
    and critical reflection 48
    features of 48
    impact of 97
    introduction of 163
    and the learning organization 170
    and organizational change 27
    and organizational learning 18–19
    and practice development 53, 54
    and reflection 59
    and social work 84
    and targets 13, 48
    and uncertainty 48, 54
Mandy, P, and multi-professional teamwork
    82
Manthorpe, J, settlements and social work
    education 89–90
marginalization, and the learning
    organization 2
Marshall, J 102
Maslow, A 3
Masschelein, J, and reflection 103
material constructivism 29
meaning perspectives 28, 31, 32, 38
    and social work 32
mediation, and the activity system 34
mental health services
    and the learning organization 77
    and modernization 7
    and multi-professional teamwork 75, 78
    and service user involvement 75, 78–9

and the Workforce Action Team 77
Mezirow, J
  and meaning perspectives 28, 32, 38
  and perspective transformation 139
  and reflection 129
Milburn, A 76, 77, 78, 81, 85
Miller, C 76
  and communication 84
  and multi-professional teamwork 82–3,
    84
mission, organizational, and supervision 14,
    15
mistakes, repetitive nature of 1
modernization
  and mental health 7
  and New Labour agenda 75, 76
Morgan, G, and organizational theory 163
Morrison, K, and reflective practice 102,
    103
Muetzelfelt, M
  and the learning context 19
  management and learning 18–19
multi-professional teamwork
  and beliefs about teamwork 83
  and brokers 81
  characteristics of 82
  and communication 84–5
  learning in and by 82–3, 86
  and the learning organization 75, 81
  literature on 82
  and local councils 77–8
  and organizational structures 77
  philosophies of 83
  and power 83–4
  and service user involvement 75, 85–6
  and shared learning 82–3
  and social work 7
  and trust 84

National Health Service, as learning
    organization 76, 77
National Institute for Social Work, and *Care
    Practice Standards Manual* 89
National Occupational Standards 92
National Science Foundation 117
  and evaluation culture 120
National Vocational Qualification (NVQ)
    101
network learning 16, 172
  and supervision 20
New Labour

and the learning organization 76, 164
  and managerialism 163
  modernization agenda 75, 76
Newman, J, and the managerial state 84
NHS and Community Care (NHSCC) Act
    (1990) 88
Nonaka, I, and innovative learning
    community 36
Nyhan, B, and the learning organization 6

O'Connor, P, reflective account of
    organizational change 157–9
O'Neill, O, and trust 84
oppression
  and critical incident analysis 108
  and race 153, 154
  and social work 106, 109
  and white supremacy 154, 155, 160
organizational learning 3, 35
  approaches to 26
  barriers to 54, 131–2, 140, 141
  and critical reflection 64, 66–9, 72–3
  and double-loop learning 47, 51, 71, 72,
    134–5, 139, 140–1, 166
  effective 50
  evidence of 44
  imperatives of
    critical reflection 173–4
    managerial practice 174–5
    service user involvement 174
    stakeholder participation 174
  and individual learning 3, 43–4, 46, 72,
    129, 136–7, 141, 170
  and innovation 26
  intentions and practice 47
  and managerialism 48
  and ownership of change 53, 171
  and power 44
  and practice 28
  and single-loop learning 47, 134–5
  and supervision 24–30, 37–8, 39
  and tacit knowledge 36
  threats to 54, 170–1
  and unlearning 86
organizational theory 163
organizations
  and change 3, 9, 23, 66–7, 163
  definition of 81
  descriptive studies 5
  development of 28
  and identity 165

impact of globalization 27
and individual learning 4, 68
and knowledge production 36
and mission 14
and politics 72
prescriptive studies 5
scientific views of 2
structure and behaviour 2
structure and learning 80–1
and supervision 15, 24
Owen, J M, and evaluation 118, 123

Papell, C, and process recording 137
parents, practitioners attitudes towards 130,
132–5, 137–40
participant observation 90
participation
and co-operative inquiry 173
and evaluation 173
and learning 80
and learning organization 53
and organizational learning 174
partnership working, see multi-professional
teamwork
partnerships, creative 87, 88–9
and joint research 90
and peer review 91
and social policy development 89–90
and staff supervision 91
and work-based training 90
Patton, M 121
and evaluation 118, 120, 126
and internal evaluation 123
Pearson, M 76
peer groups, value of 110
peer observation 98–9
peer review, role of 91
Pengelly, P, and child death inquiries 12
perspective transformation 139, 169
policy analysis 164–5
policy implementation
and critical reflection 49
and political process 165
politics
organizational 72
and policy implementation 165
portfolios
and lifelong learning 87, 92–4
and Stonham Housing Association 98
power
and assessment 113–14

and critical reflection 58–9, 68–9
and ethnicity 84
and gender 84
impact of 53
and learning 17, 19
and the learning organization 2, 83–4,
171, 172
and multi-professional teamwork 83–4
and organizational learning 44
and reflective practice 58
and service user involvement 78
practice
communities of 8, 26, 29
and context specific knowledge 4
and critical incident analysis 8
and discretion 7, 45, 50
and evaluation 126–7
and indeterminacy 19
and innovation 26
knowledge-based 27–8
and learning 4, 79
and management by target 13
and mediated activity system 34–5
multi-professional 75
organizational context 2
and organizational learning 28
prescriptive approach towards 11
and problem-solving 4
and quality movement 13
reflexive nature of 24
rule-governed 19
and supervision 2, 11, 12, 19
practice teaching 8, 169
and critical incident analysis 101–2,
106–11
and workload relief 106, 169
Practice Teaching Award (PTA) 102
practitioner research 124
characteristics of 124–5
collaborative 125–6
Preskill, H
and evaluation 118, 123
and readiness for learning and
evaluation 121–2
primary care groups 77
primary care trusts 77
problem-solving
and action-learning 3
and experience 4
and knowledge production 30
and problem-setting 4

and professional learning 1
process recording 137
professional identity
    and supervision 26
    threats to 13
    and unlearning 86
professional practice development
    continuing 77
    and critical reflection 41, 46, 51, 54
    and managerialism 53, 54
    and portfolios 87
    and reflection 58
    and supervision 2, 11, 31, 32, 37, 169
professionalism, as threat to learning
        organization 171
professionalization, and learning 2
public management ideology, and
        supervision 13
Pugh, R, and welfare fragmentation 162

qualifications, importance of 80
quality movement, and supervision 13, 14

race and racism
    and class 150, 156
    and hierarchy 154
    and identity 154
    institutional 44, 167, 171, 175
    and organizational conflict 144-53,
        155–6, 158
    and reflective accounts of organizational
        conflict
        Badwall's account 149–57
        O'Connor's account 157–9
        Rossiter's account 145–9
    and resistance to discrimination 156–7
    and white middle class women 147
    and white supremacy 154, 155, 160
Ramian, K, and practitioner research 125–6
Ranson, S, and discretion 44–5
Razack, S 154–5, 160
reflection
    and critical reflection 58
    criticism of 41, 59
    emancipatory 105–6
    and identity histories 159–60
    influence of 1
    and learning 42
    limits to 160, 171
    and organizational change 159–60
        Badwall's account 149–57

O'Connor's account 157–9
    Rossiter's account 145–9
organizational embedding 8
practical 105
process of 58
and supervision 32
technical 105
see also critical reflection
reflective change 9
reflective learning 9, 17–18, 35, 119
    application of 87
    and discretion 7
    influences on 1
    premises of 4
    and supervision 6–7
reflective practice
    benefits of 57–8, 129
    disadvantages of 59
    implementation problems 140–1
    and the learning organization 4, 59
    and power 58
    problematic nature of 102
    process of 104
    and Stonham Housing Association 95–6
    theoretical concepts 102–4
reflective teaching 9, 130–1, 168–9, 172–3
    and critical incident analysis 137
    implementation problems 140–1
    and individual learning 136–7
    and the learning organization 136–7
    and reflective change 137–40
    and systems thinking 135–6
    and theories-in-use 132–3
reflexive cycle 35
reflexivity, and supervision 21, 22
Reid, W, and accountability 117–18
Revans, R, and action-learning 3
Riessman, C K 127
risk management training 90
Ross, N, and multi-professional teamwork
        82–3
Rossiter, A, reflective account of
        organizational change 145–9
Ruch, G 102
Ruijters, M C P, and work-related learning
        81

Sackett, D L, and evidence-based practice
        104
Schein, E
    and definition of organization 81

and paradox of learning 29
Schön, D 6, 162
　and client relationship 130, 131
　and double-loop learning 134–5
　and individual learning 136
　influence of 1
　and learning 18, 26, 28, 29
　and the learning organization 129
　and organizational learning 38, 47, 72–3
　and problem-setting 4
　and productive learning 72
　and reflection 42, 102–3
　and single-loop learning 133, 134–5
　and theory of action 131, 133–4
Sealey, C, and service user involvement
　　85–6
self-assessment 87, 113–14
Senge, P 5, 6
　and individual learning 136
　and the learning organization 2, 18, 46,
　　79, 130, 141
　and organizational learning 29
　and systems thinking 135
　and teams 82
service provision, discretion and changes in
　19–20
service users
　and the expert patient 78
　influence of 165
　involvement of 8, 78, 85–6, 162–3, 172,
　　174, 175
　learning from 86
　meeting needs of 129
　and multi-professional teamwork 75
　and practitioner attitudes 130, 131,
　　132–5, 137-40
Shohet, R, and supervision 110
Simons, P R J, and work-related learning 81
single-loop learning 72, 134–5
skill transfer, limitations of 4
Skills Councils 92
Skolnick, L, and process recording 137
social construction 29–30
　and the learning organization 163
social housing, *see* housing, supported
social policy implementation theory 164
social welfare, commodification of 13
social work
　anti-oppressive 106, 109
　assessment methods 92–4
　and critical practice 33

and critical reflection 57–9
definition 24
and evidence-based practice 27, 28
and expertise 25, 26, 46
and interpersonal relationships 45–6
and the learning organization 2
and management by target 13
and meaning perspectives 32
and mediated activity system 34–5
and multi-professional teams 7
and multiple agencies 113
and power 53
self-understanding model 31, 32
and uncertainty 23–4, 46
social work courses
　and creative partnerships
　　and joint research 90
　　and peer review 91
　　and social policy development 89–90
　　and staff supervision 91
　　and work-based training 90
staff development 26
Stanley, L, and reflection 103
Stewart, J, and discretion 44–5
Stockdill, S H, and evaluation 118, 120–1,
　124
Stonham Housing Association 87, 88
　assessment methods 95
　and implementation of *Care Practice
　　Standards Manual* 87, 88, 90,
　　95–99
　and peer observation 98–9
　and portfolios for services 98
　and Practice Development Adviser 91,
　　93, 94–6, 98
　and reflective practice groups 95–6, 99,
　　168
　and service users 97
　and staff backgrounds 96
　and staff training 96–7
　training programme 89
　variation in support levels 97
structuration 29–30
supervision 6
　and accountability 6, 20–1
　administration of 14
　Australian study 15–16
　and autonomy 31
　context of 12, 19, 21
　controversy over 13
　and critical reflection 38

critiques of 11
definition 32–3
development of 30
disruption of 13
effective 12
and expansive learning 31, 33
and expertise promotion 25–7, 32
failures of 12
functions of 11–12, 15, 17, 30, 110
and innovation 7, 37
and knowledge-brokering 21, 22
and knowledge production 23, 36–9
and learning networks 16, 20
and meaning perspectives 32
and mediated activity system 35
models of 31
and organizational development 24
and organizational learning 24, 25–6,
    27–30, 37–8, 39
and organizational mission 14, 15
and practice 11, 12, 19
and practice development 2
and professional identity 13, 26
and professional practice development
    11, 31, 32, 37, 169
prospects for 19–21
and quality 13, 14
and reflection 32
reflexive 21, 22, 33–6, 39
traditions of 30–1
and transformative learning 28, 38
Supporting People programme 87, 98, 99
provisions 89
sustainable development, influence on
    evaluation 119, 121
Sweden, and knowledge-based practice 28
systems thinking, and the learning
    organization 119, 135–6

Taylor, B J, and critical incident analysis
    105–6
Taylor, I 1
Taylorism 2, 3
teamwork
    beliefs about 83
    and the learning organization 2, 53, 82
    see also multi-professional teamwork
Thatcherism, and managerialism 163
Titterton, M, and risk management training
    90
Toffler, A 3

Torres, R T
    and evaluation 118, 123
    and readiness for learning and
        evaluation 121–2
Toyama, R, and innovative learning
    community 36
transformative learning 17, 35
    and supervision 28, 38
trust
    and evaluation 120
    and multi-professional teamwork 84

uncertainty
    and critical reflection 114
    inevitability of 54–5
    and the learning organization 163
    and managerialism 48, 54
    and open expertise 25, 37
    and social work 23–4, 46
universities
    and joint research programmes 90
    and social housing 89
unlearning, and organizational learning 86

van der Knaap, P, and evaluation 118

Walker, D
    and critical incident analysis 109
    and reflection 129
Weber, M, theory of bureaucracy 2
Weiss, C, and evaluation 118
welfare services, fragmentation of 162
Wenger, E
    and brokers 81
    and communities of practice 8
    and learning communities 79
    and the learning organization 82
White, S 122, 126
Wiltshire and Swindon Users Network 85
Wistow, G, and community care 88
Woolgar, S 29
work-based learning 2, 4–5, 17, 79, 81, 90,
    101, 168
work-life balance issues 77
    and the learning organization 80
Workforce Action Team 77
workload relief 106, 169

Yelloly, M
    and competence assessment 112